SOCIETY USSIAN
REVOLU

Society and Politics in the Russian Revolution

Edited by

Robert Service

Reader in Soviet History and Politics
School of Slavonic and East European Studies
University of London

St. Martin's Press

First published in Great Britain 1992 by
THE MACMILLAN PRESS LTD
Houndmills, Basingstoke, Hampshire RG21 2XS
and London
Companies and representatives
throughout the world

This book is published by Macmillan in association with the School of Slavonic and
East European Studies, University of London, in their series *Studies in Russia and
East Europe*.
Chairman of the Editorial Board: M. A. Branch

A catalogue record for this book is available from the British Library.

ISBN 0–333–46910–0 hardcover
ISBN 0–333–46911–9 paperback

Printed in Great Britain by
Billing and Sons Ltd
Worcester

First published in the United States of America 1992 by
Scholarly and Reference Division,
ST. MARTIN'S PRESS, INC.,
175 Fifth Avenue,
New York, N.Y. 10010

ISBN 0–312–08049–2 (cloth)

Library of Congress Cataloging-in-Publication Data
Society and politics in the Russian Revolution / edited by Robert
Service.
p. cm.
Includes index.
ISBN 0–312–08049–2 (cloth)
1. Soviet Union—History—Revolution, 1917–1921—Social aspects.
2. Social classes—Soviet Union—History—20th century. 3. Soviet
Union—History—Revolution, 1917–1921—Influence. 4. Political
culture—Soviet Union. I. Service, Robert.
DK265.17.S62 1992
947.084'1—dc20   92–1009
                                                    CIP

Contents

List of Contributors

Edward Acton is Professor of Modern European History in the University of East Anglia. He is the author of a biographical study of Alexander Herzen and an historiographical survey of the Russian Revolution.

John Channon is Lecturer in Russian Economic History at the School of Slavonic and East European Studies in the University of London. He has published several articles on the peasantry in the Russian Revolution.

Stephen Jones is Assistant Professor at Mount Holyoke College, Massachusetts. At the time of the seminars he was research fellow at the School of Slavonic and East European Studies in the University of London; he is the author of several articles on Georgian social-democracy in the years before and after 1917.

Evan Mawdsley is Senior Lecturer in the Department of Modern History in the University of Glasgow. He has written a book on the Baltic fleet in the Russian Revolution as well as a history of the ensuing Civil War.

Maureen Perrie is Lecturer in Russian History at the Centre for Russian and East European Studies in the University of Birmingham. Her book on the pre-revolutionary programme of the Russian Socialist-Revolutionaries has been followed by an account of the image of Ivan the Terrible in Russian popular thought.

Christopher Read is Senior Lecturer in History in the University of Warwick. He is the author of two books on Russian culture in the revolutionary years, the first treating the pre-volutionary period and the second the post-revolutionary period.

Robert Service is Reader in Soviet History and Politics at the School of Slavonic and East European Studies in the University of London. He has written an account of the Bolshevik party after 1917, a textbook on the Russian Revolution and two out of his three projected volumes on Lenin's political life.

Howard White is Lecturer in Soviet Government at the London School of Economics and Political Science in the University of London. He has written papers and articles on the Russian Provisional Government of 1917.

Regions and guberniyas of European Russia.

by kind permission of Maureen Perrie from *The Agrarian Policy of the Russian Socialist–Revolutionary Party – from its origins through the revolution of 1905–1907*. Cambridge University Press.

1 Introduction

Robert Service

The Russian Revolution was among the most important events in twentieth-century world history. The year 1917 transformed the politics, society and the economy of the old Romanov empire. Until February, the government in Russia had been led by a monarchy which traced its dynasty back to 1613 and which, for most purposes, had retained its absolutist powers intact. From October a far-left socialist party, the Bolsheviks, held office. The intervening months had been a time of open struggles among parties. Individuals like Miliukov, Kerenskii, Tsereteli and Lenin came to the fore. There was a surge of popular enthusiasm for both universal democracy and sectional representative organisations. The privileges of the propertied social groups were under constant threat. Yet the widely-noted political optimism occurred also in the midst of the worst economic crisis experienced by Russia since the seventeenth century. The prospect of industrial and financial collapse grew steadily over the year. Nor did the Revolution happen in peaceful times. The country was engaged in the Great War on the side of Britain, France, Italy and the USA. The German and Austro-Hungarian menace to Russia's territorial integrity increased as Russia's internal turmoil swelled. The emergence of the world's first socialist state in history in all these circumstances have made historians and social scientists return perennially to the Russian Revolution in quest of explanations.

It is not only because of its consequences for Russia that her Revolution attracted investigation. The Bolshevik seizure of power in Petrograd had repercussions elsewhere. Lenin's government, having expected to act as a stimulus for socialist revolutions in Europe, found itself so friendless and helpless that a separate peace had to be signed with Germany; and Russia's early departure from the Great War had an impact on global military affairs. A political influence was also registered, especially in Europe. The revolutionary crisis in Germany, Hungary and Italy in the aftermath of the Great War was in some measure inspired by events in Russia. Even many conservative politicians in Europe assumed a more compromising attitude to their labour movements from the 1920s in order to lessen the possibility of a native Bolshevism overturning the social order.

And so the Russian Revolution has always attracted enquiry. In past years, especially from the 1930s through to the late 1960s, it was characteristic for high politics to be examined. But there is a more recent and long overdue trend to see politics in a less confined perspective. Both Soviet and Western writers have looked at whole organisations, institutions and social classes. Much is left to be done; only a small proportion of such aggregations of people have yet been written about. Yet a great deal of excellent work has already appeared, and the time is opportune to take stock of research and to gauge what remains to be undertaken. The following chapters are intended as a contribution to such an assessment. Our central themes are linked to the ideas and activity of large social groups in the former Russian empire in 1917. It is our common feeling that no book, either in the West or in the USSR, has yet brought together the considerations of modern writers on large social groups even though an increasing number of scholars believe that such groups were crucial to the development and outcome of the Revolution. In addition, the treatment of the groups in the secondary literature is uneven; some have won much fuller treatment than others, and it is sensible to try to redress the balance.

Even so, the scope of the chapters is intentionally restricted. High politics are only glanced at. The technical workings of the economy, too, are all but ignored. This is not to imply that high politics or economics are exhausted fields of research. On the contrary, political life in 1917 is woefully under-researched to this day: previous generations of scholars have only scratched the surface on several vital questions. And economic life remains virgin soil in many aspects for writers on the Russian Revolution. We still lack a comprehensive modern monograph on economic developments in 1917. In short, our principal effort is devoted to large social groups; but we hope that this narrowness of subject (if large social classes can reasonably be described as a narrow subject) has produced insights which sharpen our vision of more general aspects of the Russian Revolution.

The book grew out of a series of seminars at the School of Slavonic and East European Studies in the University of London, which was held in 1987 in order to mark the seventieth anniversary of the Russian Revolution. Each of our authors was invited to look at a specific social group and to address the problems raised by the body of writings on it. The collective aim was to summarise what had been written and argued about, and to point to areas where further research could advance our knowledge; no one was asked to produce a mini-monograph. The resultant book is offered as a tool for contemplating what has been done and what remains to be done. Some chapters, notably those on the workers and on the peasantry, contain lengthy surveys of the historiography; but others, especially the chapters on the landowners and the urban middle classes, are written about groups which have been studied to a lesser degree. There is no better way of emphasising the point that historical treatments of social classes are far from being uniform: and this differential situation should not be allowed to persist. Another feature, which is less obvious but which became evident to our audience during the seminar series, was that certain groups have been much more frequently studied in some countries than in others. For example, USSR-based scholars of the gentry have few counterparts in the West; on the other hand, Western accounts of the urban working class have covered broader ground.

In choosing social groups for inclusion, we cast our gaze mainly at those which had an overt and substantial impact on the history of the Revolution. We have mainly followed the divisions conventional in the literature. It would have been strange not to have included the workers and the peasants, the urban middle classes and the landowners, the cultural intelligentsia, the soldiers and sailors, the non-Russian ethnic groups.

We should have liked to have embraced more groups. There is no chapter, for example, on house-servants even though their numbers were not much different from those for factory workers in this period. We offer no chapter on the royal family and the higher levels of the aristocracy. Nor do we treat women (or indeed men), children or the elderly as separate groups. We do not have chapters on the unemployed, the prisoners-of-war, the clergy, the refugees, the artisans and the vagrants. Whereas we discuss the non-Russian nationalities, moreover, we have not given a chapter to the Russians themselves. Some omissions were caused by the paucity of published studies while others resulted from the limitations of the length of the series. For example, it would obviously have been helpful to know more about Christian, Moslem and other religious believers in 1917. Information about them is steadily being accumulated (although most treatments to this day deal more with institutions and ideologies than with the believers *en masse*). Such believers are included in other groups incorporated in our chapters; but they do not figure as believers in explicit terms. In summary, then, we do not claim that the following survey and agenda of research is panoptic.

Yet the chapters range widely enough to provide grounds for several tentative generalisations. Firstly, the chronology of the Revolution experienced by the various groups was variegated. A process of development between February and October which makes sense of high politics in Petrograd is not automatically applicable to all our large social groups. The rise and fall of the Provisional Government followed a particular sequence, and this sequence affected everything else (as everything else affected it); but the sequence for several groups was substantially out of time with that sequence.

Thus Maureen Perrie demonstrates that peasants were attentive to the Provisional Government's legislation and that Lenin's Decree on Land in October released a tidal wave of seizures of estates. But the growth of hostility towards the Provisional Government occurred at different paces among several other social groups – and there were few social groups which did not eventually turn against the Provisional Government. Christopher Read's account of the cultural intelligentsia describes how, in many cases, individuals made their choices in politics not in autumn 1917 but in spring 1918 or even later. Needless to add, some poets and painters opted to support the new Soviet régime while others remained staunchly antipathetic. Nor was the process a steady one whereby social groups were revolutionised (or counter-revolutionised, as the case may have been): Evan Mawdsley describes the abrupt impact exercised by the June offensive on soldiers and sailors. Furthermore, each large social group exhibited considerable internal diversity in interests and even aspirations. No group was monolithic. Terms like 'the working class' or 'the middle class' trip easily off the tongue or pen and constitute a useful shorthand; but Howard White gives due emphasis to the tensions amidst the urban middle-class elements in the early months after the absolute monarchy's overthrow.

Nevertheless these internal differences became less important than the antagonism between the proprietorial élites and the rest of the population. Social 'polarisation' was an all-pervasive fact of life in 1917. The chasm separating the countless poor wretches toiling in the factories and in the fields from the rich few had been vast for centuries and became vaster still in 1917. Hatreds quickly acquired an intensity unprecedented even under the Romanovs.

The polarisation was multi-dimensional. Conflicts of economic interest provided a decisive arena of struggle in the months before the Bolshevik seizure of power in October, and the clashes between factory workers and their employers were crucial to the process. Yet other tensions were also important. Stephen Jones, examining the Revolution's ethnic dimension, analyses the difficulties facing the Provisional Government in holding down several non-Russian regions of the old empire. He sounds a note of caution against over-simplification. Whereas a large number of Finns came to desire an end to Russian rule it is difficult to detect an abundance of anti-Russian feeling among Belorussians in 1917. Nor were ethnic struggles simply a contest between Russians and non-Russians. The Transcaucasus was a hotbed of mutual resentments of Armenians,

Azeris and Georgians; and Ukrainians, Jews and Poles held each other in distrust in the Ukraine. All such conflicts, furthermore, cannot properly be understood unless we widen our perspective beyond 1917. Ethnic rivalries were of long duration; the Revolution gave them a more overt and more highly developed expression. This is true of most other social phenomena. John Channon stresses that the gentry landlords quickly recognised that the prospect of a general peasant assault on their property was strong. They could not stand politically alone in the countryside and sank their energies into a frantic, and ultimately vain, attempt to detach the richer and property-owning peasant households from the rest of the peasantry.

Material motivations were important in getting peasants to act as they did. Most villagers, being poor, saw a chance of becoming better-off through a take-over of non-peasant land. Maureen Perrie argues that age-old attitudes and customs also influenced the peasantry. She highlights the peasant notions of social justice and self-justification. Historical writing on 1917 has increasingly accentuated factors amenable to quantification. Social attitudes, especially in an era before gallup-poll questionnaires, are inherently less easy to count; but they are no less significant because of their elusiveness.

The realm of ideas has been more intensively studied for individual politicians than for large social groups. Robert Service indicates how little we yet know about how the urban workers felt in 1917. The problems of investigation are considerable, and it should not be assumed that all contemporary ideas should be accepted at their face value. Stephen Jones focusses on this point when describing how popular support for 'socialism' in Georgia sometimes concealed an undercurrent of Georgian national feeling. Accordingly, the meaning attached to programmes, policies and slogans differed from group to group across the old empire, from sub-group to sub-group and from individual to individual. A connected issue is approached by Robert Service in his account of the workers and their political ideas. He shows that the Bolsheviks modified their public statements with the purpose of maximising their popularity among the working class. Not that Bolshevik public statements were uniform. Strong disagreements were characteristic of political parties in the Revolution, and the Bolsheviks were no exception. The different pronouncements of various Bolsheviks resulted in part from contrasting strategical conceptions. But a deliberate endeavour was made, especially by the central and local leaders, to tailor policies to perceptions of what was likely to be acceptable to working-class opinion. Analytical techniques which are commonly applied by political scientists to the study of late twentieth-century parties should not be witheld from the Bolsheviks.

The Bolshevik party's main efforts in 1917 were devoted to getting support inside the various sectional mass organisations. The Bolsheviks were hoping to capitalise on the extensive enthusiasm in the towns for involvement in politics. Debating, electing and activism of all kinds became a way of life for larger numbers of people in Russia than ever before or ever after until 1985.

Yet only a minority of Petrograd's workers participated in the overthrow of the Provisional Government in October; only a minority had taken part in the various anti-governmental demonstrations in spring, summer and autumn 1917. If this was true of the working class, it was true to an even greater extent of most other social groups. Christopher Read shows that many literary intellectuals regarded the cultivation of the arts as a much more important occupation than involvement in politics. He argues, too, that practical difficulties in everyday life (especially in the obtaining of food) eventually pushed even many apolitical individuals – and no 'group' was more individualistic than the *littérateurs* – into taking a definite viewpoint on the country's politics. As a group there was greater cohesiveness among soldiers and sailors. But their attitudes, as Evan Mawdsley demonstrates, were no less influenced by 'ordinary' matters like the provision of rations. The notion grew up vigorously among them that, unless the government could supply bread, it was not a proper government. Similar sentiments were widespread among other groups. But the danger of alienating the conscripts of the army and the navy was acute since they were equipped with weaponry. Soldiers and sailors, even if they did not rise up against the Provisional Government, could also harm it simply by refusing to rush to its defence. This was not the least important influence on the outcome of 1917. The more we learn about the establishment of the Soviet régime, the more obvious it becomes that Lenin and his colleagues were correct in assuming that power would not fall into and remain in their hands unless they acted decisively and ruthlessly; and that they had to be especially careful to neutralise any possible military counter-coup in the early days of 'soviet power'. Edward Acton emphasises that for several months Bolshevik authority hung in the balance of the fates, and that it was not until the ending of the civil war that the party's grasp on the reins of government became unshakable.

This was sensed by everyone in Russia at the time: John Channon relates that many landlords immediately after October 1917 did not give up hope that their estates would be restored to them. With Kornilov being poised to undertake a counter-revolution in 1917 and with White armies penetrating Soviet-held territory in 1918–1919 it was far from being obvious that victory would go to the Reds. Indeed a cautious approach to questions of land reform was adopted by sections of the peasantry, especially in the border areas. On the other hand, the morale of the peasants in most Russian regions was high; and, even where they were cautious, they were apparently also confident. The same cannot be said for either the upper échelons of the urban middle classes. Howard White shows how, while sympathising with vigorous right-wing policies, a significant number of industrialists and bankers were preoccupied by thoughts of transferring their finances abroad and emigrating.

Thus we have returned to our starting point: namely that the behaviour of large social groups had an enormous impact, both direct and indirect, on the Russian Revolution. Why such a consensus should have arisen among many recent scholars is attributed by Edward Acton to a variety of factors, notably the changes in world politics in the past two decades. He mentions the effects of various phenomena in countries in Western Europe and North America in the 1960s and later; and he highlights the forward strides made by Soviet scholars writing about Soviet history as the result of political reforms in the USSR under Nikita Khrushchev and Mikhail Gorbachev. Contingent circumstances of this kind will no doubt continue to affect historical writings in the years ahead. In the meantime and for the foreseeable future, scholars will need to decide on the implications of the newer data on large social groups in 1917. Much discussion already exists about 'political' in contrast with 'social' history. Somewhat extreme variants in interpretation can nowadays be found. Some writers in the 1980s have continued to treat high politics in 1917 as deserving a near-monopoly of attention in the explanation of the Revolution's development; others, reacting against such treatments, have elevated social processes close to a similar status at the expense of high politics. The first school of thought steers towards a political determinism which annexes social phenomena as subordinate territory. The second abuts on sociological determinism, allowing little decisive autonomy to politics.

For instance, suggestions continue sometimes to be made that the Bolsheviks 'won' virtually exclusively because of their combination of vastly superior organisational skill with their manipulative talents. Supposedly the party hoodwinked the 'masses' and led them by the nose. On the other side of the debate, it has sometimes been implied that the victory of the Bolsheviks had nothing to do with manipulativeness but stemmed all but totally from their development and propagation of policies which directly reflected popular opinion.

But these extremities in interpretation are surely based upon a false dichotomy. For no political event or situation is without its social ramifications. Nor does any social phenomenon lack a political dimension.

Fortunately, fewer and fewer historians engaged in the controversy over political-versus-social historiography would commend either of the two interpretative extremities. There is increasing acceptance that the Bolshevik party in 1917 was a ramshackle contraption and not a finely-tuned motor, and that several policies of the party (such as the transfer of land to the peasants and the rapid and serious opening of a peace campaign) coincided with the wishes of the great majority of the population. Nor can it sensibly be claimed that the 'masses' had no part of their own to play in the disruption and replacement of the Provisional Government's authority. Yet the selectivity of the Bolshevik central leaders in presenting their policies to the public had a manipulative dimension. Indeed Lenin and Trotskii, in arguing for the seizure of power in October, did not make it fully clear even to several of their fellow central leaders that they envisaged a soviet government led by Bolsheviks and devoid of Mensheviks. Consequently the Bolshevik party, while hardly being a machine in Lenin's total control, was nevertheless nudged towards policies that would have been much more difficult to impose if a vote had been taken in advance.

The way forward is not to counterpose 'political' to 'social' history (or, as it is often put somewhat differently, 'history from above' to 'history from below') as if they were mutually exclusive approaches. Scholarship on modern Russian history ought to exploit its advantage in arriving at the political-versus-social controversy after such controversies have already taken place among scholars of English, French and German history. The result of the preceding multi-national historiographical debate has been a widely-agreed conclusion that comprehensive interpretations require the dovetailing of the political and social timbers. Neither can be sawn away without doing damage to the other.

To call for such joinery is merely to declare an objective. There remain several unresolved issues. Among them is one which is basic to all the rest: namely the question about the respective significance to be attached to political and social factors in 1917. We are only at the beginning of this discussion. We do not yet possess a sufficient number of studies on areas which would help to link up 'high politics' with 'low-level social life'. A stronger chain needs to be forged. In the first place, the studies of central political life are not comprehensive. Even deliberations on policy in the Bolshevik Central Committee (which is the most thoroughly investigated of all Petrograd-based political bodies, whether Bolshevik or non-Bolshevik) are only patchily described. Our problems are naturally greater below the level of the supreme political leaderships. Luckily, some research has appeared on Bolsheviks in certain localities. But the lower échelons of other parties are largely uninvestigated; and mass organisations like the soviets

and the trade unions require much more attention, especially outside the
metropolitan districts, than they have received. Similarly, remarkably little
work has yet been published on local state administration. In addition, we
need further research in political sociology. The background of participants
in the Revolution, at whatever level and in whatever place, requires
investigation: their jobs, their parentage, their ethnicity, their age.

All these themes ought to be developed to the accompaniment of
expanded attention to large social groups. This book, while summarising
the achievements of recent scholarship, points to the yawning gaps which
remain. Several such groups have yet to be the subject of a single article.
Ways of life and of feeling have to be charted. The experiences of members
of these groups in 1917, in everyday life at home and at work and at leisure,
need to be identified; and the dimensions of continuity and change in the
maelstrom of Revolution await further necessary enquiry.

Economic, rather than political or social history, is as yet the most
lightly tilled field of scholarship on 1917 (although Soviet studies have
shed invaluable light on fundamental questions). Work is growing in
abundance on the changes in property rights over the year as factory
labour-forces began to impose 'workers' control' and as peasant communes
moved towards land seizures. Less is as yet available on incomes, on the
effects of taxation or even on the food-ration system in the towns. Nor is
there much material on peasant family incomes in 1917 or on the buying
and selling practices of the rural community. It is also vital to map out an
accurate geography of the various social groups across the country. And
what of the propertied élites? How well-off were the rural landlords in
the course of the Revolution? What were the financial circumstances of
industrialists, bankers and the members of the professions? These social
aspects need to be complemented by further research on the general crisis
of the national economy. Statistics on output, trade and supply which are
presently known only in approximate terms must be refined. In addition,
we must ascertain the precise variations in the provinces. It is a massive
project; but only in the light in this future research will so many interesting
and important questions be answerable.

Furthermore, the danger has to be avoided of closing up the Russian
Revolution of 1917 in a national and chronological box. The histories
of other countries in periods of revolutionary upheaval supply crucial
comparative material. So, too, do the histories of countries which did not
undergo revolutions but yet had political and social features or confronted
problems of self-development resembling those of the old Russian empire
in crucial ways.

It is also vital to construct an account of the months between February and October which is interlocked with scholarship on both earlier and later epochs in the history of Russia and adjacent territories. This is a prerequisite for gauging the nature and extent of the uniqueness of the Revolution in the framework of the Russian past; it also affords the data for judging how durable the changes wrought in 1917 turned out to be. While the current trend towards historiographical specialisation is to be welcomed, the compartmentalisation which frequently accompanies it is regrettable. One of the most difficult tasks for historians and social scientists writing on the Russian empire and the Soviet Union is to establish a sense of proportion. The country covers a sixth of the globe's land mass. No other state sprawls over such diversity in its geology, climate, density of population, ethnic composition, and material conditions of human life. Major questions about 1917 are raised, too, in regard to other epochs. What were the relative impacts of 'action from on high' and 'pressure from below' on the historical process? Did the Bolshevik Politburo under either Lenin or his successor Stalin decide everything? Or were phenomena lower down the political system and in the broader strata of society responsible for the various outcomes?

The older traditions of historiography, which are by no means moribund today, stressed the role of the individual to an enormous extent. Several recent writers have reacted against this, stressing the many administrative difficulties faced by the Stalinist central élite in the 1930s in getting policies implemented. Bureaucrats obstructed new policies. There were also technical obstacles: the country's infrastructure of communications was inadequate; the cultural training of officialdom was flimsy. No wonder, in such circumstances, that disorderliness and even outright chaos existed. Debate did not cease even in a Bolshevik party which had formally banned internal factions since 1921. Central politicians contended with each other in struggles over policies.

Yet the task for scholarship is not so much to enquire whether Soviet state and society was disorderly in the 1930s; the answer is plain enough: disorder existed. The really difficult business is to assess the scale of disorderliness. A balanced verdict will be facilitated by reference to the year of the Revolution. The chaos of the 1930s was orderliness incarnate in comparison with the phenomena of 1917. Which local Bolshevik committee dared, under Stalin, to propose its own foreign policy or to challenge the party's economic programme or to mock Stalin? Such daring was common in the early revolutionary period. And ill-run as they were in the Stalin era, how often did the railways and postal services completely break down? Again the scale of the disruptions in 1917 catches the eye. Furthermore, Stalin may well have had to modify several ideas after discussion with his close cronies; but he surely never had the exceptional difficulties confronting Lenin in cajoling his party to agree to seize power in October 1917 or in persuading it to sign the treaty of Brest-Litovsk in March 1918. Stalin mostly had his way in the policies that mattered to him most of the time. It was not for nothing that he was known as a dictator. Nor was Lenin inaccurate in 1921 when he denied that he himself had dictatorial power.

There are many reasons for broaching these controversial matters. They have their own intrinsic importance; but they also deeply pervade the post-1985 renaissance of public debate in the USSR about Soviet history. Mikhail Gorbachev's accession to power has accentuated the need for his country's native historians to address both the 'Lenin question' and the 'Stalin question'. Underlying the two questions is the theme of continuity and discontinuity. The elaboration of satisfactory answers, as this book's contents emphasise, calls for us to look not only at individual politicians but also at the gamut of political, social and economic influences at work in the post-Romanov period. High politics are not enough; we must have sociology and economics (and indeed low politics) as well.

And so to the chapters themselves. We are acutely aware that each of them raises more questions than it answers, and that research remains at a preliminary stage. A unity of purpose existed for us inasmuch as we all intended to summarise the existing historiography and to propose an agenda for future work; and the views of most of us coincide on several basic issues – but by no means on all of them. A degree of mutual accommodation has occurred since the end of the seminar series; but no single general interpretation has been aimed at: thus have the freedoms of Russia in 1917 been extended into the historiography of 1917. We hope that the pleasure we have had in holding the seminar series and in writing our respective chapters is conveyed to the reader. We have tried to make the contents accessible to people who may know only a little about Russian history. Please note that dates are given according to the Julian calendar in official use in Russia until 1918. The scheme of transliteration is in accordance with the practice of *The Slavonic and East European Review* (except for certain famous names which would have looked odd to most pairs of English-reading eyes). Lastly, our thanks are due to the London School of Slavonic and East European Studies which funded the original series; and we look forward to holding another such series on some future anniversary of the Russian Revolution and to discovering whether the enormous scholarly progress achieved in the past decade will have been repeated in years ahead.

2 The Peasants

Maureen Perrie

Until recently, the English-language literature on the peasantry in 1917 consisted virtually exclusively of Lancelot Owen's pioneering but dated work, published in 1937.[1] Since the mid-1970s, however, more studies have become available, the fullest discussion being in the chapters on the peasantry in John Keep's book on the revolution, and in the monograph by Graeme Gill.[2] Marc Ferro and Dorothy Atkinson have dealt more briefly with the peasantry in 1917, Ferro as part of a general social history of the revolution and Atkinson in the context of a study of the commune from 1905 to 1930.[3] George Yaney's idiosyncratic contribution to the subject is rather less than helpful: his discussion of 1917 is entitled 'Obscurity in the countryside', and stresses the essential 'unknowability' of the peasantry in this period.[4]

Soviet historians have naturally paid considerable attention to the peasantry, although as in most areas of Soviet historiography the gap between the tenth and the fortieth anniversaries of the revolution saw the publication of little which was of interest or value.[5] The basis of post-Stalin historiography on the agrarian revolution was laid by the veteran scholar P. N. Pershin, whose two-volume study of the period 1905–1918 was first published in Ukrainian in 1959–1962.[6] In the 1950s and 1960s many local and regional studies of the peasant revolution were undertaken by Soviet historians, and useful new works of synthesis, based on these researches, have been published since the early 1970s.[7]

These studies, both Western and Soviet, are concerned with various aspects of the rural revolution: the agrarian policy of the Provisional Government; the creation in the countryside of food and land committees, and of peasant organisations and soviets; and the agrarian programmes of the various political parties and their organisation and support in the villages. Central to most discussions, however, are the events which the Soviets term the 'peasant movement', and which Western historians refer to as 'agrarian disorders' or 'rural unrest': namely the actions which the peasants undertook against the existing agrarian order and its social relations. The 'peasant movement' in this sense will comprise the main focus of the present chapter.

The basic data on peasant disturbances consist in the militia reports, which were published in 1927 by Kotel'nikov and Meller. These were necessarily incomplete and selective, and show a total of somewhat over 4000 incidents.[8] More recent Soviet work in local archives has led to considerable and rapid inflation of estimates of the total number of incidents. Dorothy Atkinson cites Soviet works of the 1970s which give estimates ranging from 5416 (in 1971) to 11 364 (in 1977);[9] Malyavskii's book of 1981 has gone on to identify 16 298 incidents.[10]

The absolute number of incidents is in itself, of course, of little significance, since the scale of an 'incident', or its very definition, could vary so greatly. It would be more useful for gauging the extent of the agrarian unrest to know the number of estates or villages which were involved, but the sources do not seem able to provide this kind of information. Atkinson tells us that, by the end of the summer, 'over three-quarters of all districts in the country were caught up in the peasant movement, and in the more populous central regions scarcely a one remained unscathed.'[11] And yet, as Keep among others has pointed out,[12] only one village or estate in an administrative district needed to be affected for the whole district to be counted as 'disturbed'. Indirect evidence of the extent of peasant infringement of private landowners' rights is provided by an estimate, based on incomplete data for six provinces, that 15 per cent of private land had been acquired by peasants between March and October.[13] However dubious it may be, this figure is nonetheless useful in helping us to put the peasant movement of March to October into perspective, indicating as it does that the main attack on private landownership came after rather than before the October Decree on Land.

Soviet historians have displayed a concern with the periodisation of the peasant movement. The militia statistics were organised simply month by month, according to the established practice of the officials of the Provisional Government.[14] Atkinson has tabulated the monthly militia figures of 1917 against those of three Soviet works of the 1970s, and concludes that in spite of the constant upward revisions in absolute terms, a roughly constant picture emerges of the pattern over time: namely 'a steady increase in peasant activity into July, a slackening in August, and a sharp climb to new heights in October'.[15] Soviet secondary literature until the mid-1970s tended to use a four-fold periodisation which reflected this monthly pattern of incidents: the beginning of the movement in March; the steady growth of the movement from April to July; the decline in August; and the growing peasant uprising of September and October.[16] Kostrikin, however, partly on the basis of his new and fuller data for some provinces, has argued that the decline in August was not as great as the earlier statistics had implied.[17] Because of this, he put forward a new periodisation, which has the additional advantage, for a Soviet historian, of corresponding to Lenin's periodisation of the development of the revolution as a whole – namely the period of peaceful development, March to June; and the period of preparation for the armed uprising, July to October.[18] Malyavskii agrees with Kostrikin's periodisation and its statistical justification, but he further divides each of these two main periods into two sub-stages, as follows: March; April to June; July to August; and September to October.[19] Graeme Gill, by contrast, opts for a tripartite periodisation based on the changing political composition of the Provisional Government: the spring honeymoon (March to April); the summer upheaval (May to August); and the dénouement (September to October).[20]

As well as tabulating the number of incidents month by month, or period by period, exponents of the quantitative approach to the peasant movement divide the incidents territorially. The militia statistics were organised by province, in alphabetical order; the Soviet editors of the reports, however, organised their material by geographical-economic regions (Central Agricultural, Mid-Volga, etc.),[21] and this sort of regional classification has been common since then. Shestakov's calculations, based on the militia reports, showed the highest number of incidents to have been reported from the Central Black Earth region (with 1034, about a quarter of the total), followed by the Mid-Volga (902) and Belorussia (659). The smallest number of incidents (18 out of 4410) was reported from the North, where of course there was virtually no gentry landownership; next came the Baltic area, which was affected by the war, and reported only 72 incidents; the Amur region of Siberia reported 143; the remaining regions each reported between 200 and 400 incidents.[22] The inflation of totals by new data does not seem to have significantly altered this picture. Kostrikin's 1977 article still gives first place to the Central Agricultural Region, with 2270 out of 11 364 incidents, followed by the Mid-Volga with 2014. His third place however is taken by the right-bank Ukraine, with 1794 incidents, where Shestakov recorded only 284. The inflated numbers for some regions probably reflect the varying degrees of assiduity of local Soviet historians in collecting new data, as well as real underestimates by the local authorities in 1917: Kostrikin's figure for the right-bank Ukraine, for example, includes the disproportionately high figure of 1177 incidents for Podol'e province alone.[23] The geographical coverage of the new studies is in any case uneven: Malyavskii's total of 16 298 incidents supplements the 1917 militia data with the fruits of Soviet researches for only 15 out of the 48 non-occupied provinces of European Russia.[24]

The third dimension of the quantitative approach to the peasant movement, and arguably the most important, although in many ways the most problematic, is the form or type of unrest. The Kotel'nikov and Meller collection reproduces the categories used by the officials in 1917 itself; unfortunately for the sake of comparative consistency, however, these categories changed from month to month as the movement itself developed. By September, 'infringements of land rights' alone were classified under the following headings: destruction of estates (*razgrom*); arson; seizures of estates, of arable land, of meadows and hayfields, of forests, of working livestock and equipment, and of crops; illegal woodcutting; prevention of the cutting and transportation of timber; forced renting; removal of labour; and 'other wilful actions'. Most of these categories were subdivided into 'organised' and 'unorganised' forms, giving a total of 21 types of action.[25] Historians who have used these data have simplified the categories: Shestakov, for example, identifies only nine types.[26]

Soviet historians have subsequently developed increasingly elaborate and sophisticated typologies for the forms of peasant unrest. Kostrikin proposes 32 forms, under four main headings: direct actions for the restructuring of land relations; indirect actions directed towards the restructuring of land relations; various economic sanctions against landowners; and political actions.[27] Malyavskii puts forward an elaborate scheme comprising no less than 44 forms of the peasant movement, organised under six main headings: I. seizure of land, the means of working it, livestock and foodstuffs; II. the struggle against the government's punitive expeditions; III. limitation of property rights of landowners and forest owners; IV. peasant terror; V. movement of agricultural workers; and VI. anti-kulak actions and the struggle against Stolypinite separators.[28]

Two points are perhaps worthy of note at this stage in connection with the classification of forms of peasant unrest. First of all, it is very difficult to classify an incident without an understanding of the context in which it occurred – a context which is not always clear from the sources, particularly when these are in the form of the terse and often tendentious militia reports. Peasant demands for lower rents, for example, might in one context simply represent attempts to improve their conditions within the framework of existing landownership relations; in another context (perhaps more common in 1917, as we shall see) they could represent indirect attempts to undermine and ultimately overthrow private landownership.

Secondly, most attempts to categorise the peasant movement relate exclusively to incidents involving land relationships. But, as George Yaney has trenchantly pointed out, much rural violence in 1917 was concerned with – he actually says it 'centred on' – the struggle for food

TABLE 1　Forms of the peasant movement in 1917

Form	March	April	May	June	July	August	September	October	Total
Destructive raids on estates (*razgromy*)	29	11	11	7	5	16	127	144	350
Seizures of estate land	3	51	59	131	237	167	166	116	930
Seizures of meadows and hayfields	–	1	14	110	238	113	71	69	616
Seizures of equipment	–	10	7	68	94	26	35	27	267
Seizures of crops	–	–	–	–	60	68	84	22	234
Illicit woodcutting	24	30	45	119	150	89	187	280	924
Rent disagreements	–	4	1	14	27	3	10	5	64
Removal of labour	2	22	41	62	79	34	27	9	276
Other types of movement	18	87	72	47	222	166	125	71	808
Total	76	216	250	558	1112	682	832	743	4469

Source: A. V. Shestakov, *Ocherki po sel'skomu khozyaistvu i krest'yanskomu dvizheniyu v gody voiny i pered Oktyabrem 1917 g.* (Leningrad, 1927), p. 142.

rather than the struggle for land (although in practice the two cannot be easily separated). Yaney lists the following types of food-oriented violence: fights between hoarders and government agencies; attacks on estates to force them to cultivate land or give up their grain; attacks by food-collecting gangs on villages; fights between army and civilian grain purchasers; and fights between grain purchasers from different guberniyas and uezds.[29] While Yaney does not himself try to quantify these types of action, he is probably right to stress that they were an important element in 1917, although they do not feature to any significant extent in Soviet (or Western) accounts of the 'peasant movement'.

How did the nature of the peasant movement change over time? Shestakov tabulated his 4469 incidents by form of movement and by month. This showed that the most common form over the eight-month period was the seizure of estate land (930), closely followed by illegal woodcutting (924). 'Miscellaneous', rather oddly, came next (808), then seizures of meadows and hayfields (616). Destructive raids on estates were fourth overall (350), but their incidence increased dramatically in September and October, when 271 of the 350 incidents were concentrated, and when they constituted 15 per cent and 19 per cent respectively of the total number of incidents in these months, as compared with less than 7 per cent of the total over the entire period (Table 2.1).

Surprisingly, perhaps, in view of the enormous effort which Soviet historians have put in recent decades into the collection of new data on the peasant movement, no complete new cross-tabulation of incidents, by period, by type and by region, on a nationwide basis, has yet been produced to replace the calculations made in the 1920s on the basis of the militia reports of 1917. The difficulty lies not only in the incomplete geographical coverage of the new investigations, but also in the researchers' lack of agreement on the categories to be employed, which means that the data of the various local studies are not fully compatible one with another. Kostrikin in a recent article asserts that recent data on the forms of the peasant movement can be easily compared for only a handful of provinces.[30] In a limited exercise relating to ten provinces for March to June, he attempts to compare the new data with that of the militia reports, classifying the incidents under five broad headings. Both sets of statistics show the 'seizure of estates, arable land, meadows, forests, working livestock and equipment' to have been the most common form of the movement, but the new data elevate timber offences to second place (Table 2.2). Kostrikin's analysis of the changing forms of the movement over time, for nine provinces from May to October, shows a similar pattern to Shestakov's tabulation of the militia data, with a significant increase in

TABLE 2   The development of the peasant movement, March–June 1917
(for 10 provinces: upper figures are from the militia data of 1917; lower figures are Kostrikin's calculations)

Form	March		April		May		June		Total	
	No.	%	No.	%	No.	%	No.	%	No.	%
Seizures of estates, arable land, meadows, woods and equipment	– 41	– 41.4	22 162	44.9 33.0	24 266	37.5 38.3	82 359	59.4 45.6	128 828	50.6 39.9
Seizures of land for rental	– 14	– 14.1	1 74	2.0 14.9	1 51	1.6 7.5	7 73	5.0 9.3	9 212	3.6 10.2
Removal of labourers and POWS from estates	– 15	– 15.1	5 89	10.2 18.1	17 85	26.5 12.2	19 42	13.8 5.3	41 231	16.2 11.2
Prohibition of the cutting and transport of timber	2 22	100 22.2	4 128	8.2 26.1	4 215	6.2 31.1	11 217	8.0 27.6	21 582	8.3 28.1
Other actions	– 7	– 7.2	17 39	34.7 7.9	18 76	28.2 10.9	19 96	13.8 12.2	54 218	21.3 10.6
Total	2 99	100 100	49 492	100 100	64 693	100 100	138 787	100 100	253 2071	100 100

SOURCE: V. I. Kostrikin, 'Krest'yanskoe dvizhenie nakanune Oktyabrya', in *Oktyabr' i sovetskoe krest'yanstvo, 1917–1927 gg.*, (Moscow, 1977), p. 24.

the incidence of the 'liquidation of estates' in September and October.[31]

In any case, it is doubtful whether a new overall quantitative analysis of the peasant movement, by form, by month and by province, would significantly advance the cause of historical understanding and explanation of the behaviour of the peasantry in 1917. Too much of the work of the quantifiers involves excessively abstract schematisations, with little attempt being made to understand what their behaviour meant to the peasants themselves, or how it was influenced by the broader social, economic and political developments of 1917. Study of the peasantry in 1917 seems to lag behind that of the peasantry in earlier periods, by both Western and Soviet historians, where there has recently been a much more imaginative attempt to empathise with the peasantry and to understand the attitudes and mentality which underlay their behaviour.[32] There are encouraging signs, however, that Soviet historians are now recognising the limitations of the quantitative approach. The best of the recent studies which I have consulted is by Malyavskii, who relegates statistics to an appendix and examines the various forms of movement in an essentially qualitative manner, displaying an unusual sensitivity to the contextual significance of the various forms of peasant action.[33] The account which follows draws heavily on his material and typology, while presenting it within a somewhat different interpretative framework.

It is difficult to explain the peasant movement of 1917 purely in terms of specific economic grievances. Some émigré historians have even argued that the economic position of the peasantry improved during the war;[34] and, although their views have been attacked by Soviet historians,[35] the question of peasant living standards in this period remains open. There is no doubt, on the other hand, that in some areas there was real hardship among the peasantry, with pre-war problems of land-hunger and exploitative rents and wages being exacerbated by the wartime effects of inflation, requisitioning of livestock, and conscription.

Long-standing peasant aspirations for the landowners' land, which had manifested themselves most recently in the revolutionary years 1905–1907 were of course still unsatisfied in 1917. Antagonism between peasants and landowners, however, had been largely overshadowed in the last pre-war years by disputes within the peasantry itself, arising out of the Stolypin agrarian reforms of 1906 onwards, which encouraged individual peasant households to separate from the land commune. Market forces continued to redistribute land from gentry to peasantry: between 1905 and 1914 around ten million desyatinas of private land were purchased by the peasants, most of it coming from the noble landowners, who lost about a fifth of their land in this period.[36]

Wartime conditions appear to have done little to exacerbate relations between peasants and landowners. Anfimov's figures show a decline in peasant conflicts with landed gentry from 85 in 1914 to 25 in 1915 and 16 in 1916.[37] The peasant economy in fact became less dependent on that of the landed gentry in the course of the war, as the effects of conscription reduced the numbers of men who had previously relied on the large landowners for land to rent or for waged employment.[38] A considerable amount of gentry land was uncultivated by the beginning of 1917, although there is uncertainty as to whether this stemmed from the lack of available peasants to work it, or whether the rents and wages offered were inadequate to tempt the peasants. Land-rents fell during the war, in real terms, but it seems that more land could have been worked if the rents had been lowered further.[39] Certainly in 1917, as we shall see, a major demand of the peasantry was for a reduction in rents, and when the rents were reduced, often by the use or threat of violence against the landowners, there appeared to be no shortage of peasants willing to plough and sow the land.

Thus it seems likely that the main cause of the peasant movement of 1917 was the February revolution itself. The fall of tsarism revived peasant aspirations of a 'black repartition' (or a peasant-led redistribution of all agricultural land) now that the regime which had supported large landed property had ceased to exist. The revolution created an atmosphere in which the peasants felt able to test the boundaries of what was now possible and permissible within the new framework of the Provisional Government. And the presence of large tracts of uncultivated estate land in many areas, in wartime conditions of food shortage in the towns, was to provide the peasantry with an unprecedented pretext and opportunity to undermine gentry landownership.

There is general agreement that the peasantry in the countryside (as opposed to peasants in uniform) played little part in the February revolution. The first reported cases of peasant unrest occurred in March. Indeed, according to Shestakov's analysis of the militia data, there was a higher incidence of violent attacks on estates (*razgromy*) in March, in both absolute and relative terms, than in the months from April to August.[40] This March wave of agrarian violence can be explained partly in terms of a settling of old scores. Many of the incidents occurred in areas where suppression of the peasant movement of 1905–1907 had been particularly brutal; and the estates of landowners with German surnames were often singled out for arson attacks – evidence of chauvinist attitudes intensified by the war.[41] In Simbirsk province a landowner named Gel'shert was lynched by a crowd which claimed to believe that he was a traitor.[42]

After this initial spate of violence, however (which paralleled similar violent incidents in the town and in the armed forces in March), events in the countryside were more peaceful throughout the spring and summer of 1917. This in part reflected the hopes which the peasants placed in the Provisional Government for a resolution of the land question; the period was also characterised by actions which the peasants claimed to believe to be in the national interest. The peasantry seemed to feel the need for some kind of appearance of legitimacy for their actions. This aspect of the peasant movement of 1917 has been noted in passing by some historians,[43] and it was also commented upon by contemporaries. A well placed observer, A. V. Peshekhonov, the agrarian expert who led the Popular Socialist party and was Minister of Food Supplies in summer 1917, remarked that in the first months of 1917 the peasants cloaked their desires for land seizures with expressions of concern for state welfare and necessity:

> They seized land from the landed gentry on the pretext that it would remain unsown or that the crop would not be harvested; they confiscated livestock and implements, insisting that they were unused, and so on. At the same time they endeavoured in every way to characterise their actions as justified, and undertook them, for the most part, only according to resolutions of the district (*volost'*), land and other committees.[44]

The peasants' apparent striving for legitimacy in 1917 is entirely consistent with patterns of peasant behaviour long before the revolution, when they frequently claimed to be acting according to the will of the tsar. Historians have speculated about the sincerity of the peasants' professed 'faith in the tsar'.[45] Similarly, scepticism has been expressed as to whether the peasants in 1917 genuinely believed they were acting patriotically and legitimately. 'Undoubtedly,' Peshekhonov commented,

> very many peasants endeavoured in completely good faith to be guided by the common interests of the people and the state and were sincerely convinced that they were acting completely correctly. But it is also indubitable that in many, and perhaps the majority of cases, they were guided mainly, if not exclusively, by their own class interests and by selfish sectional and even personal considerations, often understanding only too well, or at least dimly sensing, the entire illegality of their actions.[46]

What Peshekhonov fails to mention is that the peasants' actions could often seem to have been justified by the Provisional Government's own policies.

On 11 April, for example, the government, concerned with the food situation, issued a resolution on the maximisation of the sown area. Whilst condemning violent actions against landowners, this document gave the local food-supply committees the right to compulsorily transfer unsown land to local farmers to rent at a 'just rate'.[47] The resolution thus provided the peasants with a patriotic motive for attempting to take over uncultivated gentry land at advantageously low rents. Sometimes the 'just rate' for renting idle land was established at zero; sometimes it was at the level necessary only for the payment of land taxes. Often the rent collected was not paid to the landowners, but retained by the committees themselves: in all of these cases, the provisions of the resolution of 11 April served as pretexts for *de facto* peasant seizure of unsown lands.[48]

The spring of 1917 saw the creation of a vast and complex array of rural organisations. The first committees to be formed were peasant executive committees at the lower administrative level, the *volost'* (or district). These emerged in many areas as *ad hoc* bodies in the course of or in the aftermath of the February revolution, but they were recognised by the Provisional Government in an instruction of 20 March. A hierarchy of food supply committees, down to *volost'* level, was created on 25 March; and a parallel network of land committees on 21 April. In practice, at *volost'* level the food-supply and land committees were virtually indistinguishable from the peasant executive committees.[49]

From April onwards, the peasant movement came to focus on gentry land which the peasants claimed to regard as idle, and hence as subject to appropriation by local peasant committees. In some cases the peasants demanded that the reduced levels of rent which had been agreed for land unworked since 1916 should also be charged for lands which they were currently renting. If the landowner refused to accept the lower rent, that land was declared to be idle, and was taken over in the same way as genuinely uncultivated land.[50] Not only arable land was taken over in this way. In Belorussia and the north-west provinces, former arable land which had been rented to the peasants, but which had been converted to pasture by the landowners before the war, was declared to be fallow land, and was taken over and returned to its former use.[51]

Sometimes estate arable land, directly cultivated by the landowner with hired labour, was also taken over by the peasants in this period. In these cases, the peasants' approach was to deprive the landowners of the labour force on their estates. Prisoners of war and refugees who had been extensively employed on the large estates, to compensate for the shortages of local peasant labour during the war, were transferred to work on the peasants' own communal holdings. This not only benefitted the peasants directly, but in some cases the estate arable land was consequently classified as idle, and appropriated by the committees in the same way as rented land.[52] Rumours were current in 1917 that estate land of this kind would not be subject to confiscation and redistribution by the Constituent Assembly (even the Bolsheviks' agrarian programme envisaged the preservation intact of capitalist estates under technical or commercial crops). It was therefore in the interests of the peasants to minimise the extent of estate arable land. Conversely, there were cases of landowners trying to extend their directly cultivable arable land at the expense of land rented to peasants, with consequent conflicts ensuing.[53]

The extension of peasant land at the expense of that of the landowners led to peasant seizure not just of arable land, but also of the means of working it – agricultural implements, draught animals and machinery.[54] Again, this might be justified in the same way as the seizure of land claimed to be idle: as a means to the patriotic end of maximising sown area and food production. The numerous cases of peasant expropriation of meadow and pasture land were sometimes linked with the take-over of gentry land and draught-animals: the extra pasture and hayfield was necessary to feed the animals expropriated in order to work the land which the peasants had seized.[55] It was comparatively rare in this period, however, for the peasants to take over an entire estate; in the few cases where this did happen, as with the property of a certain Ustinov in Penza province, the estate seems to have been genuinely 'ruined' and deserted.[56]

All of these practices were given an additional impulse by Chernov's instruction to the land committees of 16 July 1917. This to some extent restated the resolution of 11 April on the extension of the sown area, but it also expanded it considerably. It again allowed the local food-supply committees to take over unworked arable land, but they were now to pass it to the *volost'* land committees to dispose of. The land could either be worked by the land committees themselves, or rented to the local peasants at a rate to be determined by 'voluntary agreement' between the peasants and landowners, with the higher-level *uezd* and *guberniya* land committees acting as arbitrators in case of any disputes.[57] Chernov's instruction also made provision for prisoners of war to be transferred from work on gentry estates to work on peasant lands, where the food-supply committees regarded this as desirable.[58] The document permitted land committees, in consultation with the food-supply committees, to take over draught animals and equipment which were not being used by landowners, and to transfer them to 'those who need them', in the interests of maximising the provisioning of the army and the civilian population.[59]

Although the instruction was carefully framed to condemn arbitrary and unauthorised peasant actions, in many ways it seemed to legitimise the practices of indirect and surreptitious land seizure which had been under way since the spring, and it served as an additional boost to such actions. Chernov himself appeared to recognise the danger of this, when he included in the text of the instruction of the warning that the responsibility for maximising the harvest was being given to the food-supply committees *'for the sake of the maintenance of important state interests*, and not in order to fortify the peasants in their struggle against private landowner-ship'.[60] Not surprisingly this document, which could be published by the Socialist-Revolutionary party leader and Minister for Agriculture only after the Kadets had resigned from the Provisional Government at the beginning of July, was condemned by the landowners as an attempt to undermine private property. Interestingly, however, most Soviet historians are either silent about the influence of the Chernov instruction on the development of the peasant movement, or see it as designed primarily to support the large landowners.[61] This perverse interpretation derives, of course, from Lenin's view of the 'rump' Provisional Government of July as being counter-revolutionary because of its suppression of the Bolsheviks after the July Days.

The Chernov instruction was concerned not only with measures to bring unworked arable land under cultivation, but also, and more immediately, with the collection of the summer hay and grain harvest. Throughout 1917 the pattern of peasant actions was influenced by seasonal factors. Land appropriated by the peasants in April and May could still be ploughed for the spring sowing;[62] from the early summer onwards, when uncultivated land was taken over, it was prepared for winter sowing.[63] Conflicts over hayfields and pasture began to emerge as a serious issue in June, with the beginning of the haymaking season, and reached a peak in July (Table 2.1). The Chernov instruction may well have contributed to these conflicts. The land committees were permitted to transfer to the peasants, for an agreed rent, below the market rate, those hayfields which the landowners could not cut themselves. The hay harvested from these fields was to be made available to the army at fixed prices, through the supply board,[64] but it seems likely that the peasants took advantage of the situation to increase their own supplies of fodder.

Conflicts over forests and woodlands had been another area of dispute since the spring of 1917. Prices for timber had increased significantly during the war, because of the increased demand for construction materials for fortifications, as well as the use of wood as a fuel substitute for oil and coal. Private landowners were extensively cutting for commercial and speculative sale timber which the local peasants regarded as theirs by right. Peasant committees began to establish control over timber-cutting from the spring of 1917[65] and this practice was sanctioned by Chernov's July instruction, which empowered the local land committees to ensure that no 'depredatory' tree-felling took place, and that sufficient timber was available for the needs of the local peasants at prices which they could afford.[66] The militia reports indicate an increase in wood-cutting offences in June and July, when timber was presumably required for construction, and a further increase in September and October, when fuel supplies were laid in for the winter (Table 2.1).

The main agrarian concern of the government in the summer of 1917 was of course the grain harvest. A state grain monopoly had been declared by the Provisional Government on 25 March, and the resolution of 11 April had placed all sown land under protection of the local authorities; Malyavskii plausibly suggests that the peasants interpreted these measures to mean that private property in grain had been abolished, and hence that they had a right to dispose of the landowners' harvest.[67] Chernov's instruction of 16 July stated that grain which private landowners were unable to harvest themselves was to be harvested by the *volost'* (district) food-supply committees, where necessary making use of prisoners of war and troops to supplement local peasant labour. The grain was to be supplied to the state at fixed prices,[68] but in practice the peasants were likely to keep the crop for themselves. The instruction stressed that in no circumstances were the landowners to be prevented from harvesting their grain,[69] and this point was restated even more forcefully in an order from the Food Minister, Peshekhonov, of 18 July.[70] From the list of peasant actions which Peshekhonov condemned, such as seizing crops by force, or demanding payment for harvesting in kind rather than in cash, it is clear that the peasants were trying to obtain the largest possible share of the landowners' harvest for themselves.[71]

Instances of crop seizure reported by the militia increased from 60 in July to 68 in August and 84 in September (Table 2.1). In most cases, however, peasant appropriation of the landowners' harvest did not involve complete or direct seizure. Often the peasants demanded payment in kind for harvesting of one-third of the crop (the going rate before 1917 having been only one-tenth or one-twelfth).[72] In the Ukraine there were cases of the peasants taking one-third of the estates' crops for themselves, allocating a further third for the army, and leaving the landowner one-third to dispose of himself.[73] There were also cases of peasants appropriating grain stored in barns from the harvest of 1916, paying the landowner only the early summer fixed price or less.[74]

The Chernov instruction of 16 July is very revealing of the dilemmas faced by the Provisional Government with regard to the peasantry in 1917. The primary concern of the government was to guarantee the food supply to the cities and to the army; the satisfaction of the peasants' food and land needs was always secondary and subordinate to that. But in order to attempt to maximise the sown area, the government had to make concessions to the peasantry, to enable them to take over and work land which would otherwise have stood idle. Thus the peasants were able to take advantage of measures designed to remedy the food-supply situation, in order to extend their land-holdings. Yet the peasant take-over of gentry land did little to improve food supplies. There are even some reports of peasant allotment land being left unworked while the peasants established their claims to gentry land.[76] And the land which was taken over by the peasants tended to be used by them for their own consumption and subsistence needs, rather than for production for the market. This was particularly true when the land was appropriated by the poorer peasants.

The problems of disadvantageous terms of trade between town and countryside, which had affected food supplies before the February revolution, intensified in 1917. Peasants were reluctant to part with their grain for low fixed prices, especially when paper money was subject to rapid depreciation, and there was a shortage of industrial consumer goods at affordable prices. The situation was exacerbated by extensive crop failures in the Black-Earth area in the summer of 1917 – a problem which seems largely attributable to adverse climatic conditions, although the general economic, social and political disruption of the country may also have played a part. In this situation, even the doubling of fixed prices for grain at the end of August had little effect on the food-supply situation. The peasants seem to have aimed to retain as large a proportion of the harvest as possible in the villages and under their control. In many areas, peasants opposed the transport of local grain outside the boundaries of the *volost'* or *uezd*.[76] This aspect of the peasant movement clearly reflected the interests of those peasants who were net purchasers of grain. In a summer of crop failures these were obviously a higher proportion of the rural population than in a year of good harvest. (The question of the role of different strata of the peasantry is discussed more fully below, in the section on the 'second social war'.)

In the late summer and autumn of 1917, direct peasant incursions on gentry landownership increased in proportion to 'indirect' or 'surreptitious' take-overs. Possibly, as peasant disillusionment with the Provisional Government grew, there was less concern with the appearance of government legitimation of peasant actions. As the peasantry became more organised and more self-confident, the resolutions of local and national congresses of peasant soviets and other peasant organisations in favour of the transfer of gentry land to the peasants served the same function of legitimation. In addition, growing attempts by the Provisional Government to use military force to restore order in the countryside, particularly in July and August, highlighted the conflict of interests between peasants and government. The total number of incidents declined in August – a development which is usually attributed to the combined effects of government repression and peasant preoccupation with field-work in that month. Shestakov's analysis of the militia reports showed that the number of destructive raids on estates, however, which had declined between April and July, began to increase again in August (Table 2.1). Kostrikin's new data, too, lead him to conclude that although the total number of incidents declined slightly in August, the proportion of destructive raids on estates and of attacks on landed gentry increased.[77] This process continued in September and October, when violent and destructive incidents increased significantly. It must be noted, however, that these violent incidents in September and October were very localised, spreading from Tambov, in the central agricultural region, to the neighbouring provinces of Ryazan', Penza, Orel, Kursk, Tula and Nizhnii Novgorod.[78]

The first violent incident in Tambov province in the late summer was on 24 August, when the estate of Prince Boris Vyazemskii was raided by a mob of 5000 peasants. Vyazemskii himself was arrested by the crowd, and murdered by soldiers from a troop-train at a nearby station. The peasants subsequently raided the neighbouring estate of the Vel'yamin family.[79] (The Vyazemskiis and the Vel'yamins were amongst the oldest aristocratic families in Russia.) Further attacks on estates took place, particularly in Kozlov uezd, where two peasants were shot by a landowner named Romanov. (As one source describes this Romanov as a former teacher, it is unlikely that he was related to the royal family.). Romanov was murdered by the peasants, in a revenge attack, and in the following days 57 gentry estates and 13 kulak farms were raided in Tambov province alone, before the authorities succeeded in restoring order.[80] Cases of looting and arson were common.[81] It is not clear whether or how the peasants legitimised these actions, but it is not impossible that the post-Kornilov rhetoric of imminent counter-revolution played a part. Losing hope in obtaining the land from the Provisional Government, and fearful of being deprived of the gains they had made since February, the peasants on the eve of October were increasingly resorting, as they had in 1905, to their 'own means' of 'smoking out' the landowners, by destroying the property base of private landownership.

Finally, let us look briefly at the vexed question of divisions within the peasantry in 1917, or what the Soviets call the 'second social war' in the countryside. The classic Leninist analysis of the agrarian revolution identifies the 'first social war' as a struggle of the peasantry as a whole against the gentry landowners for the liquidation of the remnants of feudalism in the countryside; the 'second social war' comprises the struggle of rural proletarians against capitalist farming, whether it is conducted by gentry or by kulak landowners. This is quite a neat schema: but, as even Soviet historians now recognise, reality was rather more complex than the formula recognises.

The issue of the 'second social war' is conventionally, and conveniently, viewed under two separate headings: firstly, the movement of agricultural labourers; secondly, actions against kulaks and separators. The quantification of instances of the 'second social war' is even more problematic than that of the first, since neither of its forms was recognised by the compilers of the statistics based on the militia reports. Attempts have, however, been made by Soviet historians to quantify it and to compare it with the first social war: the results of their efforts, however, are often inconsistent and contradictory. Dubrovskii's estimate, based on the militia data of 1917, was that actions against landed gentry comprised 84.1 per cent of the total number of rural incidents between March and October; actions against kulaks and separators, 6.3 per cent; and actions by agricultural labourers, 1.6 per cent (the residue comprised: conflicts with the authorities, police and troops, 4.1 per cent; struggle against the clergy, 3 per cent; and miscellaneous, 0.9 per cent).[82] Subsequent researches by Soviet historians have increased both the total number of incidents in the 'second social war' and their weight in the peasant movement as a whole (with estimates ranging from about 20 per cent to 30 per cent for various regions), and they stress that the scale of conflicts within the peasantry intensified in the course of 1917.[83] More recently, however, Malyavskii has argued for an even higher proportion of incidents belonging to the second social war. Not only does he assert that incidents of the movement of agricultural labourers and of actions against separators have been underestimated in the past, but he argues that many other cases of divisions and conflicts within the peasantry should also be regarded as aspects of the second social war. Such a recalculation, he suggests, would indicate that over the entire period from March to October, incidents of the second social war exceeded those of the first. Nevertheless, he concludes – in good Leninist fashion – that even so, the first social war was of primary significance in 1917, since the proportion of landed gentry affected by peasant actions was higher than that of kulaks attacked by poorer peasants.[84]

In general, I am impressed by Malyavskii's approach – not because I think that concepts such as the first and second social wars and their relative importance have much significance outside the realms of ideology – but rather because his material highlights the complexity of the situation in the countryside, and the conflicting interests of different groups of peasants in different situations. Let us look in more detail at this.

Agricultural labourers as such were an important social category only in some areas of the country, mainly on the western periphery, and especially in the Baltic provinces, Belorussia and parts of the Ukraine, where capitalist commercial farming was most developed. It was only in these areas that there were significant cases of separate organisation of agricultural labourers (or 'batraks') into unions, committees and even soviets, as recommended by the Bolsheviks in 1917. The batraks' demands were mainly for improvements in wages and conditions; the demand for the eight-hour day, in conditions of labour shortage, was essentially a demand for higher wages through overtime payments. At harvest time the threat of a strike was often enough to produce concessions from the landowners; but there were also cases of actual strikes, and even isolated cases of 'batrak control' or even complete take-over of estates, with or without the sanction of the local food-supply or land committees. Such actions by agricultural labourers could be directed against both gentry and kulak enterprises, although they were more common on gentry estates.[85]

Conflicts between the communal peasantry and those who had broken away from the commune to form separate farms as a result of the Stolypin reforms were another aspect of the so-called 'second social war' in 1917. Such peasants were often forced to rejoin the commune, and their land was redivided among the communal peasants.[86] The Stolypin reforms were suspended by the Provisional Government on 28 June, which may have encouraged peasants to believe that it was now legitimate to take over separators' plots.[87] In fact, however, the resolution made no provision for the abolition of separate farms – not least because many of these farms, like the gentry estates, produced primarily for the market, and food supply was still the government's main preoccupation. Not all separators, however, were kulaks in the sense of commercial farmers employing hired labour: some were poor subsistence farmers like their communal neighbours, as even some Soviet historians recognise. The movement against separators was thus not primarily an anti-capitalist movement, nor did it necessarily reflect the 'patriarchal-communal' attitudes of the peasantry, but it may often have originated in resentments that the separators had often been allocated the best pieces of village land.[88] But if not all separators were kulaks, it was equally true that not all kulaks were separators. Many kulak farmers conducted their economy not on land which had been separated from the commune since 1906, but on privately purchased land. Such peasant landowners were often subject to the same types of attack as gentry landowners in 1917: for example, direct and indirect land seizures; removal of labour; confiscation of animals and equipment.[89]

Sometimes, however, and particularly in cases where the villages were less differentiated internally, as in the Central Agricultural Region, the most prosperous peasants in a village participated alongside their poorer neighbours in a combined attack on the gentry estates (thus typifying Lenin's 'first social war').[90] In many ways, as the experience of 1905 had shown, the richer peasants were at an advantage over the poorer peasants in such attacks. Where manor houses and outbuildings were looted, the kulaks had more carts and horses to carry away the booty; when land was appropriated, they had the equipment and draught animals to work more of it.[91] One of the most interesting and unusual aspects of Malyavskii's study, however, is his demonstration and documentation of the process by which in the course of 1917 the poorer peasants attempted to combat the initial advantages which the kulaks had in the assault on gentry landownership. The poorer peasants sought to acquire priority for themselves in the acquisition of gentry land, and where they lacked draught animals and equipment, they led the movement to confiscate and share out the landowners' inventory. The labour of prisoners of war, forcibly removed from the gentry estates, was often made available to soldiers' families whose households were suffering from a shortage of manpower. This process was facilitated by the growing dominance of poorer peasants in the local committees, which had tended to be dominated by the richer peasants in the months immediately following the February revolution.[92]

These equalising tendencies in the pre-October stage of the peasant movement foreshadowed the divisions which were to become more apparent after the publication of Lenin's Land Decree on 26 October, when peasants moved on to a more thorough share-out of the land (for there appeared to have been relatively few cases of 'black partition' under the Provisional Government). But even before October, the movement of the peasants to allocate gentry resources to themselves on the basis of need further contributed to the food supply problems of the towns, since the poorer peasants sought land primarily in order to satisfy their own consumption and subsistence requirements, while the richer peasants, like the gentry, were more inclined to produce for the market. It seems very likely, indeed, that the Provisional Government's proposals that unworked private land would be rented to peasants by the food committees were intended to secure a peaceful transfer of this land to kulak farming. The kulaks would produce for the market, and therefore their interests would coincide with those of the government. Malyavskii, however, rather perversely suggests that the government's policy was inspired by the common class interests of the gentry and kulaks, which overrode the national interest; and he argues, against all the evidence, that the transfer of uncultivated land to the poorer peasants would have satisfied not only their own food needs but also those of the workers and soldiers.[93] In practice, the poorer peasants seem to have been preoccupied with their own subsistence needs. The dilemma of how to satisfy the demand for food from the cities and the army, while simultaneously meeting the aspirations of the mass of the peasantry for land, was the major problem which the Bolsheviks inherited from the Provisional Government.

Notes

1. L. A. Owen, *The Russian Peasant Movement, 1906–1917* (London, 1937).

2. J. L. H. Keep, *The Russian Revolution; a Study in Mass Mobilisation* (London, 1976); Graeme J. Gill, *Peasants and Government in the Russian Revolution* (London, 1979).

3. Marc Ferro, *October 1917; a Social History of the Russian Revolution* (London 1980); Dorothy Atkinson, *The End of the Russian Land Commune, 1905–1930* (Stanford, 1983).

4. George Yaney, *The Urge to Mobilize; Agrarian Reform in Russia, 1861–1930* (Illinois, 1982).

5. The tenth anniversary of 1917 saw the publication of the documentary collection, K. G. Kotel'nikov and V. L. Meller, comps, *Krest'yanskoe dvizhenie v 1917 godu* (Moscow and Leningrad, 1927); and two monographs which have retained their value: A. V. Shestakov, *Ocherki po sel'skomu khozyaistvu i krest'yanskomu dvizhenyu v gody voiny i pered Oktyabrem 1917 g.* (Leningrad, 1927); and S. M. Dubrovskii, *Krest'yanstvo v 1917 godu* (Moscow, 1927). There is a German version of the latter work: S. Dubrowski, *Die Bauernbewegung in der Russischen Revolution 1917* (Berlin, 1929).

6. P. N. Pershin, *Agrarnaya revolyutsiya v Rossii*, 2 vols (Moscow, 1966).

7. See, for example: N. A. Kravchuk, *Massovoe krest'yanskoe dvizhenie v Rossii nakanune Oktyabrya* (Moscow, 1971); T. V. Osipova, *Klassovaya bor'ba v derevne v period podgotovki i provedeniya Oktyabr'skoi revolyutsii* (Moscow, 1974); V. I. Kostrikin, *Zemel'nye komitety v 1917 godu* (Moscow, 1975); and A. D. Malyavskii, *Krest'yanskoe dvizhenie v Rossii v 1917 g.* (Moscow, 1981). A useful review of works published in the previous twenty years is V. I. Kostrikin, 'Krest'yanskoe dvizhenie nakanune Oktyabrya v

sovetskoi istoriografii', *Voprosy Istorii*, 1977, no. 11, pp. 36–52.

8. Shestakov's total, based on the militia reports for March to October, is 4, 469: Shestakov, *Ocherki*, p. 142. The raw statistical tables for March to September are in Kotel'nikov and Meller, *Krest'yanskoe dvizhenie*, pp. 363–99. For discussion of the reliability of this source, see Keep, *The Russian Revolution*, pp. 187–8; Gill, *Peasants and Government*, pp. 197–8.

9. Atkinson, *The End of the Russian Land Commune*, p. 163.

10. Malyavskii, *Krest'yanskoe divzhenie*, p. 378.

11. Atkinson, *The End of the Russian Land Commune*, p. 162.

12. Keep, *The Russian Revolution*, p. 188.

13. S. L. Makarova, 'K voprosu o vremeni likvidatsii pomeshchich'ego zemlevladeniya', in *Oktyabr' i sovetskoe krest'yanstvo, 1917–1927 gg.* (Moscow, 1977), pp. 114, 116.

14. Kotel'nikov and Meller, *Krest'yanskoe dvizhenie*, pp. 363–99.

15. Atkinson, *The End of the Russian Land Commune*, pp. 162–3; cf also Gill, *Peasants and Government*, pp. 189, 197–8.

16. For example Kravchuk, *Massovoe krest'yanskoe dvizhenie*.

17. V. I. Kostrikin, 'Krest'yanskoe dvizhenie nakanune Oktyabrya', in *Oktyabr' i sovetskoe krest'yanstvo*, pp. 28–9.

18. *Ibid.*, p. 29; this is also the periodisation adopted in Kostrikin, *Zemel'nye komitety*.

19. Malyavskii, *Krest'yanskoe dvizhenie*, pp. 8, 58–9 and chapter headings.

20. Gill, *Peasants and Government*.

21. Kotel'nikov and Meller, *Krest'yanskoe dvizhenie*, pp. xxiii–xxiv.

22. Shestakov, *Ocherki*, p. 143.

23. *Oktyabr' i sovetskoe krest'yanstvo*, pp. 39–42.

24. Malyavskii, *Krest'yanskoe dvizhenie*, p. 378.

25. Kotel'nikov and Meller, *Krest'yanskoe dvizhenie*, pp. 392–3.

26. Shestakov, *Ocherki*, p. 142.

27. V I. Kostrikin, 'Massovye istochniki o krest'yanskom dvizhenii nakanune Oktyabrya i statisticheskii metod ikh izucheniya', *Istoriya SSSR*, 1977, no. 3, pp. 61–2.

28. Malyavskii, *Krest'yanskoe dvizhenie*, pp. 64–7.

29. Yaney, *The Urge to Mobilize*, p. 472.

30. *Oktyabr' i sovetskoe krest'yanstvo*, p. 22.

31. *Ibid.*, p. 28.

32. For an excellent Soviet example of work on peasant mentality, see K. V. Chistov, *Russkie narodnye sotsial'no-utopicheskie legendy XVII–XIX vv.* (Moscow, 1967); and in the West, Daniel Field, *Rebels in the Name of the Tsar* (Boston, 1976).

33. Malyavskii, *Krest'yanskoe dvizhenie*.

34. A. N. Antsiferov *et al.* (eds), *Russian Agriculture during the War* (New Haven, 1930); P. B. Struve, ed., *Food Supply in Russia during the World War* (New Haven, 1930).

35. Notably by A. M. Anfimov, *Rossiiskaya derevnya v gody pervoi mirovoi voiny (1914 – fevral' 1917 g.)* (Moscow, 1962).
36. A. M. Anfimov and I. F. Makarov, 'Novye dannye o zemlevladenii evropeiskoi Rossii', *Istoriya SSSR*, 1974, no. 1, p. 85.
37. Anfimov, *Rossiiskaya derevnya*, p. 362.
38. Ibid., pp. 92–113, 152–62, 188–96, 212–23.
39. Ibid., pp. 153–5, 214–17; cf. Malyavskii, *Krest'yanskoe dvizhenie*, pp. 69–73.
40. Shestakov, *Ocherki*, p. 142. See Table 1.
41. Malyavskii, *Krest'yanskoe dvizhenie*, p. 21.
42. Kotel'nikov and Meller, *Krest'yanskoe dvizhenie*, p. 4.
43. See Keep, *The Russian Revolution*, pp. 202, 206; Gill, *Peasants and Government*, pp. 41, 46; Malyavskii, *Krest'yanskoe dvizhenie*, pp. 77, 296.
44. A. V. Peshekhonov, *Pochemu my togda ushli* (Petrograd, 1918), p. 17.
45. Field, *Rebels in the Name of the Tsar*, pp. 208–15.
46. Peshekhonov, *Pochemu my togda ushli*, p. 17.
47. *Ekonomicheskoe polozhenie Rossii nakanune Velikoi Oktyabr'skoi sotsialisticheskoi revolyutsii; dokumenty i materialy*, part 3, *Sel'skoe khozyaistvo i krest'yanstvo* (eds, A. M. Anfimov *et al.*; Leningrad, 1967; hereafter *EPR* III), pp. 211–13.
48. Malyavskii, *Krest'yanskoe dvizhenie*, pp. 76–9, 220–21.
49. Gill, *Peasants and Government*, pp. 18–73.
50. Malyavskii, *Krest'yanskoe dvizhenie*, pp. 79, 113–14.
51. Ibid., pp. 84–5.
52. Ibid., pp. 93, 98–9.
53. Ibid., pp. 100–1.
54. Ibid., p. 144.
55. Ibid., pp. 156–66.
56. Ibid., pp. 178–84.
57. *EPR* III, p. 239.
58. Ibid., pp. 237–8.
59. Ibid., p. 240.
60. Ibid., p. 238. Emphasis in the original.
61. See, for example, Malyavskii, *Krest'yanskoe dvizhenie*, pp. 271–2.
62. Ibid., p. 85.
63. Ibid., p. 264.
64. *EPR* III, p. 239.
65. Malyavskii, *Krest'yanskoe dvizhenie*, pp. 166–78.
66. *EPR* III, pp. 239–40.
67. Malyavskii, *Krest'yanskoe dvizhenie*, p. 296.
68. *EPR* III, p. 239.
69. Ibid., p. 239.
70. Ibid., pp. 243–4.
71. Ibid., p. 243.

72. Malyavskii, *Krest'yanskoe dvizhenie*, pp. 296–300.
73. Ibid., p. 301.
74. Ibid., pp. 306–7.
75. Keep, *The Russian Revolution*, p. 216; Gill, *Peasants and Government*, p. 40.
76. Malyavskii, *Krest'yanskoe dvizhenie*, p. 306.
77. *Oktyabr' i sovetskoe krest'yanstvo*, pp. 28–30.
78. Malyavskii, *Krest'yanskoe dvizhenie*, p. 336.
79. Kotel'nikov and Meller, *Krest'yanskoe dvizhenie*, p. 212.
80. Malyavskii, *Krest'yanskoe dvizhenie*, p. 331–6.
81. Kotel'nikov and Meller, *Krest'yanskoe dvizhenie*, pp. 268–9.
82. S. M. Dubrovskii, 'K voprosu ob urovne razvitiya kapitalizma v sel'skom khozyaistve Rossii i kharaktere klassovoi bor'by v derevne v period imperializma (dve sotsial'nye voiny)' in *Osobennosti agrarnogo stroya Rossii v period imperializma* (Moscow, 1962) pp. 35–6.
83. Malyavskii, *Krest'yanskoe dvizhenie*, pp. 309–24.
84. Ibid., pp. 324–6.
85. Ibid., pp. 185–206, 309–13.
86. Ibid., pp. 209–13.
87. *EPR* III, pp. 228–9.
88. Malyavskii, *Krest'yanskoe dvizhenie*, pp. 209–10.
89. Ibid., pp. 215–16, 314–5.
90. Shestakov, *Ocherki*, pp. 160–61; Malyavskii, *Krest'yanskoe dvizhenie*, pp. 82, 346.
91. Maureen Perrie, 'The Russian Peasant Movement of 1905–1907: its Social Composition and Revolutionary Significance', *Past and Present*, no. 57, Nov. 1972, pp. 123–55.
92. Malyavskii, *Krest'yanskoe dvizhenie*, pp. 101–4, 128–38.
93. Ibid., pp. 75–6, 264–5.

3 The Non-Russian Nationalities

Stephen Jones

This chapter must begin with some qualifications. It does not represent original research and only makes limited use of Soviet sources. It attempts to assess some past and current thinking on the 'nationalities question' in 1917 among Western scholars. It is interpretative, and aims to raise questions about assumptions and approaches rather than provide answers. The chapter's first section will address some theoretical problems associated with ethnicity and national identity, and the second half, in the light of this discussion, will look at the non-Russian national movements in 1917.

The focus is on the attitudes of the mass of the non-Russian population rather than on the political leaders. The viewpoint 'from below' does not necessarily imply that the national elites played no independent role in 1917, but their visibility, organisational power and articulateness has largely overshadowed the close symbiotic relationship they had with their constituents. The traditional image of the radical *intelligenty*, who made up most of the national leaders in 1917, as being 'class marginals' isolated from the social structure and imposing a radical ideology on the confused masses is particularly inappropriate to 1917 when the ideologies and tactics of the leaders, in the Russian metropolitan centres as well as in the non-Russian borderlands, were firmly constrained or directed by their followers. Thus while not underrating the role of ideas in the 1917 revolution as 'concretized' by political parties, many recent studies have shown us that the image of a relatively homogeneous working class or peasantry being successfully manipulated or contained by revolutionary organizations is inaccurate.[1] These new sociological perspectives on the revolution demonstrate highly complex relationships between regions, parties, social groups and their subdivisions; but as yet there has been little attempt at such an analysis of the non-Russian areas during this period. It is a serious neglect since non-Russians made up 55 per cent of the Empire's population at the turn of the century.[2]

The lag in 'revisionist' attention to the non-Russians in 1917 can be partly explained by the language barrier, by problems of access to sources, and by the sheer complexity of the subject. Accurately determining the views of the anonymous and least articulate sections of the non-Russian population is extremely difficult. Eugene Weber in his study of the French peasantry remarked that 'the acts, thoughts, and words of the illiterate . . . remain largely unrecorded. Such records as exist are the work of outsiders who observed and recorded what they saw for purposes of their own'.[3] Although the situation in 1917 is a little better for the social historian because of the explosion in popular activism, we still have to rely to a large extent on inference, partisan reports and observations, petitions and partial or possibly inaccurate election results. Events in the non-Russian areas make the extraordinarily complex picture of economic, political and social conflict in ethnically homogeneous Russia look straightforward. In 1917 the Russian Empire officially incorporated over 100 nationalities and ethnic groups, which by 1926 under more accurate census definitions had risen to 194.[4] The non-Russians were extremely heterogeneous in social structure, socio-economic development, demographic dispersion, religion, history, national consciousness and race. Western historians, faced with such a demanding area of research have, it seems, shied away from a comparative study of the non-Russians in 1917. Generalisation or meaningful comparisons hardly seem attainable. In addition, one is dealing with some of the most slippery concepts – nation, ethnicity, nationalism – which attract a welter of sociological, anthropological, and historical interpretations which often seem mutually exclusive.[5] We are concerned with the subjective sphere of values, sentiments and feelings.

The field has been left to Richard Pipes's pioneering work *The Formation of the Soviet Union*, first published in 1954 (and revised a decade later), which recognises the complex socio-economic relationship with national consciousness and avoids indiscriminate use of the word 'nationalism' when referring to any collective non-Russian movement of 1917. Yet it predates the new and challenging approaches to ethnicity and national identity that emerged in the 1970s, which introduced many novel ideas about the multi-layered nature of national identity. Pipes does not cover the experience of the Baltic peoples in 1917 on the grounds that they secured independence. This is unfortunate as the Latvians and Estonians present intriguing examples of Bolshevik strength among the non-Russians and contributed, in the Latvian case, to the success of the Bolshevik revolution in Petrograd.[6]

There are numerous studies of particular non-Russian groups to supplement Pipes, but these tend to be general histories with one chapter devoted to 1917, and stress the experience of a single non-Russian group rather than the multinational context of 1917.[7] A preponderance of these studies falls on a small number of non-Russian groups, mainly the Finns, Poles, Ukrainians and Jews. There are far fewer monographs covering the revolutionary events of 1917 in other non-Russian areas.[8]

Many historians dealing with the non-Russians in 1917 use such terms as 'nationalism' and 'nation' with insufficient precision, and portray the growth of collective action among non-Russians between February and October as a spectacular bourgeoning of nationalism.[9] A careful look at the non-Russian borderlands in 1917 should convince us, however, that we must be circumspect in applying such terms to the myriad of ethnic movements that emerged (or re-emerged) after the fall of tsarism. Failure to distinguish between such concepts as 'ethnic identity,' 'national consciousness,' and 'nationalism,' can only be misleading. They may all share similar attributes, through their common cultural sentiments; but they can differ in intensity and do not necessarily provide a basis for common political action.

A sense of ethnic identity may provide a feeling of separateness based on distinct cultural ties and a sense of common origins or history, but may still be a quite vague consciousness. These feelings do not necessarily possess the emotional strength to override religious or socioeconomic sentiments. This applies to the vast majority of the non-Russian peasantry in 1917, except perhaps for the Armenians and Georgians whose long history of defence against foreign Muslim oppression, combined with distinctive alphabets, languages and autocephalous churches had created a strong sense of identity even outside the cities. There is little evidence, and this is something we shall explore further, that the ethnic community secured the primary loyalty of the Ukrainian, Belorussian, Lithuanian or Baltic peasantry for much of 1917; only after the long period of revolutionary politicization, foreign invasion, and elections did their sense of ethnicity begin to serve as a basis for political action. It might be more fruitful to explore regional or local identities in 1917, including small administrative units such as the *volost'* in the Ukraine or *pagast* in the Baltic, which often presented serious barriers to the broader national ambitions of native leaders. Ukrainians, for example, referred to themselves by a variety of regional appellations such as Galicians, Rusiny, Lenki, Hutsuli or just 'peasants' and 'Christians'. Other internal divisions within the community such as class and estate may also be equally important for identity.

If we turn to the Central Asian population, we can hardly talk of ethnic identity at all in 1917. A profound social transformation had affected all levels of native society under tsarist rule and had resulted in the decline of nomadism, the arrival of a large alien Russian population, and the growth of cities. And yet the secular native leaders in 1917 failed to replace the clannish, tribal and religious identities (primarily Islam) which continued to dominate the lives – with variations – of all Central Asian ethnic groups. There were anti Russian revolts both in 1916 (against labour conscription) and from 1918 onwards under the banner of the *Basmachi*, but these were temporary tribal unions which had little significance for the mass of the native population and were not based on any sense of common ethnicity.[10]

In contrast to ethnic identity, national consciousness, although founded on pre-existing ethnic values, is a political concept deliberately fostered by native elites, or by what Miroslav Hroch calls in his study of small nations, the 'patriots'.[11] Such patriots may come from any social group, from the clergy (Galicia) to the aristocracy (Poland). National consciousness is expressed by what Karl Deutsch, in his book *Nationalism and Social Communicaton*, terms 'material signs, symbols, devices and institutions' that make 'many members' of a people 'explicitly aware of their membership'.[12] If there is no collective attachment to ethnic symbols around which the population can be mobilised, it is difficult to talk of national consciousness. For such mobilisation to be viable, there must be a degree of communication within the community. This implies some development of schools and a press[13] (although literacy is not essential to national consciousness), a breakdown of traditional peasant parochialism and a degree of politicization. Village schools, in particular, are important to the development of a national identity among rural inhabitants. The strength of national consciousness is determined by numerous variables; and among the most influential are the activity of the elite, the homogeneity of the population and the degree of successful penetration into the countryside of the national idea by the 'patriots'.

As regards the non-Russian peoples in 1917, the majority of rural native strata would not qualify as nationally conscious. The cities, as John Armstrong and Hroch have pointed out, are crucial to the development of national identity among the population because they provide the resources and training for the 'patriots'; and many such cities were politically or numerically dominated by non natives[14]. This slowed down their development as crucibles of national culture, and reduced the chances of employment for the native intelligentsia who often had to go elsewhere; it also initially discouraged peasant migration as the city was perceived as a hostile and foreign place. Generally, the lower status positions in the cities, were filled by natives, and, although the resulting ethno-social divisions may have motivated greater national consciousness among this group (but not in Ukrainian and Baltic cities in 1917 where workers' class identity seemed stronger than ethnic concerns), the generally low level of urbanisation, the scarcity of patriotic cadres and agitational means, and the weak penetration of the market outside city environs failed to break down much of the particularism in rural areas. The market had been making inroads for some time into the countryside, but the internal communications network – trains and roads – remained skeletal compared to Western Europe. Even where the natives were a plurality in their own cities or where urbanisation was comparatively high (as among Latvians and Estonians), the 'patriots' still had difficulty in 1917 overcoming the parochial peasant mentality which saw ethnic allegiance of secondary importance to their economic interests. Ethno-social divisions in certain non-Russian rural areas such as in the Baltic provinces of Livland, Kurland and Estland or in Lithuania and the Ukraine, where alien German, Russian, Polish or Polonized landlords ruled over indigenous peasants, did not automatically produce a greater national consciousness among the peasantry even in the conditions of 1917. Alien rule does not necessarily encourage rebellion or resentment on ethnic issues. There come into play other factors such as the nature and frequency of landlord-peasant contacts; the extent of cultural differences (since rulers and ruled may share a common religion, as in Lithuania); the number of peasants who believe in the cultural superiority of their rulers, and the type of leadership provided by (usually) outsiders.[15]

Nationalism was a much more visible phenomenon than national consciousness in 1917. This is because most nationalists were literate and capable agitators. Nationalism, unlike the other two concepts we have been discussing, is an ideology and more easily identifiable. Anthony Smith defines it as 'an ideological movement for the attainment and maintenance of self-government and independence on behalf of a group, some of whose members conceive it to constitute an actual or potential "nation" like others'.[16] If we accept this definition, then there was very little nationalism in 1917. Most non-Russian national leaders and parties, until the October revolution at least, did not seek independence, but a variety of forms of autonomy within a Russian federal republic. Long association with the tsarist state had provided jobs and encouraged many elements of the non-Russian middle and upper classes to identify their interests with the continuing unity of the Russian state. As Russian citizens, they would also acquire a certain international status, but, perhaps most importantly, the Russian state would offer protection against other imperial predators such as Germany, which had ambitions in the Baltic, or the Ottoman Empire, which had designs on Armenia and Georgia. This made many nationalist parties such as the Armenian Dashnaktsutiun firmly oppose independence (as do large numbers of Welsh and Scottish nationalists today). But if we were to modify Smith's definition to read 'self government *or* independence', then clearly there were significant sections of every non-Russian elite we could call nationalist, even though they were not necessarily in the majority.

And, even if we accept that nationalist parties, according to Smith's definition as modified above, played a significant role among non-Russians in 1917, the most popular of them were equally committed to a socialist land reform programme. The parties rarely called themselves 'national' or 'nationalist' and their programmes often emphasised the radical social nature of their aims. Juri Borys remarks that in 1917 'non-socialist political parties in (the) Ukraine were not common';[17] and Miroslav Hroch concludes in his study that 'where the national movement was not capable of introducing into national agitation and articulating in national terms, the interests of the specific classes and groups which constituted the small nation, it was not capable of attaining success'.[18] Borys's remark could be applied to most non-Russian regions before October, barring Central Asia, Azerbaidzhan, the Northern Caucasus and the Volga German regions. Even the Tatar leaders formed an All-Moslem Democratic Socialist Bloc committed to the nationalization of landlords' land.[19] This fusion of nationalist and socialist ideologies in native parties, often the result of ethno-social divisions between indigenous peasants and workers on the one hand and alien landlords or bureaucrats on the other, makes it difficult to attribute native parties' popularity solely to nationalist sides of their programmes such as demands for autonomy and a separate cultural identity. Socio-economic, religious or other aspirations are often submerged within ostensibly nationalist movements, and may play a greater role than national ideals in securing popular support. This is a point I shall pursue below, but twentieth-century history has surely shown that nationalism rarely succeeds without fusing with some other ideology, either of the right or left. As Konstantin Symmons-Symonolewicz points out, nationalism is neither a uniform psychological syndrome nor a pure ideological scheme, and takes on board a variety of social or economic ideals.[20] The nature of a particular nationalism will largely be determined by the groups and classes that contribute to it.

In 1917, nationalism merged with socialism in the non-Russian border-lands because nationalist ideology was not enough by itself to secure the support of the radicalised peasantry and workers. Similarly socialist parties which specifically rejected nationalism, including the Bolsheviks, could not prosper in 1917 without some concessions to national feelings.[21] Despite being the party, *par excellence*, of 'proletarian internationalism', the Bolsheviks portrayed themselves as defenders of national sovereignty;

and non-Russian *perceptions* of the Bolshevik stance on the national question, involving a commitment to national self-determination and to the defence of national rights, were probably not unfavourable even if they were ultimately inaccurate. It was only during the civil war when the Bolshevik fight for survival led to military actions on non-Russian territory, with all that entailed in terms of food-supply requisitioning and of the various abuses by soldiers, that a distinctly anti-Bolshevik nationalism animated large sections of the non-Russian populations. Thus we may surmise that many of the followers of the highly successful Bolshevik Latvian Social-Democracy (LSD) supported the party in 1917 not only because of its radical social programme, but because they perceived that, as a native party, it would somehow ensure Latvians' control over their own lives, something the Bolsheviks had long promised.

In short, in 1917, the majority of non-Russians probably did not perceive the support of socialism or nationalism (autonomy, cultural rights) as in any way contradictory, and native parties rarely presented them with the choice of two distinct ideologies. Nationalism and socialism in 1917, far from being incompatible, provided a potent ideological mix. Socialists such as Volodymir Vynnychenko, leader of the Ukrainian Social-Democratic Labour Party (USDLP) and Noi Zhordania of the Georgian social democrats, believed like Otto Bauer that 'socialism leads necessarily to realization of the principle of nationality'.[22] Similarly, many nationalists who saw Bolshevism as the greatest threat to their rule did not reject socialism but continued to preach radical social programmes. (The internationalist Mensheviks, after all, also denounced Bolshevism). So even if we accept that there was a reservoir of support among non-Russians for nationalist policies, (and this remains debatable in rural areas) it is extremely hard to separate this from the equally strong support for socialist policies or to determine which had the greater allegiance.

The view that the conflict in the borderlands in 1917 was between the forces of nationalism and socialism was promoted by Russian Marxists and is maintained by Soviet historians who emphasise the struggle and eventual victory of 'internationalism' over 'bourgeois nationalism'.[23] An alternative conflict model popular among many Western writers, which is a development of the originally Leninist theme of a 'prison of nations,' is that 1917 represented the climactic battle of the long oppressed peoples against the dominant Russian nationality.[24] This approach is equally one-sided. First, the native populations were not all anti-Russian. Their attitudes to the Russians depended on their own socio-economic level, in relation to that of the colonisers; on the nature of tsarist policies in their area, which varied from Russification to neglect; on the types of mutual contacts with

Russians; and on their own culture's relationship to the Russian one. In 1905, anti-Russian activity in the non-Russian areas was overshadowed by class politics; and for most of 1917, there was little hostility to the Russians except in Central Asia and Poland (which in any case was German-occupied). And there was little desire on the part of most of the native elites to secede.

Second, this approach seems to be allied to the belief originally propagated by the German romantics J. G. Fichte, E. M. Arndt and others (what Anthony Smith calls the 'primordialist view') that there is something essentially organic about nations, and that the national spirit is some sort of irrepressible force. But as Hroch remarks, we should be 'on guard against the illusion that the extension of patriotic attitudes takes place automatically and in equal measure among all members of small nations'.[25] The tsarist case demonstrates that the achievement of national consciousness is not a unidirectional or natural historical process and is rarely as successful as it might seem on the surface. The emergence of national consciousness is contingent on a host of variables related to social modernisation: the growth of literacy, communications, cities, social mobility – all of which provide the new secular priesthood of 'patriots' with the organisational means to mobilise a population, increasingly divorced from the traditional village way of life, through collective symbols based on ethnic ties. Eugene Weber has noted that, until social structure was no longer considered 'absolute and immutable' by the peasantry, doctrines that advocated rebellion around issues of social change were unlikely to be successful.[26] In 1917, many of the results of social modernisation were only at an embryonic stage in the borderlands. Most of the non-Russians lacked a strong urban class (whether bourgeois or any other) and a powerful intelligentsia; the cultural and political apparatus was often dominated by foreigners; and the vast majority of the population was illiterate and lacking socio-economic mobility. Many of the native nationalist elites were simply not capable of propagating their new message, because of their small numbers or lack of penetration into the community; and large segments of the native populations were indifferent to such ideas being concerned predominantly with economic survival.

A third and related criticism of this approach is that it overestimates the power of ethnicity to unify and maintain a community's allegiance. Ethnicity must be placed in a social context; it operates alongside economic, religious, regional, and familial ties within an environment, particularly at times of revolution, characterised by significant changes in the social structure. Ethnicity will not be of primary importance in every social interaction. Before national consciousness is firmly established, choice of identity may simply be a question of expediency. Thomas Spira noted that in a plebiscite in Upper Silesia in 1921 on whether to join Germany or Poland, the Polish majority favoured Germany because of its greater economic prosperity and political attractions (since a social-democratic government was in power);[27] and Paul Magocsi claims in his study of Subcarpathian Rus' that in 1917 Rusyn intelligentsia representatives were convinced of their Slavic identity, but 'were not sure as to whether they should be Ukrainian, Russian or something unique'.[28] National identity is not always rooted in some primordial past and does not necessarily occupy a primary place in people's lives.

In the Russian borderlands in 1917, there was the greatest fluidity between economic and ethnic interests. J Rothschild, discussing the ethno-economic relationship writes:

> populations whose socio-economic subordination also correlates with ethnic stratification may respond in either class or ethnic terms . . . depending on which ideology, as presented by which counter elite, is accepted by them as more relevant under prevailing historical and political circumstances . . . [29]

Ronald Suny, in his study of class and nationality in Transcaucasia, has come to similar conclusions. He notes that in 1917 an Azeri worker 'had vertical ties based on language, history, religion and social origin with other members of his nationality . . . But at the same time he had horizontal ties to his fellow workers, based on economic interests . . . Under specific historical circumstances and in the context of what real threats to his well-being existed, the worker could shift his primary loyalty . . . from class conscious solidarity with his proletarian comrades to nationalist unity with his ethnic brethren . . . '[30]

More work also has to be done on differentiation within the non-Russian working class and peasantry. We may find, like Hroch, that there were strata within social groups, which were more inclined to nationalist or socialist activity than others. Max Weber, in his essay on the nation, contended that 'an unbroken scale of quite varied and highly changeable attitudes toward the idea of the "nation"' is to be found among any social strata and also within single groups to whom language use ascribes the quality of "nations"'.[31] Hroch's own conclusion is that the poorest strata in any social group, urban or rural, are the least likely to be involved in nationalist activity. Clearly, non-Russian national groups should not be treated as homogeneous, any more than should other social groups. If we could establish some degree of correlation between nationalist activity and economic groups among the non-Russian strata, (although it is unlikely there would be any general rule) this might help explain some of the regional differences in nationalist activity. Maureen Perrie and Robert Edelman have already applied such analysis to the question of regional variations in peasant revolutionary activity in 1905 and 1917.[32]

Before dealing more concretely with the experience of different non-Russian groups in 1917, certain caveats should be made. There were crucial factors in 1917 that worked in favour of the creation of national consciousness such as the war; the new freedoms of propaganda and agitation, the forced involvement of villages in national politics, the collapse of old values and authority and the search for new authoritative guides. Although ethnicity was still not of primary significance in the actions of the mass of non-Russians through most of 1917, this is not to deny it an important role. Yet we should still be careful in interpreting any collective movement operating within ethnic parameters as a nationalist one. As we shall see, there is sufficient uncertainty between scholars on this issue to stimulate lively debate.

It should also be made clear that, although the peasants and workers may have been indifferent to mobilisation around ethnic issues, this is not to deny the growth of significant political consciousness. In 1917, many non-Russian peasants, like their Russian counterparts, were drawn into revolutionary politics and gave new content to traditional organisational forms such as the village *skhody* and created new institutional links with organisations from the soviets to the Constituent Assembly.[33]

The above discussion challenges the assumption that nationalism was the major factor in non-Russian behaviour in 1917. Rather, as Arthur Adams suggests, nationalism was 'only one component of a complex process involving other forces, events, and ideas perhaps of equal significance'.[34] Some distinction ought to be made between mass political action that may be expressed within ethnic parameters (particularly when it is attached to socio-economic issues), and action taken on the basis of the primacy of ethnic goals. Because the Finnish, Polish and Jewish cases have been extensively covered by others, I shall only touch on these for purposes of comparison. I include the Ukraine because it represents the largest non-Russian group and is an important illustration of many of the issues we have been discussing. But clearly, for reasons of space, not all ethnic groups are included, and there is bound to be a degree of simplification in a discussion of such complex issues.

We shall begin with the Latvians and Estonians, who by 1917 were urbanised, literate, and industrialised.[35] Both had significant native working classes, growing bourgeoisies and active but small nationalist intelligentsias which from the 1860s onwards continued to expand their organisational and educative work among the native population. And yet many of the native middle class, associated with the capitalist and industrial development of Russia, were lukewarm to the ideas of nationalism and were content to assimilate. There were other obstacles to the 'nationalisation' of the population. The native provinces of Livland, Estland and Kurland had never been united into separate Latvian or Estonian territorial units and had quite distinct regional histories. Regional identities remained strong. They had no separate religious tradition since their Lutheran pastors were predominantly German; their secular literatures were relatively recent; schools and universities were subject to Russification especially from the 1880s onwards (despite partial relaxation after 1905); German domination of cultural life continued until 1917, and market growth had not broken down the regional parochialism of the peasantry. None of these factors necessarily prevents the development of national consciousness, and it can also be argued that processes such as Russification tend to stimulate it. But the historian Uldis Germanis believes that in Latvian districts on the eve of the First World War 'the general population still lacked a clear national consciousness'.[36]

Miroslav Hroch and most other students of this period, however, feel that the pattern of ethno-class division in the cities and countryside, between the German barons and indigenous peasantry, decisively promoted national consciousness among broad strata of the native population.[37] Undoubtedly, national consciousness and nationalist demands were expressed in popular bodies such as the Latvian Congress of County Representatives and All-Estonian Congress in 1905, and the Maapaev and Vidzeme Land Council in 1917. Even so, the overwhelming majority of native peasants and workers supported socialist parties, despite nationalist alternatives. This was particularly true of the Latvian regions in 1917 where the Bolsheviks secured 41 per cent of the vote in Riga's August municipal elections, 63 per cent for the rural Vidzeme Land Council and 72 per cent for the Constituent Assembly (although elections remained incomplete due to German occupation of Kurland and half of Livland).[38] In Estonian regions the socialist parties had less success but still secured 50 per cent of the vote at the Constituent Assembly elections; the Bolsheviks polled 40.2 per cent excluding the soldiers' votes which would have provided the party with even greater strength, and in Tallinn obtained 47.6 per cent.[39] The nationalist parties were stronger in Tartu and southern Estonia. The Provincial Assembly elections to the Maapaev, in May 1917 also showed considerable support for socialist parties.[40]

There are many reasons not to accept elections, particularly in the conditions of 1917, as accurate reflections of public opinion. O. H. Radkey in his study of the Constituent Assembly admitted that 'comprehension of party programmes was rudimentary and attachment to party names perfunctory'.[41] In the Maapaev elections, which were indirect, electors in rural districts were generally presented with two slates only, representing the landed and landless peasants. Alternative political choices were not available and only 30 per cent of those eligible to vote did so.[42] Yet the significant support for the Bolsheviks and other socialist parties such as the Estonian Social Democrats (Mensheviks) indicated that vast numbers of indigenous peasants and workers were not convinced by the nationalist programme and preferred to settle their economic problems first. Unfortunately, there is insufficient information on different voting patterns within the peasantry or working class to be more precise, but it is reasonable to suppose it was the poorer landless peasants who provided the main socialist cohorts in the countryside. This would indirectly support Hroch's view that the poorest strata are the least likely to be involved in nationalist activity.

Arguably, support of the socialist parties was based on the perception that they were native parties with programmes of autonomy or self rule in varying degrees. Very often, the local Bolsheviks, as in the Maapaev when they pushed for the immediate introduction of Estonian language in elementary schools, seemed to be the most radical on nationality questions. And yet it was the Bolsheviks' policies on land, bread and the war, even if propagated in Estonian or Latvian, that was emphasised by the party, and it was this that was decisive in attracting support among the predominantly landless peasants, soldiers and indigenous workers.[43] The Baltic case demonstrates, perhaps, that national consciousness, even if quite extensive, does not necessarily lead to mobilisation around national issues, and that responses to modernization among oppressed ethnic groups may lead equally to a 'socialist' reaction.

After the October revolution, power passed to Estonian and Latvian Bolsheviks without much opposition. The Executive Committee of Estonian Soviets ruled until February 1918 when they were overturned by a German invasion. There is evidence from the results of the incomplete Estonian Constituent Assembly in January 1918 that the Bolsheviks lost support in this period partly because they failed to take any decisive action on land, partly because of their repressive policies. The other major socialist parties, perhaps sensing the search for a new panacea among the Estonian population following disillusionment with Bolshevik rule, had by January 1918 adopted a positive attitude toward Estonian independence. The Finnish declaration of independence in December 1917 may also have influenced the Estonian popular strata's increasingly positive appraisal of the nationalist position. Nationalist forces, however, remained too weak to overthrow Bolshevik power. This was a task left to the German army.

The Bolsheviks in Latvia, with a solid core of support in the countryside and towns, ruled after October through the Soviet of Latvian workers' soldiers' and landless peasants' deputies (Izkolat). There was no effective challenge from indigenous nationalist forces which had a weak social base among the richer peasantry and urban intelligentsia. The German army ended this socialist-based experiment in February 1918. Latvian workers and peasants in 1917 had clearly demonstrated that at this stage in their development, national concerns took second place to social ones.

In the Lithuanian and Belorussian regions in 1917, small nationalist intelligentsias attempted to organise independent states over the heads of populations largely indifferent to ethnic politics. Such states were proclaimed in 1918, but only with the aid of the occupying German army. Most students of Belorussia agree that on the eve of 1917 the rural inhabitants, who composed the vast majority of Belorussians – 98 per cent in 1897 – hardly possessed a sense of ethnic separateness, although 75 per cent considered Belorussian (or whatever the peasants may have called their local tongue) as their native language.[44] The regions occupied by Belorussians were unfavourable to the development of national consciousness. In 1897 only one per cent of Belorussians were in urban settlements over 20 000 and literacy was low. Belorussians lacked an articulate middle class and less than 0.2 per cent were in intelligentsia occupations.[45] The towns and cities were dominated by Poles, Russians and Jews. Minsk, the future capital of the Belorussian Soviet republic had less than 9 per cent Belorussian speakers and could hardly serve as a stimulus to Belorussian national culture or provide the means for propagating the idea of national identity. The majority of educated Belorussians were successfully assimilated. In short, Belorussians were lacking all the elements of a socially-mobilised population, and were firmly embedded in village life. The miniscule nationalist intelligentsia was a leadership without an army and during 1917 Belorussian peasants preferred to give their votes to parties of all-Russian significance, mainly the Socialist Revolutionaries (SRs) and Bolsheviks. Nicholas Vakar in his study of Belorussia noted that, in the first free elections to the rural (zemstvo) and municipal governments in the spring of 1917,

> not a single representative of the nationalist groups won any popular support. Likewise in the general elections to the Constituent Assembly the nationalist ticket was not able to collect more than 9000 votes in the whole country.[46]

In Minsk, the nationalist Hromada only polled 161 votes out of 35 651 cast.[47] Thus in Belorussia, even after the German invasion in February 1918, economic rather than national interest seemed to be the primary motor of native behaviour.

Lithuania's situation was more complex. Despite the loss of independent statehood in the sixteenth century when the Grand Duchy of Lithuania was forced to submit to Poland, and the subsequent incorporation of most of its former territories into the Russian empire in the early nineteenth century, a separate Lithuanian culture expressed in folk traditions, stories and song persisted among the peasantry. On the other hand, the traditional guardians of ethnic symbols – the educated nobility and clergy – were almost completely Polonised. In the nineteenth century, despite the rise of a small nationalist intelligentsia, there were several obstacles to the development of a broader national consciousness among the population. The Lithuanians were overwhelmingly rural with almost no presence in the towns. Vilno in 1897 was 40 per cent Jewish, 31 per cent Polish and only 7 per cent Lithuanian;[48] there was no 'patriotic' urban centre and Lithuanian *intelligenty* sought work elsewhere in Polish, Russian or Prussian towns. Nor were Lithuanians gathered in a single administrative unit; they were spread over four provinces in only one of which (Kovno) they made up a majority.[49] Two hundred thousand Lithuanians lived in East Prussia, but were generally Protestant and subject to a strong Germanic influence. Lithuanians in the Russian empire shared the Catholic religion of the dominant Polish culture. Many peasants simply identified themselves as 'Catholics' when asked their nationality.[50]

In 1917, national consciousness was undeveloped among the peasantry despite work in the countryside by a Social-Democratic Party of Lithuania strongly influenced by separatist ideas. The party had also dominated Lithuanian representation in the last three Dumas and supported territorial autonomy. Anti-German feeling was stimulated by the German military occupation but it did not inspire any detectable mass sentiment for independence. A National Diet, leading to a National Council (*Taryba*) was formed (not elected) in September 1917 under German sponsorship and the deputies had to be approved by the German military government. The *Taryba* declared independence on 11 December 1917, agreeing at the same time to become a German protectorate. It possessed no legitimacy or popular support, and the declaration was politically irrelevant. Although Lithuania went on to establish independence in 1920 after successive Soviet and Polish invasions, in 1917 there was no popular nationalist base for such a move.

Transcaucasia was one of the most ethnographically heterogeneous regions in the Empire. Three major peoples had emerged by 1917: the Turkic and largely Shi'ite Azeris; the Christian Georgians; and Christian Armenians. The latter two, situated on the front line of Islamic Christian conflict, had forged over centuries of self government and defence of their faith, a strong sense of ethnic separateness. Their long national histories and the subsequent creation of independent states in 1918 has led historians of the revolutionary period to concentrate on the role of nationalism in Transcaucasia in 1917 without investigating the perceptions of different social groups across ethnic lines.[51] Although national consciousness was quite well developed among all Armenian and Georgian social strata by 1917, as in the Baltic area the nationalist reaction was not automatic. For most Armenians and Georgians until the end of the nineteenth century, nationalism had little appeal. In the Armenian case, religious distinctiveness was interwoven with ethnic survival, and the church, hostile to the rise of secular nationalism, had almost complete dominance over Armenian national life until the turn of the century. The Armenian peasant's loyalty was to his church, not his nation.

In the Georgian case, the major obstacles to the spread of national consciousness were, again as in the Baltic area, social and political divisions between peasantry and nobility; foreign domination of the towns in eastern regions, which hindered their transformation into effective patriotic centres; poor literacy (15 per cent in 1897), suppression of the Georgian language and a strong regional particularism, reinforced by distinctive languages, dialects and geographical barriers. Noi Zhordania, the leader of the Georgian social democratic organisation, declared in 1894:

> Only language and ancestry tell us we are Georgians. But our people has not yet reached that conclusion. Do the Ingilos and Mingrelians imagine themselves interdependent and united? What do the Svan and Adzharian, the Samurzakhanoeli and Kakhetian have in common? . . . Do they consider themselves one nation? . . . The regions feel more their differences than unity . . . the Georgian people lack such consciousness.[52]

And yet, the events of 1905, when Georgian peasants became involved in national politics for the first time and clashed with tsarist troops and other guardians of order defending landlords' property, and the 1914–1918 war, which led to the Turkish massacre of one million Armenians and the massive influx of refugees, politicized all popular strata. National consciousness was reinforced by ethno-class divisions between a Georgian working class and an Armenian bourgeoisie in Tiflis and other Georgian towns, and the major parties – the Georgian social-democratic organisation and the Armenian Dashnaktsutiun – became essentially mono-ethnic in composition.

Ernest Gellner has stressed that nationalism can occur when, in the process of industrialisation, a mass of newly-arrived less skilled workers, distinguished by certain markers such as language or colour, is excluded by the more skilled (such as the Russians in Tiflis or the Armenians in Baku) in the competition for scarce resources.[53] In Georgia, however, as in Latvia, the convergence of social and ethnic factors seemed to make class symbolism more meaningful to the workers than nationalism, although the two ideologies were closely intertwined. In contrast to the European experience, the proletariat was not converted to nationalism by the war. Other social groups such as white collar workers and intellectuals were the mainstay of nationalism in Georgia.

Between 1905–1918, the Georgian social-democratic organisation, which was part of the broader Russian party, prevented Georgian nationalist parties from gaining any significant following. In 1917, despite increasingly nationalist pressure from the Armenian and Azeri leaders who were forming their own national soviets and military units, the Georgian organisation maintained a stoically non-nationalist position. It had almost total support from the Georgian workers. On the other hand, because of its large non-proletarian support, it resembled a national party, and there can be little doubt that many ordinary supporters, despite the leaders' rhetoric, perceived it as a national-liberationist as well as socialist movement.[54] But only after the October revolution, which was followed by the Russian army's withdrawal and the growing threat of a Turkish military advance, were secessionist moves reluctantly adopted which finally led to independence in May 1918. For most of 1917, the Georgian popular strata were not moved directly by nationalist slogans.

The Armenian Dashnaktsutiun, though formally a socialist organisation and constituent party of the Second International, emphasised national symbols and attracted mass urban support when it defended the Armenian church against a tsarist attack on its property rights in 1903. By 1917, after the Turkish genocide, it became the principal defender of Armenian national interests and swept the board during the Constituent Assembly elections;[55] it formed army volunteer units and its own national soviet. In Baku the Armenian workers led by the Dashnaktsutiun supported the multinational Bolshevik-led Soviet but in March 1918, after a Muslim (Azeri) rebellion, Armenian-Muslim animosity led to mutual bloodletting. This was not simply an ethnic conflict, however, but a clash between a Dashnaktsutiun-Bolshevik alliance defending revolutionary gains against a conservative force of Muslims backed by Turkish units. The party never sought independence but preferred to stay under Russian protection. When this proved no longer feasible after October, the party reluctantly declared independence in May 1918. The Armenian experience in 1917 was a popularly-based nationalist one. The Dashnaktsutiun had overwhelming indigenous support; but it has yet to be shown that the socialist component in its programme was any less important than the national component in attracting Armenian working class support.

The mass of Azeris, a Turkified people with no tradition of unity or separate statehood, had no distinct national identity until after the revolution. Their loyalty was to a supranational Islam, to the *umma*, the worldwide community of Muslims. Most lived in backward closely-knit villages dominated by their religious leaders, even though there was a large proportion of Azeris among the unskilled oil workers in Baku. Literacy and mobility was low. A small number of nationalists emerged from the oil rich bourgeoisie, influenced by the ideas of Turkism, Pan-Turkism and the 'new method' of secular education known as Jadidism. After the inter-communal violence in 1905 between Azeris and Armenians, the first Azeri Muslim political organisations were formed. By 1917 the most important were the secular nationalist Musavat which commanded the greatest support of the local Muslim population, the non-nationalist and socialist Himmat which had some support among the Baku workers, and the Ittihad, a conservative Pan-Islamic organisation. The Azeri intelligentsia wrangled over questions of Islamic, Turkic and Azerbaidjani identity. And yet, according to Tadeusz Swietochowski, 'the idea of an Azerbaidjani nation state did not take root among the majority of the population; the very term *nationalism* was either not understood by them or, worse, it rang with the sound of abuse, a fact the communists exploited in their propaganda against the Azerbaidjani Republic.'[56]

In 1897, Ukrainians numbered over 22 million, the largest non Russian group in the Russian empire. Like the Belorussians, they were a predominantly rural people whose lives focused on the village. In 1897, 93 per cent of all Ukrainians were peasant; and only 2.4 per cent lived in urban settlements over 20 000, which were dominated by non-Ukranian populations. Only one seventh of Ukrainians were literate and there was no instruction in the Ukrainian language.[57] Nonetheless despite these similarities with the Belorussians, the broad strata of Ukrainians were more politicised in 1917.

The role of the Ukrainians in the revolution has been extensively studied by Western scholars[58]. Disagreements prevail, however, about the impact of Ukrainian 'nationalism' and the nature of Ukrainian consciousness in 1917. Some studies emphasise that Ukrainian national consciousness in

1917 was restricted to a small but well-organised intelligentsia; others argue that it was only over the course of the year that Ukrainian national consciousness spread into the broad strata of the population and became a significant factor in mass political action.[59] Still other students take an ambivalent and more cautious view, and are not convinced that either class or ethnic symbols predominated in the consciousness of the broad strata.[60] This position is probably the most accurate because it reflects an ambivalence among the popular strata themselves, particularly among the peasantry on whom, given the numerical weakness of the Ukrainian bourgeoisie and working class, rested the success of the nationalist movement.

As elsewhere in the borderlands, the convergence of ethnicity and class – between the Ukrainian peasants and their alien landlords (since only a quarter were Ukrainian) and between the predominantly Ukrainian countryside and foreign cities (which were dominated by Russian, Poles and Jews), meant that ethnic and class issues were intimately linked. There was clearly the basis for an agrarian movement on national lines although such a pattern was by no means inevitable as Latvia and Georgia demonstrated. Much peasant behaviour in 1917, such as the election of Ukrainian parties to the Constituent Assembly, and the support for national demands at peasant congresses, seemed to indicate this as a possible development. The peasant support for Ukrainian parties with programmes of national autonomy and Ukrainianization undoubtedly reflected a sense among peasants that those who spoke their language and were local people would best represent their interests. But it did not necessarily reflect a high degree of national consciousness. Peasant support always remained within the context of the agrarian struggle. H. R. Weinstein remarked that in the Ukraine 'no national government or any other regime could retain the favour of the peasants in the Ukraine if it failed to satisfy economic demands of the rural majority'.[61] This was the touchstone of peasant behaviour in 1917. Thus peasants abandoned the national Ukrainian governments embodied by the Rada, the Directory and Hetman Skoropadskyi in 1917–1918 largely because of their failure over the land issue. Nevertheless, the agrarian problem increasingly raised questions of broader political import and began to break down the isolation of the peasant: a pre-requisite to the growth of an effective Ukrainian national movement.

The peasant constituency was extremely volatile and its political behaviour depended on a host of variables such as local land relations; socio-economic level, the proximity of cities and the type of local leadership provided. The peasantry was not a homogeneous mass, it was divided economically and regionally, and further study on the lines of Robert Edelman's work on the peasants of the right-bank Ukraine (which was constituted by provinces on the western bank of the Dniepr river) in 1905, looking closely at peasant politics within the context of the region's particular political and economic environment, needs to be applied to 1917. Bohdan Krawchenko for example, has noted in his study of Ukrainian national development that the Ukrainian intelligentsia was disproportionately concentrated on the left bank, which accounts 'for the important regional differences when it came to the national movement's influence'.[62] O. H. Radkey has also noted in his work on the Constituent Assembly elections that 'the behaviour of the same class of the same nationality may vary from region to region'.[63] In the Ukraine, a sense of ethnicity and national consciousness were quite uneven. Kholm, and Carpatho-Ukraine were weak areas of Ukrainian national identity whereas Galician Ukraine due to the historical experience of Austrian rule, the role of religion (most Galician Ukrainians belonged to the Greek Catholic church), the greater penetration of the market and education, and conflict with the neighbouring Poles had established a broad national identity.[64] Such unevenness was reflected in 1917 and should be incorporated into any discussion of the Ukrainian peasantry's attitude to nationalism in 1917, as should an analysis of the variable levels of politicisation among different economic strata within the peasantry.

To recall J. Rothschild, a class or ethnic response by any group will depend on the particular political circumstances, the degree of ethnic awareness and the nature of the social interaction. The Ukrainian worker or peasant had to decide between a number of possible identities and allegiances and choose among Russian, Ukrainian or Polish versions of socialism and nationalism. Choices in the extraordinary conditions of 1917 with armies, rulers and parties coming and going, were highly susceptible to changing perceptions of particular events or convincing propaganda and promises, and swung wildly between what we might call nationalist and socialist directions, (even though undoubtedly the peasant saw no such stark polarities). Ethnic loyalties play a role in peasant actions in 1917, they were hardly stable enough to provide a firm basis for national government as was demonstrated by the peasantry's indifference to newly formed national institutions. The strongly local view of the peasants seriously hindered the development of nationalism in 1917. Ihor Kamenetsky notes that the peasants' 'undeveloped sense of responsibility for nationwide issues' in the civil war led them to fight for the expulsion of 'foreigners' or interlopers from their own villages or locality, but rarely did they 'exert themselves on behalf of more distant villages or larger cities which they frequently considered either foreign or hostile'.[65] The development of the *Makhnivshchyna* (a peasant movement which was restricted to the southeastern Ukraine and led by Nestor Makhno, an anarchist publicly hostile to Ukrainian nationalism) as well as the emergence of *otamans* (local commanders who controlled whole Ukrainian regions) partly reflected the continuing lack of national solidarity among Ukrainian peasants who would fight fiercely for their own local territory but venture no further in defence of other Ukrainian communities. In short, the Ukraine exhibited a complex relationship between ethnic and class politics. Although ethnic loyalties, along with regional and village identities, seemed to influence much of the population, nationalism maintained a precarious and sporadic hold on the natives, and its success was contingent on peasant perceptions of its ability to solve the land question.

Finally and very briefly, Central Asia in 1917 presented a highly intricate ethnographic picture of Uzbeks, Tadjiks, Kazakhs, Turkmen, Kirgiz and others making up about 9.5 million including the Khanates of Bukhara and Khiva.[66] Despite cultural homogeneity among the different ethnic groups, there were also social and clannish divisions which prevented the development of a broad ethnic consciousness. The vast majority of the native population were either peasant farmers or nomads; they were socially immobile and illiterate. Admittedly there was a significant urban trading class among Uzbeks and by 1914 one-fifth of Kazakhs received wages for part or all of their income;[67] but 'modernisation' was at a very early stage. The Russian authorities made little attempt to integrate the peoples of Central Asia into the tsarist state and the local administration retained primarily a military character. The major cities were dominated politically and economically by Russians; and, although a significant portion of the mining and industrial workers were indigenous, they occupied the most menial posts. In the countryside, Russian colonization led in some areas, particularly in the northern Steppe provinces, to Russian pluralities (which sometimes attained 40 per cent). But most districts remained overwhelmingly native. There were sporadic revolts against settlers' seizure of native lands, and in 1916 there was a mass revolt in Transcaspia and the Steppes against a new decree on labour conscription. There is some disagreement among scholars on the significance of the revolt although most agree, that, despite its anti-Russian character, it was a tribal and religious rather than ethnic phenomenon.[68] Thus, colonization did not lead to a significant growth in ethnic consciousness, apart from among a small number of native secular *intelligenty* propagating policies of Pan-Turkism, Turkism or Jadidism. Clannish and religious identities prevailed, and the clergy exercised strict control over Muslim village life.

This is how it remained in 1917. Small secularised native élites organised parties and attended all-Russian Muslim congresses with demands of autonomy and the redress of native economic grievances, but it made little impact on the vast majority of the population. Nationalist parties did emerge (such as the Kazakh Alash Orda) which put ethnic and territorial interests before all-Muslim ones but they lacked a firm popular base. There was a struggle against the foreigner who had taken their native land, but most of the resistance was based around the clan, village, or region. Fierce tribal rivalries and Pan-Islamic ideas encouraged by the clergy continued to present obstacles to nationalist ideas. The same could be said of the *Basmachi* revolt which began in early 1918 and lasted till the mid 1920s. To call it a national-liberation movement or nationalist, as do some scholars, is hard to justify.[69] It was a tribal alliance intent on the expulsion of Russians and restoration of the traditional order (although Enver Pasha, an exiled Young Turk turned *Basmachi* leader, envisaged a pan-Islamic empire) with little vision or political philosophy.

To conclude, the following points can be made. First, when we discuss non-Russians in 1917, we must be precise in our use of terminology. Terms such as 'nationalism' are frequently used indiscriminately to describe anything from the incohate aspirations of non-Russian peasants for self government to the policy of national cultural autonomy adopted by certain non-Russian RSDLP sections. Second, there is insufficient analysis of the social structure of non-Russian groups and the relationship of different strata (rather than classes) to the national movement. When discussing attitudes to the national movement, broad social categories such as the 'peasantry' and 'working class' often obfuscate the significant differences within these groups although the use of such general terms is often unavoidable. Is it useful to talk in such broad terms as the 'Latvian people' or 'Ukrainian peasants' without at least acknowledging the differences within such categories regarding the level of national or political consciousness? Third, not enough work has been done on the whole range of alternative identities among non-Russian groups such as regionalism, religion, kinship and class. The latter is too often seen as some sort of 'false consciousness' among non-Russians. Nationalism is a social phenomenon and only takes its meaning within a social and historical context. More discussion of nationalism's relationship to socialism and other ideologies would be useful. Fourth, more attention should be paid to new approaches and debates on ethnicity among scholars from other disciplines, such as social anthropology, sociology and psychology, and applied to 1917. Fifth, there is surprisingly inadequate investigation of party organisations 'on the ground' and the type of interraction with the popular strata at this very basic level. It is quite possible that the peasants were getting quite a different message from the provincial and local party workers than that propagated by the party leaders and theorists in the higher echelons of the party. The smaller non-socialist parties also tend to get short shrift. It is important to know what sort of alternative 'nationalist' programmes were offered to the non-Russians and why they lacked appeal. Finally, as yet there has been no attempt to follow up Pipes's now dated work. The time is ripe for a new comparative study of non-Russians in 1917 incorporating all the new theoretical and empirical advances in the field.

Notes

1.   See for example S. Smith, *Red Petrograd: Revolution in the Factories, 1917–1918* (Cambridge, 1983); D. Mandel, *The Petrograd Workers and the Fall of the Old Regime* (London, 1983) and *The Petrograd Workers and the Soviet Seizure of Power. From the July Days, 1917 to July 1918* (London 1984); D. Koenker, *Moscow Workers and the 1917 Revolution* (Princeton, 1984); G. Gill, *Peasants and Government in the Russian Revolution* (London, 1979).

2.   This figure is taken from the 1897 census and excludes the Grand Duchy of Finland. As nationality was measured by native language, it underrates the number of non-Russians as many adopted Russian as their native language. On this point, see R. Pipes, *The Formation of the Soviet Union: Communism and Nationalism 1917–1923*, Revised edn (Cambridge, Mass., 1964) p. 2. For a detailed analysis of the national composition of the Russian Empire in 1897, see N. A. Troinitskii (ed.), *Pervaia vseobshchaia perepis' naseleniia Rossiiskoi imperii 1897 g.* (St Petersburg, 1899–1905) 89 vols.

3.   Eugene Weber, *Peasants into Frenchmen: The modernization of rural France 1870–1914* (London, 1979), p. xi.

4.   Yu. V. Bromley, *Soviet Ethnography: Main Trends* (Moscow, 1977) p. 152. See also *Vsesiouznaia perepis' naseleniia 1926 goda*, 56 vols (Moscow 1928–33).

5.   For the best survey of the numerous approaches to 'nationalism' and 'nation,' see Anthony Smith *Theories of Nationalism*, second edn (London, 1983).

6.   See Andrew Ezergailis, *The Latvian Impact on the Bolshevik Revolution. The First Phase: September 1917 to April 1918* (Boulder, USA, 1983).

7.   See for example, Martha Brill Olcott, *The Kazakhs* (Stanford, 1987); Toivo U. Raun, *Estonia and the Estonians* (Stanford, 1987); Alan Fisher, *The Crimean Tatars* (Stanford, 1978); Andrew Ezergailis, *The 1917 Revolution in Latvia* (New York and London, 1974); D. M. Lang, *A History of Modern Georgia* (London, 1962).

8. The situation is improving. The Hoover Institution series, 'Studies of Nationalities in the USSR' (see Olcott, Raun, and Fisher above) is expanding our knowledge of the less well documented non-Russians. In 1986, Azade-ayse Rorlich's *The Volga Tatars: A Profile in National Resilience* (Stanford, 1986) was added to the series. Richard Hovannisian has written extensively about the Armenians during the revolution. See for example, his *Armenia. On the Road to Independence* (Berkeley, 1967); *The Republic of Armenia. From Versailles to London: 1919–1920* (Berkeley, 1982). There has also been a recent study of the Azerbaidzhanis by T. Swietochowski *Russian Azerbaijan 1905–1920: The Shaping of a National Identity in a Muslim Community* (Cambridge, 1985).

9. Marc Ferro in his *The Bolshevik Revolution: A Social History of the Russian Revolution* (London, 1980) declared that 'during the six months preceding October, the outstanding phenomenon was the rise of nationalism' (ibid., p. 94). M. Rywkin, although he sees the main divide in Central Asia in 1917–1918 as between Russians and Muslims (not between Russian and Kazakhs, Uzbeks, Tadjiks and so forth), nevertheless goes on to argue that the 'struggle in Turkestan was followed along ever increasing nationalist lines . . . ' rather than on religious (Muslim?) grounds (*Moscow's Muslim Challenge: Soviet Central Asia*, London, 1982, p. 26).

10. This is the view of most Western students of this period. See, for example, T. Rakowska-Harmstone *Russia and Nationalism in Central Asia: The Case of Tadzhikistan* (Baltimore, 1970, p. 24) who argues the 'Basmachi bands' were based on clannish and religious ties. P. A. Zenkovsky in his *Pan Turkism and Islam in Russia* (Cambridge, Mass., 1960) supports the view that among Russian Muslims in 1917 'Islam revealed itself to be stronger than any national or racial program' (p. 139). Marie Broxup in her article, 'The Basmachi' (*Central Asian Survey*, vol. 2, no. 1 (July 1983) pp. 57–77) writes that 'the Basmachi movement was a limited local revolt deeply rooted in the local environment. As a rule, the leaders had narrow local interests' (ibid. p. 61); Olcott, in her article 'The Basmachi or Freemen's Revolt in Turkestan 1918–24' (*Soviet Studies*, vol. XXXIII, no. 3 (1981) pp. 352–69) agrees that in 1917 the Central Asian Muslim population had no sense of collective identity, but feels the Basmachis did create a primitive 'common consciousness' (based on what is not made quite clear) among Turkestanis during the civil war. Pipes is more emphatic and argues that by 1920, a sense of national consciousness had begun to emerge among the Azerbaidjani, Volga Tatar and Kazakh masses (*op. cit.*, p. 191). Unfortunately, there is insufficient data to determine with any definiteness what motivated the mass of Muslims in this period, but in a backward society like Central Asia, dominated by tribal, religious, regional and clannish loyalties, the idea of common ethnicity would have little resonance for the mass of Mulsim peasants and nomads. The

likely differences between the perceptions of leaders and led should also be remembered. Beatrice Forbes Manz points out that in Central Asia, the prevalence of religious leadership did not necessarily mean that the followers were equally religious. ('Central Asian Uprisings in the 19th century: Ferghana Under the Russians.' *Russian Review* vol. 46, no. 3 (1987) p. 278).

11.   Miroslav Hroch *Social Preconditions of National Revival in Europe: A Comparative Analysis of the Social Composition of Patriotic Groups among the Smaller European Nations*, trans. Ben Fowkes (Cambridge and London, 1985), p. 14.

12.   Karl Deutsch, *Nationalism and Social Communication: An Inquiry into the Foundations of Nationality* (New York, 1953), p. 178.

13.   Bohdan Krawchenko in his *Social Change and National Consciousness in Twentieth Century Ukraine* (London, 1985) makes the same point in his introduction. Krawchenko's book is an excellent example of the application of social history to a non-Russian people, although unfortunately the revolutionary period is not well covered.

14.   See John Armstrong's study *Nations Before Nationalism* (Chapel Hill, North Carolina, 1982) especially chapters 4 and 5.

15.   There is a voluminous literature on what pushes normally passive peasants into rebellion. See for example Robert P. Weller and Scott E. Guggenheim (eds), *Power and Protest in the Countryside in Asia, Europe and Latin America* (Durham, North Carolina, 1982) and Claude E. Welch Jr. *Anatomy of Rebellion* (Albany, New York, 1980) as good overviews. Pioneering works in this area are Barrington Moore, Jr. *Social Origins of Dictatorship and Democracy: Lord and Peasant in the Making of the Modern World* (Boston, 1966); E. J. Hobsbawm, *Primitive Rebels* (Manchester, 1959); and T. Shanin (ed.), *Peasants and Peasant Societies* (Penguin Books, 1971).

16.   A. Smith, *op. cit.*, p. 171.

17.   Jurij Borys, *The Sovietization of Ukraine 1917–1923: The Communist Doctrine and Practice of National Self–Determination*, rev. edn (Edmonton, Canada, 1980), p. 74.

18.   Hroch, *op. cit.*, pp. 185–86.

19.   Zenkovsky, *op. cit.*, p. 158.

20.   K. Symmons-Symonolewicz, *Modern Nationalism: Toward a Consensus in Theory* (New York, 1968) p. 23.

21.   M. Agursky in his latest book *The Third Rome: National Bolshevism in the USSR* (Boulder and London, 1987) argues to the contrary, and like John Kautsky (see his 'Comparative Communism versus Comparative Politics', *Studies in Comparative Communism* vol. 6, nos 1 and 2, pp. 135–170), sees Bolshevism as an essentially Russian nationalist movement.

22.   Bauer, 'Socialism and the Principle of Nationality' in T. Bottomore and Patrick Goode (trans. and eds), *Austro-Marxism* (Oxford, 1978), p. 116.

23. A typical exposition of this view is in I. I. Mints *et al.*, *Velikii Oktiabr', sotsializm i natsional'nyi vopros* (Erevan, 1982), pp. 40–41; G. A. Galoian, *Rabochee dvizhenie i natsional'nyi vopros v Zakavkaz'e 1900–1922* (Erevan, 1969), p. 200; and in V. A. Demidov, *Oktiabr' i natsional'nyi vopros v Sibiri 1917–1923 gg.* Second edn (Novosibirsk, 1983) esp. chs. 3 & 4. Soviet ethnographers and sociologists present a far more sophisticated analysis of ethnicity and nationalism, from which Soviet historians should learn (see, for example, Bromley *op. cit.*). Unfortunately, until now, any attempt to reassess the role of nationalism in the borderlands or the relationship between nationalism and socialism among the non-Bolshevik parties, has not been permitted (see B. Nahaylo and C. J. Peters, *The Ukrainians and Georgians*, MRG Report no. 50, London, 1981, p. 17). Some Western historians take a similar line to their Soviet counterparts, although their sympathies are with the 'nationalists'. See, for example, Ivan S. Lubachko *Belorussia under Soviet Rule 1917–1957* (Kentucky, 1972) who portrays the major struggle in 1917 as between the 'nationalist', whom he never quite defines, and the local Bolsheviks, mostly 'Russian soldiers' or 'party workers sent to conduct propaganda among the troops . . .' (ibid., p. 13).

24. H. Carrère d'Encausse in her *Decline of an Empire: The Soviet Socialist Republics in Revolt* (trans. Martin Sokolinsky and Henry A. La Farge; New York and Cambridge, 1981) declares that by the beginning of the twentieth century, the Empire's subject peoples were 'looking for ways to escape from it' (ibid., p. 13). A. H. Arslanian and Robert L. Nichols also see an essentially ethnic conflict between Russians and non-Russians as characteristic of the period before the revolution. They wrote that 'every expression of national identity and separateness among the ethnic minorities challenged both the Imperial government and Russian national feeling' ('Nationalism and the Russian Civil War: The Case of Volunteer Army-Armenian Relations, 1918–20', *Soviet Studies*, vol. XXXI, no. 4, (1979) p. 559). But in many cases, the Russian government actually encouraged national identity (as in Georgia in the 1840s) or granted significant autonomy or cultural rights (Finland before 1901). The degree of Russian-ethnic minority conflict before 1917 was overshadowed by social divisions within ethnic groups and by inter-ethnic conflict between the minorities themselves (Armenians versus Azeris, Latvians versus Germans). The social configurations of such inter-ethnic conflict often put ethnicity into a reinforcing but secondary role.

25. Hroch, *op. cit.*, p. 12.

26. Weber, *op. cit.*, p. 276.

27. Spira in M. Palumbo (ed.), *Nationalism: Essays in Honor of Louis Snyder* (Westport, Connecticut, 1981), p. 43.

28. Paul Magocsi, *The Shaping of a National Identity: Developments in Subcarpathian Rus' 1848–1948* (Cambridge, Mass., 1978), p. 18.

29.   J. Rothschild, *Ethnopolitics: A Conceptual Framework* (New York, 1981), p. 55.

30.   R. G. Suny 'Nationalism and Social Class in the Russian Revolution: The Cases of Baku and Tiflis' in R. G. Suny (ed.), *Transcaucasia: Nationalism and Social Change* (Ann Arbor, 1983), p. 241.

31.   *From Max Weber: Essays in Sociology*, trans., edited, and with an introduction by H. H. Gerth and C. Wright Mills (London, 1977), p. 174.

32.   Maureen Perrie, *The Agrarian Policy of the Russian Socialist-Revolutionary Party from its Origins through the Revolution of 1905–1907* (Cambridge, 1976) and R. Edelman *The Revolution of 1905 in Russia's Southwest* (Ithaca, 1987).

33.   For some debate on this issue, see Graeme Gill 'The Mainsprings of Peasant Action in 1917' (*Soviet Studies* vol. XXX, no. 1 (1978) pp. 63–86) and the reply by John Kress, 'The Political Consciousness of the Russian Peasantry: A Comment on Graeme Gill's "The Mainsprings of Peasant Action in 1917"' (*Soviet Studies* vol. XXI, no. 4 (1979) pp. 574–80).

34.   A. Adams, 'The Awakening of the Ukraine,' *Slavic Review*, vol. XXII, no. 2 (1963) p. 218.

35.   Twenty two per cent of the population in Estonian regions was urban in 1913, with Estonians making up 69.2 per cent of the major city populations. The urban population in Latvian regions was just under 30 per cent in 1897. In Riga, Latvians comprised 38.8 per cent of the population in 1913. Among Estonians, by the end of the century, almost 100 per cent over the age of 10 could read; in Latvia a provincial census of 1881 found 92.9 per cent of rural Latvians could both read and write. In 1908, Estland and Livland (mainly Estonian, but partly Latvian in composition) ranked fourth and fifth in per capita industrial production among the 50 provinces of European Russia. In 1900, there were 86 000 industrial workers in the Baltic provinces which represented 3.6 per cent of the total population. The comparable figure for the whole of the Russian Empire in 1905 was 1.6 per cent. For these figures, see Raun, *op. cit.*, pp. 90–91, 133; also his 'The Revolution of 1905 in the Baltic Provinces and Finland,' *Slavic Review*, vol. 43, no. 3 (1984) p. 457; Alfred Bilmanis, *A History of Latvia* (Princeton, 1951) p. 16; E. C. Thaden (ed.), *Russification in the Baltic Provinces and Finland, 1855–1914* (Princeton, 1981), p. 224, 290.

36.   Uldis Germanis, 'The Idea of Independent Latvia and its Development in 1917', in *Res Baltica: A Collection of Essays in Honour of the Memory of Dr Alfred Bilmanis 1887–1948* (Leyden, 1968), p. 30.

37.   Hroch, *op. cit.*, p. 85; Stanley W. Page *The Formation of the Baltic States* (Cambridge, Mass., 1959) esp. chs. 1–3; V. Stanley Vardys and R. J. Misiunas (eds), *The Baltic States in Peace and War: 1917–1954* (Pennsylvania State University and London, 1978), pp. 1–12; Thaden, *op. cit.* chs. 13–21.

38. Ezergailis, *The 1917 Revolution, op. cit.*, p. 145; also his *The Latvian Impact, op. cit.*, p. 79, 87–88; and O. H. Radkey The Election to the Russian Constituent Assembly of 1917 (Cambridge, Mass., 1950), p. 33, Note 26.

39. Raun, *op. cit.*, p. 103.

40. Olavi Arens 'The Estonian Maapaev during 1917', in *The Baltic States in Peace and War, op. cit.*, p. 23.

41. Radkey, *op. cit.*, p. 61.

42. Arens, *op. cit.*, p.22.

43. Raun 'The Revolution of 1905', *op. cit.*, p. 457.

44. See for example Pipes, *op. cit.*, p. 73; S. L. Guthier, 'The Belorussians: National Identity and Assimilation 1897–1970', *Soviet Studies* vol. XXIX, no. 1 (Jan. 1977), pp. 37–61; N. P. Vakar in *Belorussia. The Making of a Nation: A Case Study* (Cambridge, Mass., 1956) referring to the period at the end of the nineteenth century, wrote that 'when asked who he was, the Belorussian used to answer that he was neither Russian nor Polish, but *tutejsi* or *tutasni* (local), that is, one of the native race. He seldom used the term Belorussian, and when he did, he was rather ashamed of it. Indeed what little he knew of civilization now was associated with 'Russian' in his mind . . .' (ibid., p. 74).

45. Guthier, *op. cit.*, pp. 43–45. According to Lubachko (*op. cit.*, pp. 9–13) the literacy situation improved between 1905–1910 when there was a 23 per cent increase in pupils in elementary and high schools.

46. Cited in Guthier, *ibid.*, p. 58. See Vakar, *op. cit.*, p. 97.

47. Pipes, *op. cit.*, p. 75.

48. Alfred Senn, *The Emergence of Modern Lithuania* (New York, 1959), p. 42.

49. Hroch, *op. cit.*, p. 95.

50. Algirdas Budreckis, 'Demographic Problems of Vilnius Province,' in *Eastern Lithuania. A Collection of Historical and Ethnographic Studies* (Chicago, 1985) p. 312. He goes on to say that 'a large number of Lithuanian peasants lost their identity and became Belorussians' (ibid., p. 313). Senn, in contrast, takes a more positive view of Lithuanian consciousness on the eve of 1917, although he recognises there was no significant national movement among the broad Lithuanian strata. The centre of the Lithuanian national movement was abroad in Switzerland *op. cit*, pp. 15, 17, 23.

51. Pipes, *op. cit.*, pp. 98–107; Serge Afanasyan, *l'Armenie, L'Azerbaidian et la Georgie de l'independence a l'instauration du pouvoir sovietique 1917–1923* (Paris, 1981); R. Hovannisian in his works (*op. cit.*) also tends to neglect the social bases of ethnicity and nationalism among Armenians. R. G. Suny, however, in his *The Baku Commune 1917–1918: Class and Nationality in the Russian Revolution* (Princeton, 1972) as the title suggests, puts nationality firmly within its social and class context.

52. N. Zhordania, *Ekonomiuri tsarmateba da erovneba* (Paris, 1937),

pp. 21–22. The Ingilos, Mingrelians, Adzharians, Samurzakhanoelis and Kakhetians are all regionally based but ethnically Georgian groups living in Georgia.

53. See his *Thought and Change* (London, 1964) and the more recent *Nations and Nationalism* (Oxford, 1983).

54. Akaki Chkhenkeli, a prominent Georgian social-democrat declared that in 1905 (it could equally apply to 1917), although Georgians were united 'behind the flag of Georgian social democracy', the protest was 'in the minds of many against national oppression' *Shurduli* (Catapault), Tiflis, no. 3 (4 September, 1908), p. 2.

55. Radkey, *op. cit.*, pp. 16–17.

56. Swietochowski, *op. cit.*, p. 193. See also his 'National Consciousness and Political Orientations in Azerbaijan, 1905–1920', in Suny (ed.), *Transcaucasia, op. cit.*, pp. 209–32, where he seems to present a more positive assessment of national consciousness among the broad strata of Azerbaidjanis (ibid., pp. 231–32, where he talks of the 'emergence of a nation' by 1920).

57. S. Guthier 'The Popular Base of Ukrainian Nationalism in 1917', *Slavic Review* vol. 38, no. 1 (1979) p. 31.

58. John Reshetar Jr., *The Ukrainian Revolution, 1917–1920: A Study in Nationalism* (Princeton, 1952); Michael Palij, *The Anarchism of Nestor Makkhno, 1918–1921: An Aspect of the Ukrainian Revolution* (Seattle and London, 1976) Taras Hunczak (ed.), *The Ukraine, 1917–1921: A Study in Revolution* (Cambridge, Mass, 1977); James Mace, *Communism and the Dilemmas of National Liberation: National Communism in Soviet Ukraine, 1918–1933* (Cambridge, Mass., 1983); Arthur Adams, *Bolsheviks in the Ukraine: The Second Campaign, 1918–1919* (New Haven and London, 1963); Borys, *op. cit.* and Krawchenko, *op. cit.*

59. The first view is best exemplified by Arthur Adams in 'The Awakening of the Ukraine' *op. cit.*, and the second by Guthier, 'The Popular Base of Ukrainian Nationalism', *op. cit.*

60. Reshetar and Borys seem to take this view.

61. H. R. Weinstein, 'Land Hunger and Nationalism in the Ukraine, 1905–1917.' *Journal of Economic History*, vol. 2, no. 1 (1942), p. 35.

62. Krawchenko, *op. cit.*, p. 36.

63. Radkey, *op. cit.*, p. 23.

64. For an analysis of the growth of Ukrainian identity among Galician Ukrainians, see Jan Kozik, *The Ukrainian National Movement in Galicia: 1815–1849* (Edmonton, Canada, 1986).

65. Ihor Kamenetsky, 'Hrushevskyi and the Central Rada: Internal Politics and Foreign Interventions,' in Hunczak, *op. cit.*, p. 41.

66. E. Allworth (ed.), *Central Asia. A Century of Russian Rule* (New York and London, 1967), pp. 93–4. Other studies of Central Asia covering this period include R. A. Pierce, *Russian Central Asia, 1867–1917: A Study in Colonial Rule* (Berkeley and Los Angeles,

1960); T. Rakowska-Harmstone, *op. cit.* Alexander Benningsen and Chantal Lemercier-Quelquejay, *Islam in the Soviet Union* (London, 1967); E. E. Bacon, *Central Asians under Russian Rule: A Study in Culture Change* (Ithaca, 1966); Alexander Park, *Bolshevism in Turkestan, 1917–1927* (New York, 1957); Olcott, *op. cit.* and Zenkovsky, *op. cit.*

67. Olcott, *op. cit.*, p. 92.
68. Pierce, pp. 271–96, Helen Carrère d'Encausse in Allworth (ed.), *op. cit.*, p. 213; Zenkovsky, *op. cit.*, pp. 130–38. Marie Broxup takes the most emphatic stand on this point. She writes that the Basmachi movement was the 'attempt of a rural community, threatened and essentially ruined, to preserve its traditional spiritual values and way of life. It was neither an authentic liberation movement, nor a war against a foreign invader . . . nor was it a holy war. The Basmachis had no clear idea of their national identity and never reached the level of Pan–Turkestani consciousness' (*op. cit.*, p. 62)
69. Pipes, *op. cit.*, p. 256 and M. Rywkin, *op. cit.*, p. 43.

4 The Urban Middle Classes

Howard White

It is perhaps not surprising that Western interest in the social history of the Russian Revolution has not yet extended to the middle layers of society. The forging of the new order has naturally been of greater concern than the collapse of the old, and in this the middle layers may seem to have played no part. It may also appear that there is less need to employ detailed sociological analysis to explain their political behaviour: if some historians rebel against such determinism, most assume the correlation is obvious and need not detain them. It must also be said that such sociological analysis would in any case be no easy task. There was little effort at the time to collect data about the middle strata or debate their characteristics. Nor has much interest been displayed by Soviet historians, upon whose access to archives much Western literature relies. The one exception to this unconcern, the vexed question of the kulak (rich peasant), indicates that there are considerable problems of interpretation even where data are more plentiful: whether wealthy peasants constituted a separate social grouping as a 'rural bourgeoisie' is still hotly disputed. Yet, despite these biases against systematic investigation, there has been some attention paid to Russia's 'middle class'; indeed, several distinct approaches can be identified in the literature.

The dominant theme is that of class struggle between the proletariat and the bourgeoisie. This is of cardinal importance to Soviet historians, who interpret the whole Revolution in class terms. Even so, their attention has always tended to focus more on the proletariat than the bourgeoisie. When the bourgeoisie does make more than a token appearance, even the most scholarly works on the subject tend to convey to the Western reader a certain desperation – to locate an enemy worthy of the working class, and to explain developments in terms of direct social confrontation. Soviet literature which directly addresses the question of Russia's 'middle class' is mostly devoted either to its economic struggle against the proletariat,[1] or (more recently) to its involvement in political counter-revolution.[2] These themes have been taken up by Western scholars too, although in examination of economic struggle the emphasis once again has been on the working class;[3] as regards counter-revolution, the Kornilov affair exerts a perennial fascination.[4] It should be noted that all of these approaches are partial: only the French historian Marc Ferro has tried to provide an overview. His analysis of the failure to mount a successful counter-revolution touches upon the collapse of traditional social and political institutions, while still drawing heavily (and perhaps uncritically) on Soviet writings on the class struggle.[5]

The subject of class struggle ought in theory to have focused Soviet minds on the question of the petty-bourgeois. The 'official' interpretation of the Revolution is to acknowledge that Russia was an overwhelmingly petty-bourgeois country, and to point to the success of the Bolsheviks in 'neutralising' this dominant element, preventing the grande bourgeoisie from commanding their allegiance. While Soviet historians do sometimes engage in demonstrating this, they tend to do so on the level of generality – presenting as a self-evident truth the claim that the Bolsheviks' principal socialist rivals, the Mensheviks and Socialist-Revolutionaries, were petty-bourgeois parties. Only in works on the peasantry is there usually an effort at detailed analysis. The urban petty-bourgeoisie has not been paid much attention, an exception being an interesting study by N. A. Vostrikov.[6] Western writing on this stratum is virtually non-existent.

If class struggle is still the dominant theme in the literature, it has nonetheless been augmented by a number of other approaches. The rediscovery of private sector entrepreneurship by Western economic historians has been complemented by a growing interest in the emergence in Russia of a business élite, although no-one seems to have pursued this subject right up to 1917.[7] The relationship between the business élite and the state on economic issues has also received new attention from both Western and Soviet historians.[8] A third approach to have attracted the interest of Western historians is the emergence of professions in Russia: the medical profession has received most attention, but there has also been interest in lawyers, statisticians, teachers, army officers and (from a slightly different perspective) civil servants.[9] Finally, there are some political histories by Western scholars which do pay close attention to the 'middle class', most notably William G. Rosenberg's study of the Kadet Party and Lewis H. Siegelbaum's monograph on the War-Industry Committees.[10]

The general neglect of the middle layers of society is quickly apparent when any attempt is made to quantify them. This is a process which requires attention to definitions as well as adroit statistical footwork: Soviet historians have not put sufficient effort into either. Vostrikov's computation of the petty-bourgeoisie, which is to say the least rough-and-ready, is effected by taking the known urban population (27 million) and subtracting the working class (10 million) and the grande bourgeoisie including landowners and high officials (3 million), giving a total of 14 million.[11] It will clearly require much burrowing before adequate statistical data can be located, if indeed this is possible at all, but it is evident that the middle layers form a sizeable sub-section of the population. It is also clear that this sub-section is not the relatively homogeneous middle class usually identified in industrial society (although this concept is itself problematic). Consequently any serious attempt to relate political behaviour to social position and experience requires that discrete sub-groups be identified within it.

Sub-dividing the middle layers of society is necessarily contentious because of competing modes of analysis. The formal social estates (*sosloviya*) of tsarist Russia are clearly inadequate by the early twentieth century. Soviet historians naturally employ economic criteria to identify social groups. At their most subtle they distinguish between grande bourgeoisie, petty-bourgeoisie, intelligentsia and employees (*sluzhashchiye*). While conceptually clear, their scheme is hard to employ empirically: thus the boundaries between the grande bourgeoisie and the traditional social elite, or between the grande bourgeoisie and the intelligentsia, are not easy to draw. Most Western scholars would seek to introduce additional criteria. The most sensible working solution is that applied by Laura Engelstein in her study of Moscow in 1905: a mixture of the legal, economic and subjective.[12] Drawing on her methodology, it would seem sensible to identify three distinct groups: a business élite; a professional/intelligentsia stratum; and the urban middle strata of traders, artisans, employees, etc.

It will become evident that there are definite limitations even to this simple classification. Attention must be drawn at the outset to the competing 'frameworks of meaning' available to individuals. There are modern orientations ('business', 'professional') and the perceptions generated in the socialist movement ('bourgeoisie', 'intelligentsia'). The *Sosloviye* system, however obsolete as an objective categorisation, offered identities as 'honoured citizen' (*pochyotnyy grazhdanin*), 'merchant' (*kupets*), 'artisan' (*remeslennik*) and 'common townsman' (*meshchanin*). These legal identities had institutional reinforcement: most of these categories had their own organisations which still played a role in local government as well as in regulation of the working life of each group. A further identity on offer was that of 'educated society' (*obshchestvennost'*), usually counterposed to 'the state power' (*vlast'*). It conjured the image of a progressive, enlightened and civilised social elite – nobles, businessmen, professionals – which deplored the primitive and bureaucratic ways of the tsarist state. An equally powerful identity for some was that of the 'third element' (*tret'ii element*), denoting originally the specialists employed by the zemstvos (rural local government) such as teachers, statisticians, veterinarians. Their image was that of the radical intelligentsia: educated persons who devoted their lives to the welfare of the common people, to social justice; the spiritual heirs of the populists of the mid-nineteenth century, often close to revolutionary politics. To stress their identification with the common people they sometimes adopted the label 'democratic intelligentsia', linking themselves to another identity: the 'democratic elements' (*demokratiya*). This was usually counterposed to the 'enfranchised elements' (*tsenzovye*) who had greater electoral rights under tsarism – although this could not be a precise criterion since the franchise was exceptionally complicated. The *demokratiya* was an emotive concept, implying the social and political unity of the lower orders and their moral superiority; it too drew on nineteenth-century populist conceptions, and was broad enough to embrace the radical intelligentsia. In 1917 it came to denote the 'mass organisations': soviets, factory committees, soldiers' committees and similar bodies.

Despite these complications, it is possible to use the three simple categories indentified above to discuss the social position and experience of the middle layers of society during the last years of tsarism, the First World War and the Revolution of 1917. It should be added that this discussion is impressionistic: it is a first survey, to identify points of interest and gaps in our understanding. It will not include the clergy, which clearly requires separate treatment.

The first social group to which the literature draws attention is the business élite. Alfred J. Rieber's major study of Russia's merchants and industrialists concludes that, as a group, they were still very segmented in the early twentieth century. Although clearly identified (and despised) by state officials and professionals as a breed apart, they had little sense of solidarity and little organisational unity. Ethnic, cultural and regional diversity was reinforced by the official divisions of the *sosloviye* system, and by the differences of outlook and interest between those whose livelihood depended on the state and those who were entirely independent of it. A further complication was introduced by the presence of foreign capital and entrepreneurship. Nonetheless, Rieber and others suggest that a modern business élite was beginning to emerge around the turn of the century. They identify five regional groups: Petersburg, in state-financed heavy industry; Moscow, in textiles; the Southern mining and metallurgical industries; the Urals mining industries; and the sugar-beet processors of the South-West.[13]

There are certainly signs of modernity in the business activity of these regions, with growth in the scale and complexity of production, and the development of monopolistic tendencies. There are grounds, however, for caution in considering whether this promoted a distinct and united commercial-industrial middle class. Account must be taken of probable ties to the traditional social élite, particularly in the Urals and South-West, as well as of continuing ethnic and sectoral divisions. Our knowledge of most of these five regional groups, with the exception of Moscow, remains sketchy. Thomas C. Owen and Jo Ann Ruckman have made studies of the emergence of a Moscow business élite which was to develop close links with professional and intelligentsia circles in the city, and to give birth to the Progressist Party. Both authors note the limits of this process. Even in Moscow, most of the business élite turns out to be a small group of families with a distinct élite culture. P. A. Smirnov, the vodka magnate, was not a part of it, despite his immense wealth. The dominant ideological heritage of the group was not *laisser faire* liberalism but religious nationalism; this, and their distinctively local orientation, hindered ties with business communities elsewhere.[14] The continued existence of division in the Russian business élite is illustrated by the inability to establish a genuine nation-wide organisation to represent commerce and industry. The Council of Congresses of Trade and Industry posed as a national body, but was unable to unite and co-ordinate the 175 employers' organisations that existed by 1917. The pre-war years witnessed considerable debate about the role of the state in the economy: manufacturers argued about government hostility to syndicates, about labour legislation and about expansion of state economic activity.[15] The most obvious political development involving the business élite was the appearance of the party of the Progressists, but this was the creation of the Moscow group and not by any means an all-Russian business party. Certainly the business community dominated municipal government, although in smaller towns this was a preserve of the traditional merchantry rather than modern business. Even in the larger towns, the party system was weak; most dumas (municipal councils) had 'progressive' and 'right' fractions rather than parties, and membership cannot be neatly related to social position as businessmen were predominant in both.[16]

During the First World War there was a definite consolidation of the business élite. The war furthered economic concentration and promoted an even stronger *modus vivendi* between big business and the state. At first there was considerable dispute over whether to apply state regulation or voluntary regulation of the war economy, but the pattern which emerged was for the government and manufacturers to agree to control distribution rather than production. This was not appreciated by traders, except where there were syndicates involving both manufacturers and traders (as in milling).[17] The war seemed to bring politicisation to business through the War-Industry Committees set up to assist the war effort; but Lewis H. Siegelbaum has warned against overestimation of this. He shows that the central apparatus of the War-Industry Committees were dominated by the Moscow business élite, but underneath it was not a united structure; and there was no clear picture of large sections of business being drawn into Progressist radical politics. Thus on the contentious issue of labour relations, the Moscow manufacturers championed the formation of Labour Groups (worker delegates attached to the Committees to promote co-operation), while their Petrograd counterparts advocated militarisation. There was also considerable dispute over a continuing role for the Committees during demobilisation.[18] A further wartime development to be noted is the spread of speculation and corruption in business. Although hard to quantify, it did occur – and more important was perceived to be occurring on a phenomenal scale.[19] The position of the business élite during 1917 was undermined by this wartime reputation, and that of the widespread evasion of conscription. This was a reputation earned by most 'middle-class' groups: Allan K. Wildman has estimated that there were 1 200 000 upper and middle class persons eligible for military duties, of whom 200 000 served as officers and 500 000 in vital services, leaving a missing half million.[20]

Divisions in the business élite continued into 1917, with rival national centres emerging in Petrograd and Moscow, and a general pattern of mushrooming of business organisations. This was despite the general economic crisis and the related political problems faced by the élite as a whole in their economic activity. The first set of problems arose from coping with the workers' movement, which had to be faced on the morrow of a February revolution that had involved widespread strikes. The pattern of events has been documented by the Soviet historian P. V. Volobuyev, endorsed with reservations by S. A. Smith.[21] Konovalov, as Minister for Trade and Industry in the Provisional Government, promoted a policy of concession to immediate worker demands. He was successful in Petrograd and Moscow, although elsewhere there was resistance, and a new labour politics began to emerge. It was based on the 8-hour day, wage increases, recognition of factory committees and arbitration of disputes, and appeared to be quite successful during the spring. Smith dates a change in climate to June, both among the employers and in the government: as the economic crisis deepened, excessive wage demands were attacked and a policy of punitive lockouts began to appear. It is still unclear how many factories were deliberately closed for this reason rather than because of the fuel crisis, but the *lokautchiki* were a big issue in working-class politics – especially after Ryabushinskii's provocative speech to the All-Russian Congress of Trade and Industry in early August, in which he threatened the workers with the 'bony hand of hunger' and the militarisation of labour. In the autumn, manufacturers began to make a noticeable effort to curb the factory committees, with the support of the Provisional Government: circulars by the Menshevik Minister of Labour, unfortunately coinciding with the Kornilov affair, limited their rights and powers. This became a major issue between employers and workers in the autumn, along with plans in Petrograd for the evacuation of industry. By the autumn, the business class presented a far more united front – but too late.

The second set of political problems faced by businessmen in 1917 concerned the course of government economic policy. These have been analysed by the Soviet historians P. A. Volobuyev and V. Ya. Lavyorychev.[22] The first was the question of a state grain trade monopoly. As with the earlier wartime interventions of the state, manufacturers sometimes saw advantages, but there was also some resistance. In particular, the Provisional Government's system of Food Supply Committees gave preference to co-operatives and public organisations over private traders, which led to a prolonged dispute between the government and business circles. The All-Russian Union of Trade and Industry became particularly alarmed when it approached forty-one food supply organs with offers of help and found that eleven responded by rejecting 'collaboration with the trading bourgeoisie'. Business circles began to demand that representatives of commerce and industry take over the system, and that the expertise and capacity of private trade be exploited. Bankers also undermined the government's system by withholding finance without extensive treasury guarantees, and by demanding higher rates of interest. As the Provisional Government from May 1917 onwards began to move into supervision of production as well as distribution, conflict between manufacturers and the new socialist-dominated Ministry of Labour deepened. In the Donets, state supervision was extended even to the financial transactions of mineowners, under pressure of the miners and the fuel crisis. As the months passed, the government was forced to declare more and more state monopolies. As the Provisional Government became more resolved to resist worker's demands, the situation eased a little. In the summer the government set up a Supreme Economic Council and Conference to run its growing state regulatory apparatus, which heard proposals for labour conscription, compulsory arbitration and fixed wages. But manufacturers argued with the government about demobilisation and the post-war economy, with many wanting the private sector to take over from the War-Industry Committees and the other 'Voluntary Organisations' (the Union of Municipalities and the Union of

Zemstvos) as fast as possible; meanwhile Zemgor (the joint committee of the local government Unions) was already switching production from military supplies to spades and other 'items of prime necessity' for the civil population. The Provisional Government set up a commission under Manikovskii to merge the Voluntary Organisations into the state apparatus (as Chief Administrations of the War Ministry).[23]

The political picture is thus one of apparent initial harmony between the government and the business elite gradually dissolving. The harmony was encouraged by the Moscow industrialists who were represented in the Provisional Government by Konovalov, and were active with Kadet professionals in the Moscow Committee of Public Organisations (where S. N. Tret'yakov and P. A. Buryshkin were amongst its commissars). It was, however, a sort of temporary hegemony of the Moscow business élite – and was untypical. It appears that businessmen did not rush to join the Provisional Government's apparatus, either centrally or locally. Nor did they necessarily align with the Kadet Party, which was widely seen as the basis of the first Provisional Government. In Moscow, Tret'yakov and Buryshkin stood on the Kadet slate for the municipal duma, but a separate slate of manufacturers was entered under the name of Liberal-Democratic Union.[24]

The role of the business élite in counter-revolutionary politics is still one of the major issues of the secondary literature.[25] Although the government's tougher stand after the July Days appeased some, it seems that many had given up on it. Whether alarmed by the economic situation or agitated by Lenin's suggestion to the first Congress of Soviets that it might be productive to 'hang 50 or 100 of the richest millionaires', a number of businessmen began to flirt with the idea of military dictatorship. The Soviet historians' account of the Kornilov Affair is by now complex and sophisticated, with room for different emphases on the role of Kerenskii in particular; but there is still a great lack of hard evidence. It is clear that Putilov's Society for Economic Recovery was a big-business propaganda fund, and that there were links with Kolchak's entourage and then Kornilov, but much of the Soviet case rests on equating sympathy with actual conspiracy. There is little evidence of serious counter-revolutionary activity outside Petrograd and Kornilov's immediate staff, but it is clear that after the Kornilov affair the business élite was universally identified with counter-revolution. Workers identified a dual campaign of economic pressure in the factories and political conspiracy. With the climate turning against them economically and politically, many of the more wealthy businessmen began to think of escape – although in the midst of war this was not easy to arrange.

Nor, by comparison, was the intelligentsia in an enviable position: it is a truism of the secondary literature to observe that Russian intellectuals were very different from any Western bourgeoisie, and had little in common with commercial and industrial circles either in social origin or culture. Nonetheless, a more modern 'middle class' consciousness may have been developing: businessmen were becoming more educated, professional and 'cultured'; the intelligentsia was becoming more of a social than a political category. A convergence of mentality was promoted through the concept of 'educated society' and the institutions which supported it: elected local government and the 'liberal' political parties. There has been a growing interest among historians in the theme of professionalisation, a process which might conceivably turn an *intelligent* into a *bourgeois* and support the rise of a Western middle class. And yet their conclusion is similar to that of those who study the business élite: the process was far from complete in the late tsarist period.

Medicine is an important example of this: a field expanding both in numbers and quality of personnel, with an effective professional organisation in the Pirogov Society of Russian Doctors. Nancy M. Frieden has chronicled efforts to build up a professional identity around the personnel and the ethos of zemstvo medical care, but notes how this was thwarted. The growth of private practice and of curative scientific medicine (rather than preventive public health medicine) led to a visible split between public and private sector doctors, including a tendency to division in political outlook.[26] John F. Hutchinson suggests that there was resistance to professionalisation from both political wings of the public sector: some doctors had a 'bureaucratic' paternalist attitude (the doctor as a civil servant), while others clung to the 'populist' ethos of the zemstvo (the doctor as a servant of the people).[27] Frieden agrees that the tradition of state service was a brake on the assertion of professional autonomy, most doctors being employees of the state and sharing to some extent a 'service ethos'. She further points out that the experience of 1905–1907 was very damaging to morale and unity, leaving the activists of the Pirogov Society exposed as a radical clique without majority support.[28] Samuel C. Ramer identifies a further problem: the 25 000 doctors in the Empire were diluted by large numbers of (mostly female) paramedics – 27 000 *fel'dshery* and 14 000 midwives; their mutual relationship was uneasy.[29] Finally, in seeking to draw political implications out of professionalisation, the suggestion of Peter F. Krug should be noted: he argues that professionals came relatively easily to an accommodation with the Bolsheviks, in the belief that they were committed to expanding health care and would allow the specialists to control it.[30]

Education was less professionalised than medicine, although the process was underway. Jeffrey Brooks notes that by 1915 there were 157 000 primary school teachers in European Russia, together with a smaller number of secondary school teachers, and that there had been the beginnings of organisation with congresses held in the pre-war years. But the teacher was not ideal material for professionalisation. There was little in common between primary and secondary school teachers, the former tending to be of lower (mostly peasant) social origin and more limited education. Most primary school teachers worked in rural schools, in considerable isolation; most were women, often working for a short period before getting married; their pay was extremely low, and they had to be careful not to offend the local peasantry and officials. This did not prevent many teachers from harbouring radical political views, but as with the doctors this tended to work against rather than for the development of a sense of professional identity.[31] The Empire's 4240 academics were a small group, very much polarised politically (although a largely conservative political colouring was ensured by state interference); the 180 000 students in secondary and higher education were exposed to a strongly intelligentsia tradition, which many would carry into their working lives.[32]

The law was significantly 'professionalised', if again not completely. Alongside the 11 000 'sworn' advocates were 2000 'private' advocates who were not members of a bar. These were mostly untrained, many being junior or retired state officials supplementing their incomes. The 'sworn' advocates were heavily concentrated in larger towns, while their bar provided a formal professional organisation encouraging a strong sense of solidarity. Lawyers were highly politicised: the Petrograd bar had a core of 20–30 radicals around Kerenskii, and once again such elements tended to adopt a 'radical intelligentsia' rather than a 'middle class' self-image. Their presence also meant that the bar was regarded with great suspicion by the authorities, who in most fields were quick to suspect sinister political intent behind autonomous professional organisation and acted to curb it.[33]

Engineers form a final major 'professional' group, with some 60 000 members; but very little is known about them. Anecdotal evidence would suggest that theirs was not a high-status occupation, and that many engineering posts were filled by foreigners. There seems to be little trace of concerted professional activity, but this may reflect an absence of political commitment.[34]

Be that as it may, the evidence suggests that the emergence of a new 'middle-class professional' identity was far from complete. The total numbers involved remained very small. It is likely that the division noted by Laura Engelstein between 'educated society' and 'radical intelligentsia' professional orientations in 1905 was still significant in 1917, the former being the self-image of higher-paid and higher-status groups such as lawyers, doctors, academics.[35] Many sources confirm the persistence of the radical 'third element' identity among lower-status professionals, associated with the socialist inclinations which surfaced in 1917. Yet the distinction was clearer in the minds of the lower-status groups than in those of the higher. This is suggested by William G. Rosenberg's analysis of the Kadets, who belonged to a party of higher-status professionals and clung to the image of the intelligentsia, above class and serving the people. They rejected the label 'bourgeois' and tried to keep a certain distance from commercial and industrial circles.[36]

The literature throws up a few suggestions about the impact of the First World War upon professionals. Call-up and hardship had an inevitable impact on the activity of professional bodies. War service brought isolation to many professionals, and perhaps took many back into 'civil servant' attitudes as they became state employees. Professionals worked on a large scale in the Voluntary Organisations, where contact with like-minded members of the business elite and exposure to the general political issues of the war effort promoted the 'educated society' outlook. And yet, there also seems to have been a drive by 'third element' members to organise within the Voluntary Organisations, leading to clashes with the upper hierarchy. One example is the hospital strike which affected the Union of Zemstvos in Minsk in 1916. this may have pushed the Voluntary Organisations to the left; but it may also have reinforced the sense of a gap between a leadership which thought of itself as belonging to 'educated society' and the 'third element' identity of the rank and file. This did not, of course, diminish the popular perception that the educated were engaged on evasion of military service on a massive scale – a perception which is likely to have fuelled basic class antagonisms during 1917.[37]

Very little in the way of social history has been written on the professionals and the intelligentsia in 1917, even though relevant social interpretations underlie both Soviet and Western analysis of the Revolution as a whole. From a sociological perspective, the February revolution was a triumph for this stratum. There was an explosion of organisation and activity. A crude account of the composition of the first Provisional Government is itself revealing: two lawyers (G. E. L'vov, Kerenskii), two doctors (Shingaryov, Godnev), two professors (Miliukov, Manuilov), and an engineer (Nekrasov); only two industrialists (Konovalov and Tereshchenko since Guchkov was regarded as a professional politician); and one landowner (V. N. L'vov). The Provisional Government recruited its central apparatus in its own image: new senior officials brought into the Ministry of Internal Affairs included two doctors, two lecturers, one lawyer/law lecturer, one local government professional.[38] To staff his Ministry of Justice, Kerenskii summoned a meeting of the Petrograd bar, gave an emotional address to his 'teachers and dear comrades', and handed out portfolios. The advocates in effect took over the ministry and the judicial system as a whole.[39] Examination of what passed for a local government apparatus of the Provisional Government produces exactly the same picture: the district commissars for Vladimir province in the spring of 1917 comprised 2 advocates, a court investigator, a magistrate, a gymnasium teacher, an engineer, a former land-settlement commission official, and an ensign of the 21st Reserve Infantry; for Ekaterinoslav province, a school inspector, a zemstvo doctor, a zemstvo vet, an engineer, a tax inspector, two zemstvo chairmen, and a skilled metalworker. It is evident that commerce and industry was not well represented at local level.[40]

There is a problem, however, in trying to draw conclusions from this. There is also evidence of non-participation by the *intelligenty*: a Congress of local Commissars organised in April heard several complaints that they could not persuade people to participate in the urgent tasks of organising the new order and educating the masses.[41] Moreover, a glance at the composition of local soviets or the new socialist-dominated municipal dumas reveals a substantial intelligentsia presence too. The First Congress of Soviets apparently contained 100 junior officers and many doctors, teachers and vets. The new Moscow City Duma contained only 39 workers out of 200 councillors, but 13 professors, 19 doctors, 18 lawyers. It is clear that much of the active intelligentsia was socialist in orientation; indeed by August a substantial proportion of the Provisional Government's local Commissars were socialist too.[42]

It is evident that the Provisional Government did not draw much on commercial or industrial elements, but that both it and the *demokratiya* drew heavily on the professional and intelligentsia stratum. This might be interpreted as a potential source of unity behind coalition politics. The *demokratiya* was a distinctly blurred concept at its upper edges: in Moscow a Soviet of Deputies of the Working Intelligentsia represented 100 organisations and 100 000 members; its counterpart in Petrograd declared itself to be part of the proletariat.[43] Allan K. Wildman has proposed the idea of a 'committee class': a radical stratum of educated people (including Mensheviks, SRs and Popular Socialists) who formed an intermediary layer between the upper classes and the masses, controlling the organs of the *demokratiya*.[44] We certainly have the image of leadership in the *demokratiya* passing into different hands later in the year: Sukhanov's 'utterly crude and ignorant people' who crept 'out of the trenches and obscure holes and corners' to take their seats in the Second Congress of Soviets.[45] But is this too close to Lenin's insistence that the Mensheviks and Socialist-Revolutionaries were both essentially petty-bourgeois parties? It does not seem that we yet have the data from which to judge.

The professional and intellectual stratum experienced two further changes in the course of 1917: economic decline, and an identity as *burzhui* (the opprobrious corruption of 'bourgeois') increasingly imposed upon them. As early as May the government received reports from Oryol that 'every day in the skhody [village meetings] you hear calls not to trust students and *intelligenty*'. A lawyer described attending a peasant meeting where a soldier told those assembled that England was Russia's true enemy and accused him of being a *pomeshchik* (landowner). 'I said I was a writer; he said "a writer is even worse: don't believe *intelligenty*, don't take newspapers from them, don't read what they write, don't drink tea with them".' Yet there seems to have been considerable local variation: not all peasants were hostile to the rural intelligentsia. Our picture therefore remains confused.[46]

Two further 'professional' groups merit attention: army officers and civil servants. The October 1917 Army Census listed 128 000 officers and 21 000 officials at the Front, 26 000 and 43 000 respectively in the Rear.[47] Peter Kenez and M. Mayzel have written on the professionalisation of the officer corps, which may have followed a similar process to that in the civil professions, perhaps assisting their eventual accommodation with the Bolsheviks.[48] Yet the limits to professionalisation are also striking: most officers by 1917, particularly junior officers (who messed separately) were not career soldiers but belonged to the wartime intake. Wildman describes them as 'not intellectuals in uniform but literate shoots from the *narod* [common people]'.[49] It is very evident that the officer corps was politically fragmented. On the right there were many who moved instinctively towards counter-revolution: they had not necessarily opposed the February Revolution, but they wanted the Army to be depoliticised and left to get on with the war; many sympathised with Kornilov, but a few were active – there was an atmosphere of helplessness and passivity. In the centre, there were many officers who were active in support of the Provisional Government, providing many of its Commissars. On the left, many officers were active in the *demokratiya*, there being socialists even among senior commanders, such as the aptly-named General Marks in Odessa. These divisions meant that the officer corps did not fulfil its potential to be a major political force in the rear. It might also be true that the lower calibre of rear officers was important: witness the sad story of Colonel Timchenko, commander of the

149th Infantry stationed in Ekaterinburg (having been transferred from the front for incompetence), who was persuaded to stand for election to his command, received no votes at all, and shot himself.[50]

Senior civil servants were very much a separate caste, with a distinct ethos. Their social and attitudinal ties were to the traditional élite rather than to an emergent middle class. The most senior (or most obnoxious) of them were removed from office in 1917, but their immediate juniors stayed on to serve the Provisional Government. There is little evidence of them having any political impact on government policy; indeed no major political role until the anti-Bolshevik strike after the October Revolution, which itself was only partially supported. The traditional distance between 'official Russia' and 'society' seems the key to their behaviour, not really overcome in 1917.

The third social category to which the literature draws attention can be labelled the urban middle strata, comprising rentiers, traders, artisans and employees. Together, these groups must have formed a sizeable proportion of the urban population, especially in non-industrial towns; but they have attracted very little scholarly attention. There is some treatment of the employees in the Western and Soviet literature on the working class, but only the vaguest impression can be garnered of the other groups.

Most elusive of all are the rentiers, many of whom surface as the 'houseowners' (*domovladeteli*) who strongly influenced small-town politics before the Revolution, to whom D. A. Brower has drawn attention.[51] Many would appear to have been gentry who had sold up and moved to the towns; others were pensioners. Yet most were neither wealthy nor well-educated: there is at least *prima facie* reason to group them with traders and other urban property-owners. Brower uses a 1913 survey of urban taxpayers to show that only 9 per cent of those who paid property taxes had more than elementary education, which corresponds closely to the percentage of officials and professionals in the population; 27 per cent were recorded as illiterate. He also notes that the average value of property owned was low. During 1917 the 'houseowners' continued to be a major force in local politics, often mounting slates of candidates in the municipal elections. They suffered from inflation and the collapse of the local economy, both directly and as the result of strikes by concierges (*dvorniki*) and non-payment of rent by tenants.[52]

Traders (*torgovtsy*) and artisans (*remeslenniki*) are a more obvious feature of Russian urban life, but still relatively little investigated. There are some grounds for considering them as one group, even if the concept of 'small business' may seem anachronistic. In most towns both would identify themselves as *meshchane*, the separate estate organisation for artisans (*remeslennoye upravleniye*) surviving in only 29 towns, and their social experience before and during 1917 has many features in common. There were some 1 300 000 private traders in Russia, urban and rural; they formed what was still very much a hereditary caste, and very much divided ethnically. Most were businessmen on a very small scale; at least half were unable to vote in pre-Revolutionary municipal elections. A similar picture can be drawn of the 214 000 owners of handicrafts enterprises, half of whom had either one or no hired workers, and 90 per cent less than five. It may be unwise to presume that handicrafts enterprises were in economic decline in the last years of tsarism, although competition was growing from industrial manufacturing and from conversion to semi-industrial labour. (The Singer Co. apparently operated a 'putting-out system' in many towns, hiring out sewing machines.)

The experience of traders and artisans during the First World War might be considered as involving immediate profit at considerable political cost. The number of traders apparently grew: invalids, widows, refugees and laid-off workers sought a living in this way, often without official permits and therefore without participation in the formal apparatus of communal administration.[53] This dilution of the group was accompanied by the rise of considerable popular antagonism towards it. Its members seem to have gained a reputation for evading conscription: in the summer of 1917 the Petrograd Committee on the Review of Deferments found 900 workers at the Petrograd Post Office and 50 at the VKE Artillery Works who were actually owners of businesses; similar investigations at the Putilov Works prompted 2000 men to depart 'voluntarily' for the army.[54] They also gained a reputation for profiteering, which fuelled the existing hatred of peasants for private trade. Peshekhonov told the All-Russian Union of Trade and Industry that the trading class 'had so compromised itself during the war as to raise all other classes up against it'.[55]

During 1917, traders and artisans suffered considerable economic pressure. Even if their exclusion from participation in the state procurement system was incomplete in practice, the disintegration of the local economy caused them considerable hardship. Inflation was a critical problem, furthering the collapse of material and fuel supply. V. P. Anichkov, manager of a bank in Ekaterinburg, recorded the process with a professional eye: the co-operatives rushed to expand to fill the demands of the state procurement system, but on credit; his bank was faced with requests for credit from Urals manufacturers (140 million roubles), co-operative banks (6 million), the municipal administration (2 million). The effort to soak up paper money in the form of the Liberty Loan was not a success; there was a money shortage, particularly as the new 'Kerenskii' (or 'bath-house' – from the picture of the State Duma) notes were not trusted. After the Kornilov affair the stock markets collapsed, as panic set in.[56] Meanwhile it was impossible to collect taxes: the 1917 tax receipts of the Vladimir provincial zemstvo were 50 per cent of the assessment, with less than 10 per cent of taxes on peasant land and less than 50 per cent of the trade and industry taxes collected.[57]

Much less can confidently be said about the political activity of traders and artisans in 1917. In big-city politics they seem to have had little presence, perhaps in deference to the business elite. They do appear, with the 'houseowners' in small-town electoral blocs (often, of course, along ethnic lines); they also appear as deputies to soviets, especially in non-industrial small towns. There seems to be little evidence of any marked divergence between traders and artisans in political life. Vostrikov argues that the group was effectively 'neutralised' by the Bolsheviks, who promised to restore the local economy without attacking small property: only the rich would suffer.[58] However, in the absence of further evidence about local Bolshevik propaganda and its impact, it would be rash to assume that the October Revolution was won on such an 'NEP ticket'.

Employees (*sluzhashchiye*) form a large and discernable group, totalling perhaps 2 million. They are likely to have been held together both by attitudes and social experience as providers of hired non-manual labour, although they can be subdivided into a number of distinct elements. The principal categories were state employees, above all in the post and telegraph service (113 000) and on the railways; municipal employees; commercial employees (865 000) and shop assistants (314 000); industrial employees (25 000); technicians and other specialists, such as pharmacists; and concierges. Although there are few detailed studies, it would appear that they considered themselves distinct from manual workers, as a semi-educated caste even though their incomes were often directly comparable (or, in the case of state employees, lower). Their education, employed status and ethnic complexion also tended to make them distinct from traders and artisans. The group had been expanding rapidly in the last decades of tsarism, presumably recruiting both from the peasantry and the *meshchanstvo*. Although it included a large female contingent, less likely to be organised, the group boasted a strong tradition of trade-union organisation dating back to 1905.[59]

The First World War brought extreme impoverishment to employees, above all those in the public sector. Wages did not keep pace with inflation, the housing crisis eroded their living standards, and most were ineligible for social insurance. This impoverishment encouraged high expectations of the February Revolution, and considerable militancy when these were not realised.

During 1917, the employees' experience of economic life was mixed. S. A. Smith shows that industrial employees had some success in organising against employers, for example compelling Petrograd manufacturers to agree minimum wage-rates, although there were also cases when employees came into conflict with manual workers in the course of the 'democratisation' of the factories.[60] Economic collapse brought growing unemployment to private-sector employees. Two particular elements merit attention. The pharmacists are a unique category: a study of their militancy in 1905 describes them as having employee status but intelligentsia aspirations; they went on strike in most towns in the autumn of 1917, demanding the municipalisation of the pharmacies (which was conceded at least in Petrograd).[61] Another unexpectedly militant group were the concierges, who went on strike over pay in many towns; in Moscow, the Committee of Public Organisations responded by ordering all houseowners to employ a concierge at a fixed rate, in the interests of public health, but this was declared illegal by the Provisional Government.[62] Smith records a great deal of unionisation amongst employees in Petrograd, which seems to have been true elsewhere. The first organisations in the city were of the traditional *starosta* type (elected elders, as in a village), but soon there were 30 unions, eventually merging into 15.[63]

Political patterns are again hard to determine in the absence of detailed research. Soviet sources identify employees as supporting the Popular Socialists, Edinstvo, or the SRs – which seems rather too neat; voting SR in any case may indicate a sense of solidarity with manual workers. As in 1905, many employees apparently considered themselves workers: those at the Petrograd Skorokhod shoe factory declared in *Pravda* that they were '*Rabochimi intelligentnogo shtata*' (implying, 'workers, but by brain'). Others were decidedly more moderate: the Union of Employees of Credit Institutions even elected a bank manager to its Council, attracting great scorn.[64] Vostrikov suggests that the Bolshevik Municipal Programme (the centrepiece of Bolshevik agitation for a period in the autumn) had some appeal: the Bolsheviks promised municipalisation of enterprises, controls on rents and food supply, and were prepared to see employees as a part of the working population. It is certainly true that there was a Bolshevik presence in employee unions, particularly of the post and telegraph service: the Petrograd Post Office's weekly journal had Bolshevik editors; a Bolshevik political club for post and telegraph personnel, in which Lenin's wife Krupskaya was active, organised concerts and excursions to places of revolutionary significance such as Shlisselburg Fortress and Kronstadt.[65]

Predictably enough, a general survey of the middle layers of Russian society elicits little sign of a united 'middle class'. Some of the internal divisions were essentially social; but there were regional and ethnic factors too. Perceptions of group identity were always fragile, conflicting loyalties abounded, and within any social group there was a great deal of political fragmentation. It can be argued that no nineteenth-century industrial society had generated an integrated middle class.[66] Yet Russia's position seems to have been extreme. War and revolution did not act as a catalyst for integration. Many members of the middle layers seem to have drifted along with the Revolution until forced to assume a new identity by opponents. It is not hard to understand why it proved so difficult for any group to place itself at the centre of a nationwide counter-revolution and rally extensive support.

Even amongst the business élite, social experience is not a sufficient guide to behaviour. An example of this is provided by the Ekaterinburg bank-manager, Anichkov. Not a monarchist, he welcomed the February Revolution, but was alert from the start to the dangers of anarchy; he accepted office in the local Committee of Public Organisations with reluctance, finding it distasteful to be called 'citizen' instead of 'your excellency', but he devoted himself to trying to make this rudimentary democracy work. His 'leftist colleagues' in this venture were an SR lawyer, a number of radical junior army officers, a Jewish Kadet intellectual – all of whom he clearly despised. The Committee 'died a natural death' after three months, when the local soviet formally proposed a merger. Even though this would have given the Committee a minority position, Anichkov voted in favour, hoping to be able to exercise a moderating influence. After the October Revolution he was dragged into putting his expertise at the disposal of the Bolsheviks, which he did grudgingly: he would doubtless have stayed, had not civil war begun to threaten the region. Learning of an order for his arrest, he vanished into the Siberian forest . . . and ended up in San Francisco.[67] The ability of many 'middle-class' elements to come to an accommodation with Bolshevism is one of the many interesting phenomena which need further investigation: we have little idea of how many did so, although presumably quite significant numbers were involved. For some, it was doubtless simply a matter of survival; for others a fatalistic realism – even in the spring of 1917 many were resigned to the view that land redistribution was essential.[68] Others still may have been drawn in across a 'populist bridge' – the idea of serving the people,[69] or out of a feeling that they must 'preserve the cultural base' of Russian society.[70]

It is to be hoped that more research will be undertaken into this unfashionable region of the social spectrum, both to understand the collapse of pre-Revolutionary society, and to understand its successor:

the 'democratic intelligentsia', employees and professionals surely did have some hand in its making.

Notes

1. The best scholarly expositions are P. V. Volobuev, *Proletariat i burzhuaziya Rossii v 1917g.* (Moscow, 1964); R. Sh. Ganelin and L. E. Shepelev, 'Predprinimatel'skiye organizatsii v Petrograde v 1917g.', in *Oktyabr'skoe vooruzhennoye vosstanie v Petrograde* (Moscow, 1964); V. Ya. Lavyorychev, *Po tu storonu barrikad* (Moscow, 1967).

2. Recent scholarly examples are N. Ya. Ivanov, *Kontrrevolyutsiya v Rossii v 1917 godu i eyo razgrom* (Moscow, 1977); V. I. Startsev, *Krakh Kerenshchiny* (Leningrad, 1982).

3. Particularly S. A. Smith, *Red Petrograd. Revolution in the Factories 1917–18* (Cambridge, 1983).

4. Particularly George Katkov, *The Kornilov Affair. Kerensky and the Break-up of the Russian Army* (London, 1980).

5. Marc Ferro, *October 1917. A Social History of the Russian Revolution* (London, 1980).

6. N. A. Vostrikov, *Bor'ba za massy. Gorodskiye srednye sloi nakanune Oktyabrya* (Moscow, 1970).

7. The fullest account is Alfred J. Rieber, *Merchants and Entrepreneurs in Imperial Russia* (Chapel Hill, 1982).

8. S. O. Zagorsky, *State Control of Industry in Russia During the War* (New Haven, 1928), first raised themes more recently pursued e.g. by Ruth Amende Roosa, 'Russian Industrialists and "State Socialism", 1906–17', *Soviet Studies*, XXIII (1972). A recent Soviet treatment is V. Ya. Lavyorychev, *Gosudarstvo i monopolii v dorevolyutsionnoy Rossii* (Moscow, 1982).

9. An impression of this literature can be gained from several of the contributions to Terence Emmons & Wayne S. Vucinich (eds), *The Zemstvo in Russia. An Experiment in Local Self-government* (Cambridge, 1982). Recent monographs include Nancy Mandelker Frieden, *Russian Physicians in an Era of Reform and Revolution, 1865–1905* (Princeton, 1981); M. Mayzel, *Generals and Revolutionaries. The Russian General Staff during the Revolution* (Osnabruck, 1979); and on the civil service Dominic Lieven, *Russia's Rulers under the Old Régime* (Yale, 1989).

10. William G. Rosenberg, *Liberals in the Russian Revolution. The Constitutional Democratic Party, 1917–1921* (Princeton, 1974); Lewis H. Siegelbaum, *The Politics of Industrial Mobilization in Russia, 1914–17. A Study of the War-Industries Committees* (London, 1983).

11. Vostrikov, *op. cit.*, p. 15. Earlier attempts to discuss and quantify the bourgeoisie include I. F. Gindin, 'Russkaya burzhuaziya v period kapitalizma. Eyo razvitie i osobennosti', *Istoriya SSSR* (1963);

L. K. Yerman, 'Sostav intelligentsii v Rossii v kontse XIX i nachale XX v.', *Istoriya SSSR* (1963).

12. Laura Engelstein, *Moscow, 1905, Working-class Organization and Political Conflict* (Stanford, 1982), p. 16.

13. Rieber, *Merchants*, passim.

14. Thomas C. Owen, *Capitalism and Politics in Russia. A Social History of the Moscow Merchants, 1855–1905* (Cambridge, 1981); Jo Ann Ruckman, *The Moscow Business Elite: A Social and Cultural Portrait of Two Generations, 1840–1905* (Illinois, 1984).

15. See Roosa, 'Russian Industrialists'; Lavyorychev, *Gosudarstvo*.

16. M. F. Hamm, 'Kharkov's Progressive Duma, 1910–1914: A Study in Russian Municipal Reform' *Slavic Review*, XL (1981), esp. pp. 18–20; R. W. Thurston, 'Urban Problems and Local Government in Late Imperial Russia: Moscow, 1906–1914', Ph.D. thesis, University of Michigan (1980), esp. ch. 3.

17. See Zagorsky, *State Control*; Siegelbaum, *Politics*.

18. Siegelbaum, *Politics*, esp. ch. 7 and conclusion.

19. Zagorsky, *State Control*, pp. 261ff. Compare the account of an American procurement agent in Russia, Negley Farson, *The Way of a Transgressor* (London, 1935) chs. 17–18.

20. Allan K. Wildman, *The End of the Russian Imperial Army. The Old Army and the Soldiers' Revolt, March–April 1917* (Princeton, 1980), p. 102.

21. The following account is drawn from Volobuev, *Proletariat*; Smith, *Red Petrograd*. See also Ziva Galili y Garcia, 'Workers, Industrialists and Mensheviks: Labour Relations and the Question of Power in the Early Stages of the Russian Revolution', *Russian Review*, XLIV (1985).

22. P. A. Volobuyev, *Ekonomicheskaya politika Vremennogo pravitel'stva* (Moscow, 1962); V. Ya. Lavyorychev, 'Gosudarstvenno-monopolisticheskie tendentsii v prodovol'stvennom dele pri Vremennom pravitel'stve', *Voprosy istorii* (1979).

23. G. S. Akimova, 'Rossiyskaya burzhuaziya v gody pervoy mirovoy voyny', *Voprosy istorii* (1974).

24. Information on Moscow is drawn from *Moscow, Tsentral'nyy Gosudarstvennyy Arkhiv Oktyabr'skoy Revolyutsii (TsGAOR)*, f.1788 Ministerstvo vnutrennykh del Vremennogo pravitel'stva, op. 2 d. 114. See also Galili y Garcia, 'Workers'. P. A. Buryshkin, *Moskva kupecheskaya* (New York, 1954), although a valuable source on the Moscow business elite, is rather uninformative about 1917.

25. The following discussion is drawn largely from Ivanov, *Kontrrevolyutsiya*; Startsev, *Krakh Kerenshchiny*; Katkov, *Kornilov Affair*; Ferro, *October*. Startsev's interpretation of Kerenskii's position is more subtle than Ivanov's.

26. Frieden, *Russian Physicians*, esp. p. 314.

27. John F. Hutchinson, 'Society, Corporation or Union? Russian Physicians and the Struggle for Professional Unity (1890–1913)', *Jahrbucher fur Geschichte Osteuropas*, XXX (1982).
28. Frieden, *Russian Physicians*, epilogue.
29. Samuel C. Ramer, 'The Zemstvo and Public Health', in Terence Emmons and Wayne S. Vucinich (eds), *Zemstvo*, esp. pp. 292–8.
30. Peter F. Krug, 'Russian Public Physicians and Revolution: the Pirogov Society, 1917–1920', Ph.D. thesis, University of Wisconsin-Madison (1979), cited in Frieden, *Russian Physicians*, p. 322.
31. Jeffrey Brooks, 'The Zemstvo and the Education of the People', in Terence Emmons and Wayne S. Vucinich (eds), *Zemstvo*; Scott J. Seregny, 'Revolutionary Strategies in the Russian Countryside: Rural Teachers and the Socialist Revolutionary Party on the Eve of 1905', *Russian Review*, XLIV (1985).
32. Figures from Vostrikov, *Bor'ba* pp. 14–15.
33. A summary of the pre-Revolutionary Bar system can be found in Eugene E. Huskey, *The Formation of the Soviet Advokatura* (Princeton, 1986). An important source on the Petrograd Bar is the memoirs of N. P. Karabchevskii, *Chto glaza moi videli*, vol. 2 (Berlin, 1921).
34. Vostrikov, *Bor'ba*, p. 15.
35. Engelstein, *Moscow, 1905*, p. 18.
36. Rosenberg, *Liberals*, ch. 1.
37. For example Siegelbaum, *Politics*.
38. *TsGAOR*, f. 1788, op. 2, various entries.
39. Karabchevsky, *Chto glaza*, pp. 118ff.
40. *TsGAOR*, f. 1788, op. 2, d. 64.
41. *Ibid.*, d. 8.
42. *Ibid.*, dd. 16, 114.
43. Vostrikov, *Bor'ba*, p. 51.
44. Wildman, *End of the Russian Imperial Army*, p. xix.
45. Carmichael's translation: N. N. Sukhanov, *The Russian Revolution 1917* (Oxford, 1955) p. 635.
46. *TsGAOR*, f. 1788, op. 2, d. 73.
47. L. M. Gavrilov and V. V. Kutuzov, 'Perepis' russkoy armii 25 oktyabrya 1917g.', *Istoriya SSSR* (1964) pp. 90–1.
48. Mayzel, *Generals and Revolutionaries*; Peter Kenez, 'A Profile of the Pre-revolutionary Officer Corps', *California Slavic Studies*, VII (1973).
49. Wildman, *End of the Russian Imperial Army*, p. 101.
50. *Stanford, Hoover Institution Archive*, MSS memoirs of V. P. Anichkov.
51. D. R. Brower, 'Urban Russia on the Eve of World War One: a Social Profile' *Journal of Social History*, XIII (1980).
52. From reports in *TsGAOR*, f. 1788, op. 2, dd. various.
53. Material on traders and artisans is mostly from Vostrikov, *Bor'ba*.
54. Vostrikov, *Bor'ba*, p. 21.; Smith, *Red Petrograd*, p. 22.
55. Lavyorychev 'Gosudarstvenno-monopoliticheskie tendentsii', p. 42.

56. *Hoover Institution Archive*, Anichkov memoirs.
57. *Doklady Vladimirskoy Gubernskoy zemskoy upravy ekstrennomu Gubernskomu zemskomu sobraniyu* (Vladimir, 1918) p. 21.
58. Vostrikov, *Bor'ba*, ch. 6.
59. Material on employees is drawn mostly from Vostrikov, *Bor'ba*; Smith, *Red Petrograd*. Shop assistants were, not surprisingly, the least organised element; for grim contemporary description of their life see A. M. Gudvan, 'Essays on the History of the Movement of Sales-Clerical Workers in Russia', in Victoria E. Bonnell (ed.), *The Russian Worker, Life and Labor under the Tsarist Regime* (Berkeley, 1983).
60. Smith, *Red Petrograd*, pp. 134ff.
61. Jonathan Sanders, 'Drugs and Revolution: Moscow Pharmacists in the First Russian Revolution', *Russian Review*, LXIV (1985); Vostrikov, *Bor'ba*, p. 178.
62. *TsGAOR*, p. 1788, op. 2, d. 114.
63. Smith, *Red Petrograd*, pp. 135–6.
64. *Ibid.*, p. 137; Vostrikov, *Bor'ba*, pp. 43, 146.
65. *Ibid.*, pp. 153ff.
66. For example W. D. Rubinstein, 'Wealth, Elites and the Class Structure of Modern Britain', *Past and Present*, 76 (1977).
67. *Hoover Institution Archive*, Anichkov memoirs.
68. One example being a non-socialist District Commissar in Kazan province, in June: *TsGAOR*, f. 1788, op. 2, d. 103.
69. The expression used by Christopher Read in his contribution to this volume (Chapter 5).
70. The message in the editorial of the final issue of the 'third element' journal *Volostnoe zemstvo* (1918) pp. 35–6.

5 The Cultural Intelligentsia

Christopher Read

From the time of its origin the intelligentsia had thought and breathed revolution to such an extent that this orientation was usually regarded as basic to its definition. Whether one took Lavrov's position that they were 'critically thinking people' or the populists' 'mind, honour and conscience of the people' or the less poetic but more precise definition that they were the 'verbally articulate critics of tsarism', the theme of social change in general and revolution in particular was central to their existence. The optic had been approached from every conceivable angle. Every imaginable tactic or strategy had been put forward. In the early twentieth century even liberals defended the revolutionary tradition of the intelligentsia and its great figures. It comes, then, as something of a surprise that the year 1917 displays no more than a minor unevenness in the intelligentsia's development, that in 1917 the intelligentsia did nothing in particular and did it very well. Where one might have expected it to be at the centre of the development of the revolution in general, in fact it became preoccupied with its own life and its own world. In this world, surprisingly little changed after the February revolution. There was no sign of a great upsurge in intellectual activity or fundamental alteration in their way of life.

A couple of examples might help to illustrate this. For the liberal intelligentsia, university reform had long been an important issue. Higher education policy had been a constant source of friction between liberals and the autocracy since the mid-century. The collapse of the autocracy did not, however, result in an outburst of university reform. Certainly, professors who had been dismissed from their posts shortly before the war, as part of the continuing political reaction of the 1906–1914 period, were reinstated. The Provisional Government even set up a commission to elaborate a reform programme, but (and in this it faithfully mirrored its parent) the commission's progress was slow. University autonomy was proclaimed but, by and large, this was a front for the consolidation of professorial power in universities. Wider objectives were not achieved. The social composition of the student body was not changed. There was continuing powerful resistance to the admission of women. In January

1917 there were 28 women students in Moscow University. In January 1918 the number was still only 202. The student body grew only from 7000 to 8500 in the period. A comparison with figures for the following years is a rough measure of comparison of the pace of cultural revolution in 1917 itself and in the early Soviet period. In January 1919 there were 23 000 students including 6500 women.[1]

Artistic life and high culture also show continuity with the past rather than a radical break in 1917. Like the university professors, the cultural élite saw the February revolution as an opportunity for replacing state control and influence over the arts (which was not so great anyway) with their own. The suggestion that the Provisional Government should include an arts ministry was greeted with howls of opposition. The arts, it was argued, did not need bureaucratic direction from above. Instead they needed their own autonomous grass-roots organisations – and, as subsequent events unfolded, these were destined not to materialise.

As a result, mainstream cultural and artistic life went on in 1917 as 'normally' as it could. Publishers published, painters painted, exhibitions were held, critics criticised as best they could. All this has been confirmed by Lapshin's indispensable account of artistic life in Moscow and Petrograd in 1917.[2] His picture suggests that cultural life was continuing, as the Russians say, 'from inertia' or that people were simply going through the motions. As an extremely rough indication of the relatively even tenor of artistic life through 1917, Lapshin's chronology of events devotes about the same amount of space to each month of the year except for the summer months, especially August, which are mentioned only briefly presumably because they constituted the traditional vacation period. Though one should not put too much stress on this piece of evidence the impression given by other sources is very similar.

It must, however, be emphasised that the 'normality' prevalent before and through 1917 is the 'normality' of the war years, not of the pre-war period. The effect of the war had been to create a sombreness and thinness in intellectual life in general. Conscription had drawn many younger intellectuals into the armed forces. Enrollment in universities fell. A glance at any of the intelligentsia journals shows the effects vividly. They ceased to be 'thick' journals and became physically thinner, the quality of paper deteriorated but the range of contents narrowed even more spectacularly. Continental Europe was, of course, divided into three intellectual blocks: one centred on Paris, one on Vienna-Munich-Berlin and, a poor relation, on Moscow and Petrograd. Contact among them was sparse. Very little news filtered through. Interchange between them, such a vital part of intellectual life, was very restricted. Only a few enclaves of contact – Switzerland and, for a while, Italy – survived. Like the radical political intelligentsia, the Russian artistic intelligentsia, and its young avant-garde above all, was itself divided among these groupings. Kandinskii, Altman, Chagall and Tatlin had recently returned from the West and were caught within the virtual cultural blockade while Bakst, Goncharova, Larionov, Livshits and Soutine were at the heart of the Russian avant-garde emigration in Paris.

As a result an unaccustomed parochialism descended on Russian intellectual life. Editors strained to make something of any local events. Happenings abroad were usually limited to brief reports, often based on unreliable sources. The only areas to benefit, if that is the right word, were war art and the beginnings of official poster art which are to be found in the war years rather than in 1917 or after.

Most of these effects are well-known from, for example, the last few pages of the memoirs of Benedikt Livshits – *The One-and-a-half-eyed Archer* – who brilliantly described the transition from peace-time Petersburg to war-time Petrograd.[3] He recounted his own willing transformation into a soldier, the schism in the community produced by mobilisation and the disruption to other areas of life. The university, for instance, was handed over to the garrison. Livshits put it as follow: 'The university became (not in the metaphorical sense but in the literal sense of the word) a nidus of infection.' This came about not least because, as he describes, soldiers seemed to get a particular pleasure out of defecating on the main staircase. This, not unnaturally, tended to put a damper on the life of the university.

Putting such hazards aside, however, it was certainly the war and its implications that had affected intellectual life before February 1917 and continued to do so for a long time afterwards rather than the question of revolution. The chief concern of centrist, right-wing and not a few left-wing intellectuals continued to be the war. Most took a patriotic position and shared the hope that the February revolution would mainly be a step towards victory over Germany. Very few seem to have gone much beyond that. Peter Struve was an exception in that in the first post-February edition of *Russkaia mysl'* he emphasised the vital importance of maintaining the integrity of the army if the aims of the Provisional Government were to be fulfilled.[4] Very few (apart, of course, from Lenin in Zurich) were aware of the possibility of a second revolution so early on. Others like Leonid Andreev took a patriotic line and only later became aware of the growing social revolution which filled him with dismay. In March he wrote: Thus, in the struggle on two fronts – with Nicholas inside Russia and with the Hohenzollerns without – the Russian has obtained the right to be a citizen in his own land.[5] The main threat to this new freedom, for Andreev, was the 'dark people' to whom he appealed in an increasingly shrill way to perform their patriotic duty. By the end of summer he was drawing a distinction between revolution – the noble step forward of February – and *bunt* – the growing social revolution which, he feared, would create chaos. As early as April he had asked the populist intelligentsia 'And where is the *narod* whom you served so tirelessly and honourably? It has forgotten you.[6]

Perhaps it would be truer to say that intellectuals like Andreev had forgotten the *narod*. The general pattern was that intelligentsia life only changed gradually in 1917. Even so, an exception is visible among those intellectuals who set out not to deplore the dark people but to educate them. This was an area in which the fall of tsarism had a clear impact. While the autocracy existed societies for adult education among the urban poor were very suspect. The slightest infringement of the rules could result in closure.[7]

However, the overthrow of the police system led to growing possibilities in this area. Both the Provisional Government and the soviets became involved. Many soviets had cultural sections. Political parties organised parallel activities of their own. One of the best known activists in this area was Nadezhda Krupskaya who had a lifelong interest in worker education. Her first meeting with Lenin had been at a committee for literacy in the 1890s. In 1917 and after Krupskaya continued to work in this field. After she and Lenin returned to Petrograd from Switzerland she threw herself into work at the grass roots in the Vyborg district which she much preferred to the boring tasks she had been assigned in the Bolshevik Secretariat at the Party's headquarters in the Ksheshinskaya mansion. At a Petrograd city conference Krupskaya claimed to have upstaged the popular Provisional Government deputy minister Countess S. V. Panina. The latter's report admitted the Provisional Government's plans for education were not being fulfilled while Krupskaya claimed that the Bolsheviks and the people themselves had great achievements to their credit.[8]

Ideas began to develop about bringing all this work together and achieving co-ordination. One attempt was made by the cultural-educational section of the Moscow Soldiers' Soviet in early 1917. An appeal was made to 'painters, sculptors, artists, poets, musicians and architects', who were called upon to respond to the enthusiastic upsurge of interest in and opportunities for cultural advance. It was hoped that, in the special circumstances of the sin of the great war between peoples, those responding to the appeal would throw art a lifebelt.[9]

Initiatives of this sort led to the formation of Proletkul't in the days immediately preceding the October revolution. Its chief luminaries, Bogdanov and Lunacharskii, had been involved in cultural-educational work in a variety of ways. Lunacharskii's most notable contribution took the form of mass lectures in the Cirque Moderne. His favourite theme was scientific explanation of various religious cults and practices. At the beginning of October the first Petrograd conference of proletarian cultural educational organisations was held and it was from this that Proletkul't grew. In addition to Lunacharskii and Bogdanov, Krupskaya showed some interest but never played a significant role. The Central Committee of Petrograd Proletkul't met for the first time on 17 November. 1917 and established the different departments which the organisation retained throughout its existence. These were theatre, literature, clubs, lectures, fine art, music, school and extramural education.

For all their differences, one feature is shared by all these various types of activities. They were all very predictable in that they arose from ideas and convictions held by the *intelligentsia* involved prior to 1917. The revolution and its aftermath were, not surprisingly, assimilated into pre-existing world views. Andreev had never been an admirer of the *narod* and therefore came to see the unfolding events as a justification of his views. Struve had long before drawn attention to the importance of the state as a focus of a civilised and orderly life, hence his warning about the catastrophic effects of the disintegration of the army. Krupskaya, Lunacharskii and Bogdanov had long been advocates of mass cultural work and threw themselves into it. All this leads us to the perhaps depressing but nonetheless inescapable conclusion that intellectuals seldom change their minds once they have made them up. This characteristic no doubt added to the continuity and inertia already noted. Blok himself remarked on this phenomenon in 1917 in a letter to Zinaida Gippius (which was never sent).[10] The divisions in the intelligentsia, he commented, had their roots in 1905, not in 1917. Certainly the experience of revolution only twelve years earlier had crystallised intellectuals' ideas but, as in 1905, it was not the first revolutionary year, 1917 itself, which brought about such re-evaluations and re-alignments as there were. Above all, it was the subsequent years of reflection and analysis which had this effect.

It is worth noting, before we outline the changes which eventually occurred, that the October revolution did not instantaneously change the situation any more than the February revolution had done. The 'inertial' process still had a little way to run before profound changes began to transform Russia's cultural, intellectual and artistic scene. The universities continued to function as best they could. In fact there was little attempt at direct state intervention before September 1918 even though arrests of individuals began to increase. Books continued to be published. Theatres tried to maintain performances. But conditions were becoming more and more difficult.

The ambiguity of the period was caught in a debate held at the Writers' Union in Petrograd at the time of the signing of the Brest-Litovk treaty in March 1918. On the one hand the theme of the debate, 'The Tragedy of the Intelligentsia', implied that the current situation and prospects were disastrous while, as one correspondent reporting on the debate said, the occasion itself gave the impression 'that no such tragedy had befallen either the intelligentsia or Russia as a whole. The same people were on the platform and the audience had hardly changed'.[11]

This was perhaps the last moment at which even a vestige of 'normality' could be detected as transforming forces were at work. It becomes even more difficult after this point to talk about 'the intelligentsia' rather than about, on the one hand, those who were casualties of the new situation and, on the other, those who were its beneficiaries even though these latter, including nearly all intelligentsia Bolsheviks, were eventually to be casualties themselves.

What were the forces bringing about this division? At first one thinks of deliberate political pressure and the various systems of reward, or, more frequently, punishment through the agency of the Cheka, which were brought to bear. These were certainly real enough. Anti-parasite laws, universal labour obligations, waves of political arrests: all fell heavily on the intelligentsia. Furthermore, the intelligentsia as a whole, cultural, professional and technical, began to fall into a role that was increasingly fatal to it. It was becoming a kind of surrogate bourgeoisie. Bolshevik ideology fanned the flame of class struggle in Russia but one of the prime requisites – a powerful and oppressive bourgeoisie – was missing. It was even harder to find in 1918 since those with wealth and property had deserted the Soviet areas if at all possible, rifled their company safes, sold what they could, picked up the family valuables and gone for White protection or into emigration. This left employees and intellectuals to be seen, however unfairly, as a prominent component of the old élite within Soviet-occupied areas. If class struggle had to be prosecuted and the real class enemies – capitalists, bankers, landowners and so on – were on the run, then the intelligentsia were the best the militants could find in their place. Something of this dogged relations between the non-intelligentsia party left and the educated classes throughout the 1920s.

Political processes alone, however, do not explain what happened. A major transforming effect came about through what might be called the *perestroika* or re-structuring of the economic base of intellectual life at this time. The political economy of the major intellectual institutions – the press, publishing, the theatre, concert halls, cinemas, universities, schools and so on – was falling to pieces.

The chief sources of intellectual incomes – profits from performances; private patronage, sponsorship and purchase; the tsarist state budget, especially for higher education; the book market; newspaper and journal readerships – were all breaking up and suffering from economic collapse themselves. Most *intelligenty* were not well paid and had few reserves to fall back on. Those with savings soon lost them through the depreciation of paper money. This economic hurricane wreaked greater havoc among intellectuals than the direct political pressure of the fledging Bolshevik state. Many intellectuals were reduced to manual labour, to cultivating small plots of land, to flight, to starvation. Where the economic situation was particularly bad, in Petrograd for example in 1919, the death toll among intellectuals appears to have been enormous. Eminent, elderly and undernourished scholars had little resistance to cholera and typhus. Memoirs recall the frequency of death and funerals in this period. Younger people, too, were affected as Zamyatin grimly portrays in his story *The Cave* in which the stove-god in the apartment of an unemployed intellectual couple swallows up their furniture, reduces them to stealing firewood and a few potatoes to live on; but eventually they give in and commit suicide.[12] This fictional tragedy was being repeated in real life.

However, one of the key features of intelligentsia life in these stormy years was that the effects of political and economic pressure were far from even. Some intellectuals suffered heavily, some hardly at all; a few thrived and prospered. Some semblance of traditional intellectual life survived in the most unlikely oases. This was partly because of pure chance, particularly for those in the provinces where local attitudes sometimes moderated the effects of central policies; partly as a result of intelligentsia self-defence against the situation and partly as a result of state policies and decisions which offered some protection to parts of the intelligentsia. Let us therefore turn now to the fate of the intelligentsia in 1918–1920 as the revolutionary process deepened and impinged on it more directly. Bearing in mind that the intelligentsia was increasingly divided into a non-Bolshevik and a more pro-Bolshevik part, the experience of each would be better dealt with separately.

For non-Bolsheviks, various forms of self-defence against the new conditions began to emerge. Some of them – flight and emigration – are obvious and require little elaboration here. Sporadic active political resistance also occurred but after the summer of 1918 this was increasingly rare as political repression was stepped up in the wake of the Socialist-Revolutionary uprising and the shooting of Lenin. Self-defence under these circumstances meant fighting to preserve existing institutions, setting up new ones that met the new conditions and, less easily measured, a change of consciousness.

These three things can be summarised by saying that the intelligentsia became more aware of its own *separate* class position than had been the case before. It increasingly saw its own *value* to society – a feeling far removed from the guilt associated with its privileges by earlier generations – and began to demand appropriate respect for itself as a class. This was summed up by a speaker in the 'Tragedy of the Intelligentsia' debate. For 130 years, he argued, the intelligentsia had considered itself to be outside or above class and to be in the service of the whole people. 'The revolution,' he said, 'had shown this to be a laughable self-deception.'[13]

Once again this was a process which had been underway before 1917, particularly in the war years, when, to oversimplify, populism lost further ground to nationalism among the educated classes. Nationalism had begun to be purged of its obscurantist, tsarist, Slavophile and anti-Semitic tones in flavour of a more honourable and respectable patriotism legitimised by the national duty of defence against Germany and by the discrediting of the hated, traditional system in this struggle. Struve had been the prophet of this process after 1905. Miliukov was its high priest in the Duma and the February Revolution, when loyalty to country rather than Tsar, was invented by more and more members of the élite as a justification for defending their own interests by means of ditching the dynasty. For intellectuals of the centre and right the new democratic Russia was a worthy object of nationalist sentiment where the old one had not been. Defencists on the left had felt the same way. Even Bolsheviks, of course, adapted some of these arguments after October.

These two elements of intelligentsia consciousness – the growing sense of their class interests and their creative role in the service of the nation rather than the *narod* – found expression in a variety of ways. In the forefront of these was a series of trade-union type organisations devoted to protecting and promoting the professional interests of creative intellectuals and of workers in the cultural and educational institutions. The general pattern these went through is rather similar. They set out with 'labourist' demands – for the right to work, defence of working conditions and such specific grievances as each group felt – and then moved on (if they survived) into a more limited form of assertiveness and were usually subjected to a growing degree of party control. It is notable that even in their early and more militant days, such organisations described their aims as 'organisation and defence of the labour of members and improvement of their economic and legal standing' or 'the defence of the professional and spiritual interests' of their members'.[14] References to the political and social duties of intellectuals towards the people were rare, almost non-existent.

In addition, attempts were made to defend old institutions as much as possible. One of the most interesting and surprising rear-guard actions was put up by the universities in the summer of 1918. Narkompros (the People's Commissariat of Enlightenment) had wanted to inject more adult, working-class and political education into the universities, open them to women on an equal basis and provide for the election of professors. The universities refused most of this, conceding only that some courses on socialism should be taught and that there would be very limited democratisation of university administration. They insisted on including the word autonomy in the proposed definition of a university. Narkompros was temporarily defeated but began to implement its proposals in a piecemeal fashion in the following years.

Finally one should make brief mention of a variety of lesser bodies, private publishers, writer's co-ops, bookshops which provided a fragile haven for disparate groups. Gershenzon's Writers' Publishing House, set up in 1918, published 111 titles in its first year, ranging from Bogdanov to Rabindranath Tagore.[15] Mikhail Osorgin remembered the bookshop he ran in these years as 'not only the anchor of our personal safety but also a small cultural centre for Moscow'.[16]

The non-Bolshevik intelligentsia did not, of course, simply retreat into its shell and take on a purely defensive attitude. Various platforms of reconciliation, thoroughly, perhaps excessively, documented by Soviet scholars also began to appear. In this sphere an initial sorting came about on the basis of usefulness to the regime. From early 1918 Soviet policy was geared towards incorporating needed skills and expertise of the old educated classes. Doctors, managers, engineers, army officers and senior administrators headed the list. While this to some extent blunted direct hostility to part of the educated class, the creative intelligentsia proper did not benefit. The advent of embryonic planning commissions and the Commission headed by the rector of Moscow University, M. Novikov, charged with making an inventory of Russia's natural resources, provided employment and some protection for academic economists, scientists and statisticians. But only a handful were involved. Many, were left out. Those with skills which were in demand were fortunate to the extent that the new authorities needed them and were prepared to support them, though this was a somewhat mixed blessing if, like Dr. Zhivago, you were conscripted at gun-point and carried far into the distant reaches of the Civil War.

The creative intelligentsia was only coincidentally the beneficiary of these processes. More important to them were the establishment of food aid, rations, for prominent cultural figures. A surprisingly broad range of prominent persons was included in the list. The rations were usually distributed by the intellectual organisations themselves though the total number was decided by the state. While there was a great deal of lobbying to get on the list, most accounts suggest that delivery of the promised provisions was erratic and, for some, never arrived. Nonetheless, it provided a lifeline for many unemployable prominent intellectuals in the worst years.

The same could be said for publishing which, especially in the case of Gorkii's World Literature project, provided a system of outdoor relief for writers who were prepared to translate and edit volumes intended for it. But this brings us into contact with the second part of the intelligentsia, those who were prepared to work more actively with the regime.

For many of them the experience of the early Soviet period opened up new opportunities and undreamed-of power and influence. The cultural explosion of the revolutionary avant-garde is sufficiently well-known not to require elaboration here. I would, however, like to make a few observations about the social and institutional underpinnings of this phenomenon and say a little about the overall 'consciousness' behind much of this work.

As the traditional sources of funding of the arts dried up and markets contracted and patrons emigrated, the new Soviet authorities began to channel some resources into the arts. At first glance it seems odd that they would do this at all at a time when the regime was financially so stretched. However, much funding was intended to support almost utilitarian objectives: the effective propagation of the ideals of the new regime and the raising of the cultural level of the working class. The former led to the well-known flourishing of poster art, street demonstrations, commissions to produce monuments appropriate to the new values, new plays (most of which seem to have been written by Lunacharskii) and so on. Proletkul't engaged in a campaign to develop artistic and cultural skills among factory workers and peasants through their network of studios. It took on mainly the education of literate workers. Contrary to a widely held misconception, it was not especially iconoclastic and was happy to employ non-proletarian specialists such as Belyi and Bryusov to give lectures and help workers develop their creative talent and to begin to acquire the rudiments of the history and appreciation of culture as well as its re-interpretation in the light of the official new values.

Proletkul't, like many other lesser groups, depended on the central patronage institution, Narkompros, for its budget. In these early years Narkompros was a rather sprawling and uncontrolled bureaucracy with a set of tasks far beyond its means. Trying to conciliate the almost uniformly non-Bolshevik teaching profession and, simultaneously, sovietise school education made life very difficult. The former objective made compromise

over the latter inevitable and proposals for a radical reform of education – the Unified Labour School – were beaten off within Narkompros
and replaced by a less ambitious scheme. Scientific research, publishing,
adult education, technical and higher education were also its responsibility.
In the Civil War years it did not operate in a coherent and harmonious fashion but rather through a series of crises and priority campaigns which drew
the attention of Lunacharskii, Pokrovskii, Krupskaya and its other leading
figures hither and thither wherever the next difficulty was cropping up.

The atmosphere within Narkompros tended to be one of bitter factional
conflict and this was true of the new institutions as a whole. As a general
rule they were riven by faction fighting and bureaucratic empire-building
as different groups sought to gain access to the relatively limited sources of
patronage. Intellectual groups set out to colonise parts of the new system
and set up their dominion within it. This pattern of cultural politics, noted
by many observers looking at the 1920s, was equally intense in these early
years. Many of them have mistakenly concluded that the very scope and
intensity of the struggles show that the party and the authorities were
not heavily involved in them at this time. The degree of control which
emerged later was not born complete in the October revolution; but it is
wrong to conclude that, because the entire system was not in place, then
the party was taking a more liberal line. In the first place, the party and
government controlled the flow of patronage on which the battles depended
and around which they raged. Many groups were, from the outset, excluded
from participation in these struggles. Centre and right-wing intellectuals had
no place in them. All those involved were, in some sense, revolutionary,
so the spectrum had been cut down from the outset. There are three main
reasons why party intervention was not even greater at this time. First, the
new Soviet authorities were relatively weak in these years; secondly their
attention was focussed on more critical issues like defeating the Whites and
re-ordering the economy and, thirdly, they had no policy to implement. In
these years there were three different, even competing, generators of party
cultural policy – Lunacharskii and his allies in Narkompros; Proletkul't
and, the one which was eventually the most important, the cultural (i.e.
largely publishing and agitprop) sections of the Central Committee. Battle
lines formed between them even though each of them still contained
different groups within. It was these factors which created the puzzling
pluralism of the Civil War years in which one can find more survivals
of pre-revolutionary culture than at any other time in Soviet history (e.g.
in higher education); terrible suffering and starvation among intellectuals;
and the brilliant achievements of the avant-garde.

In the background the authorities were beginning to move themselves into a position from which they could intervene in and end this chaos. It is typical of the time that the first blows were struck, not at the right-wing of fledgling Soviet culture, but at its left, Proletkul't. In 1919 its project for a Proletarian University was ruthlessly rejected and amalgamated into the party's own Sverdlov University. In 1920, though it was not wound up, Proletkul't itself was virtually broken by a resolution of the Central Committee which asserted direct party control over it.

To conclude, however, it might be appropriate to look briefly at the career, in this period, of an individual who typifies many of the processes I have referred to. Many such individuals could be chosen and are frequently chosen for this purpose – Blok, Gorkii, Belyi, Bryusov, Mayakovskii, Lissitskii, Malevich, Tatlin. These are all people who, in a special way capture something of this early revolutionary moment. One person who is less frequently thought of in this context, to the detriment of an understanding of the period and of his work as a whole, is Marc Chagall. His career mirrors some of the changes mentioned above. There was some evolution in his life and art when the war began but the main turning point came in late 1917, up to which time he had been living and exhibiting in Petrograd, the summer of 1917 finding him in the country busy painting landscapes. Byt the time he returned to the city late in the year the situation had so degenerated that he withdrew to his beloved Vitebsk, his native town situated near the Polish border. In August 1918, with Lunacharskii's approval and funding, Chagall opened his famous Vitebsk Art Academy which was devoted to bringing art to the people and, literally, bringing it into the streets, the decoration of which for the first anniversary of the October revolution was one of Chagall's first major projects there. To that extent the anniversary had more immediate impact in Chagall's life than the Revolution itself. His enthusiastic organisation ran quickly into the faction-fighting and struggle for patronage which reached even into the backwaters of Belorussia. Through superior bureaucratic organisation he was, of course, defeated by Malevich, his former pupil Lissitskii, Puni and the Suprematists who took over the Academy. He returned to Petrograd and was commissioned to decorate the Kammernyi State Jewish Theatre, which settled in Moscow in November 1920. This occupied much of his time before he left Russia in summer 1922. One of the main forces which had driven him out were the changing economic circumstances, as a result of which the state patronage he had enjoyed during the civil war had dried up. Artists no longer received grants; the state no longer had money to buy his paintings, nor did anyone else in Russia and, like many other intellectuals, the NEP transition to economic accounting and profitability blew a chill wind of market forces through the intellectual life of the country which brought chaos to many artists and institutions. Such state support as there was began to be channelled to members of the realist school rather than to members of the avant-garde.

Above all, Chagall's flirtation with the Revolution, and his subsequent work, remind us of one of the fundamental forces distinguishing those, like himself, who worked with the Bolsheviks from those who remained neutral. What Chagall saw in the revolution, for all its faults, was a step forward in the life of ordinary people. He was not terrified and appalled by the 'dark people' as Andreev had been: he loved them and tried to bring his art closer to them. Populism should take its place alongside the whimsicality, optimism, false naïveté and Jewishness always associated with Chagall. It remained with him long after. In the mid-1930s his triptych 'Revolution', depicting an acrobatic Lenin standing on one hand in the middle of a carnival, referred back to the joy felt by Chagall in the heroic years. His painting 'White Crucifixion' of 1936, inspired by the worsening plight of Jews in Germany, has, as a symbol of hope, a rag-taggle Red Army composed of the *narod* appearing in the background as liberators.[17]

It was a similar populist impulse that brought Blok, Gorkii and many other intellectuals to overcome their repugnance at the dictatorial tendencies of Bolshevism and to ally themselves, if not fully with the party and state, at least with the hope the Revolution had aroused, They were also responding to another somewhat overlooked aspect of October: namely that, for all its proletarian form, it also retained its dimension as an intelligentsia enterprise, led by a part of the intelligentsia which had traditions at least as much Russian as they were internationalist and Marxist. The broad populist impulse – understood as the desire to fight on behalf of the oppressed – was strongly present in the Revolution. The word *narod* came readily to the new rulers. Even the government was composed of *narodnye kommissary*: people's commissars. The officially-desired linking of workers with poor peasants and later with the entire peasantry was almost a disguised reconstitution of the *narod* as the very basis of the Revolution. One would imagine that a study of workers and peasants in 1917 would show a greater degree of consciousness of themselves as the *narod*, or the labouring masses, as it would of them as workers or peasants. Oddly, no one has tried to find this out. Be that as it may, from the point of view of intellectuals, the populist impulse was a powerful bridge between themselves and the new authorities, as well as having an impact on Bolshevik intellectuals themselves. This populism reminds us that those intellectuals who sympathised with the Revolution saw that the Bolshevik project itself, no matter how flawed, emanated in part from the intelligentsia tradition itself. It is also interesting to note that it was only when the intelligentsia Bolsheviks had lost influence that the Revolution reached its nadir in the mid-1930s.

This examination of the intelligentsia's experience of Revolution suggests several conclusions both about the intelligentsia at this time and about the wider contemporary processes of social revolution. First, the intelligentsia revolution was not chronologically in step with the political revolution. For intellectual life the Revolution only began to bite in early 1918 rather than in February or October 1917. Up to that point, the war rather than the political revolutions had been having a greater impact on intellectual life. It follows from this that, in its first few months of office, the 'effectiveness' of the Bolsheviks does not contrast as sharply with the 'ineffectiveness' of the Provisional Government over a similar time period. Deep processes of social revolution were occurring which were beyond anyone's control. Different sections of society were participating in this process to greatly differing extents at different times. The peaks and troughs of peasant revolution, for example, coincided neither with the political turning points nor with the pace and direction of intelligentsia revolution.

Secondly, the intelligentsia became divided more clearly, but not completely, into liberal-nationalist and populist sub-groups. The former begin to evolve a more specific intelligentsia 'class' consciousness which asserted its independence, its rights and its value to society through the pursuit of its own skills and interests. By and large the intellectuals in this camp did not welcome the October revolution but exhibited a wide range of responses from a pragmatic agreement to work with the new Soviet authorities to outright hostility. The populist group by contrast were more enthusiastic about the Revolution in the long term arguing that, for all its faults, many of which were attributable to the evils of tsarism anyway, the Revolution did offer some hope of liberation to the ordinary people of Russia. In a sense, those intellectuals within the party can be assimilated to this group as well as sympathisers with the Revolution outside the party's ranks. It should be remembered also that some intellectuals exhibited characteristics of both these groups. Though quantification is hazardous, there can be little doubt that the majority of established intellectuals drifted into the former camp. Within this group, the traditional distinction between creative intellectuals and mental labourers began to break down as both rallied to the defence of their material interests and to nationalism rather than to the *narod* or to intellectual and spiritual causes. Incidentally, Machajski's fashionable prediction that the intelligentsia would use revolutionary socialism as a class ideology in which to conceal its material interests showed no sign of coming true. The opposite was happening. Those who were most adamant in asserting class interest drifted furthest away from socialism. Similarly, the more powerful the Soviet system became, the weaker the intelligentsia influence within it. Equally, there was no evidence that the ordinary people systematically turned on the intelligentsia in these years. If anything, they turned to them. If they met a blank or hostile response they might well become more bitter towards them; but there is no sign of widespread anti-intellectual pogroms at this time. Gershenzon's opinion of 1909 that the bayonets and prisons of tsarism were protecting the intelligentsia from the wrath of the people proved to be an exaggeration.

A third conclusion worth emphasising is that the divisions within the intelligentsia were not created in these years but were a development of earlier arguments and attitudes. They resulted from pre-existing differences being drawn out rather than from mass conversions to new principles.

Fourthly, the Civil War years, and particularly 1918–1919, were a period of decisive struggle for hegemony in the new society, not just militarily but also socially. The fight of civil society (i.e. social organisations outside the formal state system) for independence, a key feature of 1917 with links going back to 1905, was resulting in the triumph of the new state at the expense of the embryonic institutions of civil society – soviets, trade unions, political parties and, with regard specifically to the intelligentsia, its independent organisations such as the Pirogov Society, the Imperial Free Economic Society and its own trade unions. In many respects it was the civil war, rather than 1917, that was the time of the real revolution in Russia. Really it would be better to think of it as the Russian revolutionary war.

Fifthly, it was in the years 1920–1922 that the victors in this struggle for hegemony organised themselves. The party-state apparatus began to dominate areas previously outside its control. In intellectual life the central party bodies gained the upper hand over Proletkul't and Narkompros. Gosizdat (the State Publishing House) dominated book production, the censorship (Glavlit) was founded, university autonomy was brought to an end and potentially troublesome and ideologically 'unsound' intellectuals were forcibly expelled.

Sixthly, economic hardship and the dislocations caused by the social revolution were a more important source of erosion of intellectual life than direct political pressure, particularly in the early years. The cultural economy collapsed rapidly from early 1918. This facilitated the growing influence of the state because it was left as the sole arbiter of patronage and controller of the cultural economy. There is no denying that the party intervened extensively in intellectual life in this period, the most prominent example being over Proletkul't, but across the whole spectrum its impact grew as alternative organisations died out.

Finally, it should not be forgotten that the Bolshevik leaders themselves were affected by the intelligentsia tradition and shared at least a degree of respect for cultural values even though they were usually contemptuous of the creators and purveyors of those values, the intellectuals themselves. It was only after the death or defeat of Lenin, Trotskii and Bukharin that the Revolution moved into its most barbaric phase. Thus the intelligentsia and the intelligentsia tradition had an impact on the Revolution as well as the reverse. Although its open expression has been difficult, many aspects of the humanism of the old intelligentsia – respect for free intellectual development, devotion to high moral and ethical standards, service of the people and respect for culture – have survived in Russia in the minds of reformers, critics and dissidents. They can even be traced in recent developments in the Soviet Union. In rhetoric at least, and probably in substance too, the intelligentsia tradition still has a role to play in the Soviet Union.

Notes

1. Materials from the Provisional Government Commission on the Reform of Higher Education and the First Narkompros Commission: archive reference F 2306. 2. 12.

2. See V. P. Lapshin, *Khudozhestvennaya zhizn' Moskvy i Petrograda v 1917 g.* (Moscow, 1983).

3. B. Livshits, *The One-and-a-Half-Eyed Archer* (Newton, Mass-achusetts, 1977), pp. 243–5.

4. P. B. Struve, 'Osvobozhdennaya Rossiya', *Russkaia mysl'*, no. 2, 1917, p. xii.

5. L. Andreev, *Pered zadachami vremeni* (Benson, Vermont, 1985), p. 36.

6. *Idem*, p. 99

7. See L. M. Kleinbort, *Ocherki rabochei intelligentsii*, vol. 1 (Petrograd, 1923).

8. See N. Krupskaya, *Memories of Lenin* (London, 1970), pp. 307–8; R. McNeal, *Bride of the Revolution* (London, 1973), p. 177.

9. See Lapshin, *op. cit.*, p. 138.

10. A. Blok, *Sobranie sochinenii v vos'mi tomakh*, vol. 7 (Moscow, 1960), p. 335.

11. A. I. [*sic*], 'Tragediya russkoi intelligentsii. (Na mitinge soyuza pisa-telei)', *Vechernie ogni*, 1 April (19 March) 1918.

12. A translation of this grim story can be found in Evgenii Zamyatin, *The Dragon and Other Stories* (Harmondsworth, 1978).

13. A. Red'ko, 'Tragediya russkoi intelligentsii', *Russkoe bogatstvo*, no. 1/3, January–March 1918, p. 264.

14.   Union of Workers in the Arts (Rabis) archive: F 5508. 1. 4. 8 and F 5508. 1. 93. 1.
15.   A. Nazarov, *Oktyabr' i kniga* (Moscow, 1968), pp. 128–30.
16.   M. Osorgin, 'Knizhnaya lavka pisatelei', *Vremennik obshchestva druzei russkoi knigi*, no. II (Paris, 1928), p. 21.
17.   The fullest account of Chagall's life in this period is to be found in F. Meyer, *Marc Chagall: Life and Work* (New York, n.d.), pp. 217–314.
      There are black-and-white reproductions of the two items mentioned here on pp. 392 and 417. See M. Chagall, *My Life* (London, 1966).

6 Soldiers and Sailors

Evan Mawdsley

The new writing on the Russian revolutionary era has brought out two related themes: broad social forces and events outside the capital.[1] Both these themes have been reflected in recent Western research on the Russian armed forces, and the goal of this chapter is to look at some of the most important examples.

Some recent general accounts of the traditionally 'central' (political) events of the revolution have made interesting points about the armed forces. For example, George Katkov's history of the February revolution, *Russia 1917*, suggested that a critical part was played by the 'aide-de-camp generals' revolution'. The current standard account of February, by Tsuyoshi Hasegawa, also has much to say on the army, and about the complex interactions of time and events involving officers and men both at the Supreme High Command and in the Petrograd garrison. Alexander Rabinowitch's history of the October revolution emphasised the importance of the early Bolshevik control over the garrison.[2] Getzler and Raleigh's non-metropolitan studies provide useful information about specific internal garrisons.[3] The emphasis is the present chapter, however, will be on works which concentrate on the armed forces themselves.

In looking at these military-oriented works a broad view will be taken of the time-span that made up the revolutionary era. Although February–October 1917 is still the pivotal period, interesting and related points about the armed forces have emerged from specialised studies of the preceding years.[4]

The best work on the Russian Army in 1917 is Allan Wildman's recently completed *The End of the Imperial Russian Army*.[5] The author makes much of the links between the soldiers and Russian peasant traditions. 'The peasants in gray coats, the cells that made up the living tissue, had acquired a "conscious" life and strength of their own . . . '; once the goals of Soviet power and peace 'had in their eyes been consummated, the millions of cells became simply peasants, anxious to be repatriated to their families and accustomed way of life . . . '[6]

The author's main stress is on the great schism in Russian society. In the war years the critical cleavage was not that between the autocracy and the political forces, but between the 'cultured and non-cultured layers'. The soldiers of the Russian Army were

> scions of a peasant culture with its indigenous parochial concerns. The war was simply one more intrusion into this private world of the demands of the [traditional] holders of political and social power, robbing them [i.e. the soldiers] of their lives and substance.[7]

This notion relates, of course, to the influential concept of 'dual polarisation' developed by Leopold Haimson, which is a thread running through much of the new historiography of the revolutionary period.[8]

Most originally, in historiographical terms, Allan Wildman argues that this cleavage in the army existed, too, between 'those groups . . . that found a new identity in the cause of the war' and 'the alienated masses'; and he affirms that part of the radical intelligentsia belonged to the first group. The men who were thrown up by the February revolution to man the higher-level committees in the spring of 1917, the 'committee class', were more oriented towards the patriotism of the Provisional Government than to the demands of their own constituents; only the grass-roots committees, at regimental level, kept their links with the soldiers, and this explains many of the developments of 1917.

One way of looking at trends in various sectors of Russian society is to focus on the relationship between 'politicisation' and 'democratisation'. 'Politicisation' might be taken to mean the general political awakening of 'the masses' to the main currents of civilian politics, 'democratisation' the change in the conditions of day-to-day life. For Allan Wildman politicisation and democratisation are very closely related: 'The peasants in uniform strongly sensed that the end of the monarchy and of the hierarchical order of authority were the same, whether at the front or in the country at large . . . ' This perception was not introduced by the Bolsheviks, but simply speeded up by them. There had been a multi-dimensional 'revolution of consciousness' as a result of the overthrow of the Tsar; the soldiers saw that they had power.[10] As with a number of other new works on the revolution (for example, on workers), Allan Wildman stresses that politicisation came in part from the consciousness-raising experience of democratisation, the changes in the immediate condition of life.

Like others, Allan Wildman makes much of the role of the spontaneous mass action, right from the February 1917 Revolution:

> The end results of 'Bolshevism' and 'Soviet power' were far more a reflection of the spontaneous forces of revolution, as opposed to the

rational constructs of ideologues and political leaders, than either Soviet or Western historiography have characteristically acknowledged.[11]

Spontaneous action was determined in part by a particular mass view of the Russian situation:

The soldiers' assumption that the Revolution signified the definitive end of landowning society and its unjust laws was clearly expressed from the very first weeks of March [1917] . . . This underlying assumption of a radical inversion of all former social and political relationships can be regarded as the leitmotif of this study . . . ' [12]

The Bolsheviks advanced 'on the crest of this Revolution', thanks to the bankruptcy of their rivals; those rivals could not come to terms with the revolution that had already taken place. The author follows this up by stressing that the changes in the army came about, throughout 1917, from within, not because of external agitation. He repeatedly makes an important distinction between 'party-oriented' Bolshevism and Bolshevism of the 'marching company-trench variety'.[13]

The End of the Russian Imperial Army says less about the Tsarist officer corps than about the rank-and-file soldiers. It does not stress high command politics; the officer plots of 1916 are seen as 'marginal' to the study, and the main events of the Kornilov affair are left out for reasons of space. The work does, however, demonstrate that the myth of the aristocratic army officer should not be accepted. The old army was largely destroyed in 1915; its junior officers were killed and replaced by wartime subalterns (*praporshchiki*), who were often educated peasants.

All told, Allan Wildman's two volumes represent a most remarkable work of scholarship, with excellent sources and an original interpretation. There is perhaps a problem of balance; all the stress on the early months of the revolution (in vol. 1) means that the treatment of the April–December 1917 period (in vol. 2) is much compressed; such important events as the Battle of Riga and even the Kornilov affair could only be outlined. And the suggestion that the book's interpretation should somehow be hidden is misjudged. It seems extraordinary for the author to argue that 'My object has been to convey as much of the original stuff of the Russian Revolution in the Army as possible without tainting it with preconceived views . . . ' [14] Given the stimulating nature of the author's argument it would have been very valuable had he pulled it together more at the end of the final volume.

John Bushnell's *Mutiny amid Repression* is perhaps the second most impressive work on the revolutionary Russian army in English.[15] Of course, 1905–1906 was not 1917. The crisis in the army was less deep than in the First World War. The structure of the army was less badly damaged by the fighting. Most importantly, the central authority of the Tsar was not altogether discredited: a basic point of the Bushnell book. In contrast with 1917 the soldiers' rebellion was eventually contained in 1905–1906 (although the crisis in the army lasted considerably longer than in 1917). Nevertheless many of John Bushnell's reflections are useful for the 1917 revolution, especially since he, like Allan Wildman, is looking at broad (and vague) concepts of mass psychology. (Indeed, John Bushnell's research began as a study of rear organisations in 1917 and – as often happens – the first introductory chapter was expanded into something different.)[16]

Like Allan Wildman, John Bushnell sees cleavages in Russian society, although his are even deeper. There was a gap between 'peasant/traditional Russia' and 'European/polite Russia'; and most of the urban revolutionaries were included in the second part rather than the first.[17] For John Bushnell soldiers (and sailors) were peasants, part of peasant Russia. They had a traditional peasant world-outlook. They had a particular view of authority. The mutinies they undertook in 1905–1906 were out of phase with the revolutions by civilians in Russia's cities in 1905–1906; 'the soldiers' revolution of 1905 and 1906 was a special case of Russian peasant rebellion'.[18] Their way of life had much in common with the peasant economy, notably the so-called 'regimental economy' of everyday labour and self-supply in army units.

For John Bushnell politicisation and democratisation are closely linked, but not identical. Democratisation was a central concern. This was one of the earliest demands of the rebels, to take away the operation of 'the regimental economy' and 'the web of controls over their movements and activity'. In fact, one of the problems was the gap between the democratisation-centred revolution of the soldiers and the politically-centred revolution of the revolutionaries.[19]

Mutiny amid Repression is mainly about politicisation, although politicisation of a different type from that of 1917; this was 'stop-and-go' politicisation. What it tries to explain is why Russian soldiers could play a dual role in 1905–1906, first rebelling and then putting down rebellions ('mutiny amid repression'). What counted, according to the author, was mass psychology, the extent to which the soldiers believed in the myth of the autocracy. That was why the October (1905) Manifesto, conceding the Duma and visibly reducing the emperor's authority, was followed by mutiny in the forces.

Further research is needed to say whether what John Bushnell says could apply fully to later developments in Russian history. He would presumably agree with Allan Wildman that the end of the autocracy in February 1917 eliminated any real restraint on soldier-peasant rebellion and made a radical outcome to the revolutionary crisis inevitable.

Possibly, however, using Bushnell's logic, the hypothetical victory of a Kornilov would have led to a greater deference to authority; certainly the middle path of Provisional Government was no formula for success. (But if the firmness of the autocracy in November–December 1905 suppressed the soldiers disorders and led them to suppress the Moscow Uprising, why did not the firmer Provisional Government line following the July Days have the same impact in 1917?) And it might be a useful way of explaining why, in 1918–1919, the Soviet government was able to create a large conscript army; it says something about the value of the officer model (patriarchal) and perhaps the value of preserving the ancient capital in Moscow. Lenin used roughly this argument against the 'Military Opposition' among Bolsheviks early in 1919 when he called for 'iron discipline': 'If you say that this is an autocratic feudal system and protest against saluting, then you will not get an army in which the middle peasant will fight'.[20]

On the other hand, John Bushnell – and Allan Wildman – may be going too far in stressing the limitations of the peasant horizon, the peasants' alienation from educated society. The result is a rather deterministic view of the future development of the Revolution. Peasants were reconscripted back into service in 1918–1920 on both sides of the Civil War fronts, and it is doubtful that *kolkhozniki* were any less alienated in Stalin's army of 1941–1945.

There are a number of other works on the forces in 1917. The late Mikhail Frenkin's two émigré monographs on front-line and rear garrisons are full of information and are more outspokenly anti-Bolshevik than anything written in the West nowadays.[21] He is especially good on the Bolshevik manipulation of the various 'revolutionary committees' in the army. Mikhail Frenkin's interpretation is rather different from Allan Wildman's view of more-or-less spontaneous radicalisation (although Wildman rightly thinks highly of Frenkin, and even dedicated his first volume to him). Mikhail Frenkin's general view is different inasmuch as he assumes a considerable ability of the Bolsheviks – through their unscrupulous manipulatory tactics – to control the soldiers' organisations. His approach seems near to that of John Keep with the stress on the manipulation from above of workers' and peasants' mass organisations; from research evidently conducted quite independently, Mikhail Frenkin came up with conclusions which neatly complemented *The Russian Revolution: A Study in Mass Mobilization*.

One other point brought out by Frenkin that has been largely ignored in other sources is the role of the nationalities movement in the army. The breakdown of the army in 1917 came not only from radical politics but also from 'Ukrainization' and similar concessions to ethnic demands.

Despite significant differences in interpretation, Wildman, Bushnell and Frenkin are alike in not making a great deal of the role of the officers. This gap is to some extent made up by Matitiahu Mayzel's *Generals and Revolutionaries*, which is good on the role and *esprit de corps* of the General Staff officers.[22] More research needs to be done on the corporate sense of certain groups in the officer cops. Peter Kenez and David Jones have written valuable articles pointing out how different the commanders of 1917 were from those of 1914,[23] but there is room for a more comprehensive work.

William Fuller's monograph on civil-military conflict deals with the period 1881–1914 and is primarily on legal and budget matters. It is however founded on an extraordinarily good archival basis, and makes some interesting points about the reluctance of military 'professionals' (or such military 'professionals' as there *were* in the Russian army) to get involved in politics. By implication it relates to another aspect of the Haimson 'dual polarisation' theory: 'The incapacity of the Imperial government . . . to digest military professionalism . . . represented one of the gravest weaknesses of tsarism . . . '[24] Likewise, *Civil-Military Conflict* argues that this related to the fall of the Tsar in February ('the abdication . . . can in part be construed as a military coup'). It also hints at the attraction for the officers of 'national Bolshevism'.[25]

In general, historians of late Imperial Russia need to look more at officer politics. One of the most surprising features of Russian politics was the small role played by the army. After the palace coups of the eighteenth century and the Decembrist Revolt of 1825, the army high command played no independent part in Russian politics until February 1917, and the only period of military rule came in White territory from November 1918 to November 1920. Richard Pipes, in his *Russia under the Old Regime*, discussed the weakness of the nobility, the church, and educated society in the face of apparently all-powerful autocracy; but it is surprising that he did not also talk about the frailty of the army.[26]

To be specific, there is a need for more detailed work on the army high command in the winter of 1916–1917, and especially for a definitive treatment of the Kornilov affair. The work of Katkov goes some distance in this direction, but more needs to be said.[27]

The Russian Navy was different from the Russian Army. Pavel Dybenko probably the best-known revolutionary from the Baltic Fleet, recalled that 'The sailor always felt that he was superior to the soldier, to the worker, and therefore he felt obliged to be in the vanguard'.[28] My own work on the 1917 military concerned the Baltic Fleet; historians, like biographers, tend to become devoted to their own subject, and I must confess that the naval point of view seemed very attractive.[29] The navy was much the junior service to the army, no matter from what perspective the armed forces are examined. In 1917 there was only one sailor for every twenty-five soldiers. Nevertheless the published sources for 1917 are richer for the navy than the army, the fleets make coherent case studies, and no one would deny that political importance of the Baltic Fleet for events in Petrograd in 1917. The navy was also a particularly volatile force; it is 'no accident', as they say, that the revolutionary era in the Russian armed forces began with mutiny of the battleship *Potyomkin* of June 1905 and ended with the Kronstadt uprising of March 1921, both naval – rather than army – mutinies.

Can conclusions be reached about the fleet that are different from conclusions about the army? Does research on the fleet correct some of the conclusions reached about the army? First of all, the mass of conscript sailors of the Imperial Russian navy seem to me to be something more than workers (and some peasants) in uniform; they formed a distinct social group, with characteristics of its own. The sailors were mostly young men in their early twenties, one of whose main experiences had been several years' service in the fleet. They were a particular selection from the population (in terms of age, geographical origin, education, and occupation), and they had been conditioned – on average for several years – by a certain series of experiences.

They were also not soldiers in blue uniforms; they were younger, with a different social background, and better education. But the points made above about the navy's distinction from civilian society could arguably also be made of the much larger army *mutatis mutandis*. Opinions vary here; Allan Wildman and John Bushnell stress the affinity between peasants in and out of uniform; nevertheless the line taken by Marc Ferro, at least as regards the early months of the revolution, seems more convincing:

> During the 1917 revolution the troops behaved quite as much like old soldiers . . . as they behaved like peasants in uniform . . . This is hardly surprising. They were young and the war was their first overwhelming experience . . . [30]

The other side of 'society' in the navy were the officers. The difference between the typical naval officer and the typical army officer, especially at the junior-commander level, was probably greater than between the enlisted sailor and the enlisted soldier. Neither could, except by the simplest analysis, be identified with the 'bourgeoisie', and even an identification with the landlords is crude. Many of the navy's officers belonged to a hereditary non-propertied service class. This is not to deny, however, that there were not cultural differences between officers and men, differences more profound than between the common *soldaty* and the low-born army *praporshchiki* promoted in 1915–1917.

Another point that seems to me to emerge from research is the importance of the specific. The unusually bloody events in the Baltic Fleet in February 1917, especially the mutinies at Kronstadt and Helsingfors, are interesting because they point to the chancy nature of historical events, at least at the 'micro' level. With roughly the same social mix, there were violent mutinies among naval units at Kronstadt and Helsingfors, but little bloodshed at Reval (Tallin) or the smaller bases (and little in Imperial Russia's smaller fleets). It was in part a specific flow of information – in particular the timing of news from the capital – that created the explosive situation at some bases. In the post-February period, too, there were interesting variations among the various bases. If the navy is aggregated into an abstract, then events would have proceeded at a fairly uniform pace. In fact, despite being less than a hundred miles apart, the three main Baltic naval bases developed in different ways, at least in the first six months after February 1917. The differences can only be understood by looking at the specific units stationed at each base.

More broadly, this question of how historical events actually unfold shows differences between historians. Some, especially when they see events as shaped by the social bedrock, take a view which tends toward determinism; Allan Wildman perhaps goes too far in his judgement on the failure of government punitive forces in the February days:

> The historian . . . cannot attribute decisive significance to fortuitous circumstances or speculate on hypothetical variations of the actual facts . . . In effect, to assume that [during the February days] there could have been energetic leadership that could have led to an opposite result would be to ignore all the deep-seated social and political reasons that led to the isolation of the monarchy . . . [31]

It is interesting that John Bushnell, whose views on the social cleavage of 'dual polarisation' are similar, is more prepared to look at the role of accident. He stresses the importance of mass perception, and this can in his view be affected by relatively small events; for example, had the Social Democrats prepared the workers' organisations to protest the dissolution of the Duma in mid-1906 it might have finally shaken the credibility of the régime in the soldiers' minds.[32] In any event, there is certainly a cleavage between historians who lay stress on the overwhelming importance of generalised forces and historians who stress the continued importance of tactics (Bolshevik manipulation, or whatever).

In analytical terms, it seems useful to keep the processes of politicisation and democratisation more separate. These two *are* related; the democratisation of naval administration, for example, took power from the conservative officer corps and gave it to the committees, and those committees then used their power to back radical political moves on the wider civilian stage. Control of all movements by the fleet committees made it possible to send detachments of sailors to Petrograd to take part in various demonstrations and in the October armed uprising. But democratisation is also interesting in its own right, both in terms of military sociology and in the way it affected the fleet as a 'war-fighting' organisation. In this connection, a third theme might be added to politicisation and democratisation: military efficiency.

Looking first at politicisation, Bolshevik organisation in the navy was weak before the February 1917 Revolution, despite what Soviet historians have alleged. More surprising, perhaps, is one feature of early politicisation at all the bases: the non-partisan nature of politics, populism with a small 'p'. Many sailors could simply not understand why the revolutionary masses should divide their forces into competing parties; they did not understand, and they mistrusted, the dogma of civilian agitators. Even at Kronstadt the non-partisan 'party', with SR-Maximalist overtones, was a considerable force. This sentiment continued even after all the headway made by Bolshevik and SR agitation over the eight months of 'free Russia'; it was shown after the October revolution by the desire for an all-socialist government, rather than one dominated by the Bolsheviks. In general, it is too easy for historians (partly following the Soviet historical model) to assume clear-cut political horizons with modern parties and a sophisticated mass political understanding.

On the other hand, non-partisan radicalism was still radicalism, and another feature of life in the fleet was a shift to the left among all groups, the Bolsheviks, the SRs, and even the Mensheviks, with the emergence of left factions – hostile to the war and the Provisional Government – as the most powerful. Soviet historians might disagree with the notion that many sailors saw no especial need for parties, or that when they moved to the left it was not necessarily into the Bolshevik party. There are, however, areas where one must agree with Soviet memoirists and historians, although this runs counter to some notions of (more traditional) Western historiography. In the first place, there is no doubt that the end result of the eight-month revolutionary process in the fleet was *radical* politicisation and that this meant being pro-Bolshevik. The Baltic Fleet elections to the

Constituent Assembly were an important – though imperfect – test, and the Bolsheviks' majorities showed the victory of left-radical sentiments.

Radicalisation was not, however, simply a spontaneous process, brought about by a cleavage in society or by lessons learned from work conditions. Lenin was right in 'What is to be Done?', and a strong role was to be played 15 years later by the quality of middle-level Bolshevik organisers, civilians who came to the fleet from the outside and who, through the strength of their commitment and their energetic use of the press, were able to make a deep impression among the sailors.[33] Why it was that Bolshevik agitators should have proven to be so much more energetic than their rivals is a most interesting question, but it was certainly true at the various Baltic bases.

Politicisation in the fleet affected the sailors much more than their officers. The rise of SR, Bolshevik and 'non-partisan' groups among the sailors, and the participation of a minority of them in political action, was not matched by the political organisation of the naval officers. There were officers' 'unions', some officers turned to the Kadets, and in the early months some tried to use the SR consensus; but, as the officers admitted in their memoirs, they were really over their heads when it came to politics, and they could not compete with radical civilian organisers.

Politicisation in action, the famous revolutionary events of 1917–1918, brought out a number of interesting developments. One thing that is striking is the way that revolutionary actions were so often seen by their planners and participants as defensive. In October 1917, especially, the sailors were brought out on the pretense of defending what had already been gained by the people's revolution. Another point is that too many studies have built up to 25 October 1917 without looking at the aftermath. Indeed the year from October 1917 to November 1918 was one of the most interesting – and formative – in Russian political and social history, and little has been written about it. This period deserves intense study as it shows, among other things, a process of 'de-politicisation'.

Democratisation is the second general theme. In the navy the ship committees matched what was happening in many other parts of Russian society, the creation of collective organisations replacing the old tsarist hierarchies. But this general process took a specific form in each area of Russian life. The sailors had a great interest in their conditions of service, of their lives as servicemen in the Russian Navy. They were not simply workers in uniform.

The spread of democratic institutions, ship committees and the like, did not proceed entirely from naval demands. The liberal and socialist politicians who dominated the Provisional Government, and some officers, realised that no matter what they did the old ways of the navy, the unthinking discipline, could not be brought back – at least not in the short run – and the only hope was to channel the movement. There were 'progressive' officers who saw the need to act with the sailors, and some elements in the government, notably Aleksandr Kerenskii, had real confidence in the 'revolutionary creativity' of their masses. Unfortunately the sailors' committees could be used either to maintain order or to take all power into the hands of the sailor's representatives, and they ended up doing the former.

In the first months of the revolution the two currents did not flow at the same pace: democratisation actually moved faster than politicisation. From hindsight it seems clear that those who favoured a continuation of the war and support for the Provisional Government should have followed a more cautious approach to committee control, but they did not. Later, of course, the two processes were more synchronised.

The post-October 1917 period, interesting for politicisation, is also interesting for democratisation. The sailors continued for some time to believe in the possibility of a democratised navy, even after the Bolsheviks began to move in the opposite direction. The naval committee came into conflict with centrally-appointed commissars dispatched by the Soviet centre. There was a progression from mass democracy, to committee control, to centrally-nominated commissars, all in the space of a few months, and this mirrored developments in Russia as a whole. Taking the question of democratisation to its limits, it could even be argued that the Kronstadt mutiny of 1921 should be seen partly as a narrow service issue rather than as an expression of peasant rage at *prodrazverstka*.[34]

Politicisation and democratisation do not make up the whole history of the revolutionary Baltic Fleet in 1917 (or of the armed forces as a whole); there is also military efficiency to consider. Russia in 1917 was not only undergoing a deep social revolution, it was also engaged in the worst war in its history. There is still no history of the Russia's war effort after the February revolution. The main purpose of military organisations is not to take part in revolutions or even to form committees, interesting as those processes are. The purpose of military forces is to fight, and it is a valid line of research to look at how this role was affected by the revolutionary upheaval. Military history is a substantial branch of historical science, although not a very fashionable one; military historians have a lot to learn from their colleagues in political and social history, but political and social historians do also have something to learn from the military side.[35]

Post-1941 Soviet scholars, when they talk about the sea war in 1917, stress the patriotic sentiments of the sailors. It does seem that in the case of the navy, at least, there is a certain truth in their argument that the defeat was brought about not just by revolution. The backwardness of the economy had left the Russian navy completely outnumbered in the Baltic. And some military efficiency survived in the navy over six months of revolutionary confusion. Only a few weeks before the October revolution the Baltic Fleet fought with some tenacity in the Battle of Moon Sound, and even a few months after the Revolution the remaining crews carried out a difficult evacuation through the ice of the Gulf of Finland – to the relative safety of the rear bases at Kronstadt and Petrograd. The Moon Sound battle brought out some specific features of naval warfare, which make it different from land warfare. Warships are centrally controlled; a few individuals on the bridge can determine the direction of movement.

Also of note, however, was the failure of revolutionary navy (and the armed forces in general) to fulfil their combat potential in the demoralisation of the winter of 1917–1918 – especially during the renewed fighting with the Central Powers in February 1918. What became fully clear at this time was the fragility of the armed forces, especially technically-advanced such forces, in times of political and economic crisis. Armed forces are consumers rather than producers, and when the economy collapses they starve; navies are particularly vulnerable as they depend on constant maintenance and on adequate supplies of fuel.

Finally, research on the Baltic Fleet raised the question of morale. Morale is something that seems to concern military historians (and military commanders) more than social-political historians, and yet it is exactly at the interface between politicisation, democratisation, and military efficiency. What constitutes 'mood'? What makes military personnel prepared to risk death? Anti-war sentiment and demoralisation might be expected to be strongest among those units which actually had to bear the grind of active patrolling, and where conditions were physically most uncomfortable. In fact, however, in the Baltic Fleet it was the active ships that had the best morale, for a considerable period at least, and it was on the small ships, destroyers and minesweepers that *esprit de corps* was most developed. The most active base, Reval, was the only one which would produce patriotic 'Battalions of Death' for the land front.[36]

The years before 1914 provide useful insights on the military-revolutionary process in 1917, and much the same can be said about the Civil War years. One thing which was *un*common in the Civil War, however, was disintegration of the kind which occurred in the Provisional Government's armies in 1917. Prominent exceptions to this were the collapse of Admiral Kolchak's army in Siberia in the autumn of 1919 and the uprising in the Soviet Navy at Kronstadt in 1921.

The civil war can be seen as the largely Great-Russian officer corps and the Cossacks fighting against almost everyone else and doing remarkably well. Given the chaos of 1917 it is interesting that anyone was able to raise armies in 1918–1921. General Kornilov failed in his 'action' of August 1917 and yet created the potentially very effective Volunteer movement in 1918. General Kutepov, who failed in the streets of Petrograd with his February 1917 punitive detachment, became a key leader of the Volunteer Army in 1919. General Krasnov, who failed to retake Petrograd after the October 1917 uprising, created a large and effective cossack army less than a year later. Admiral Kolchak, who threw his ceremonial sword into the sea in mid-1917, rather than give way to Black Sea Fleet committees, became commander of an army of over 100 000 men. Did the Provisional Government have military options that it did not consider seriously enough, including the reduction of the army's size and the creation of a more professional force?

The armed forces are an important topic for any study of the revolutionary era. There were more soldiers in Russia than workers; there were more military officers than metalworkers. The soldiers and sailors may have tipped the balance in the great instability of 1917. If the army had stayed passive at the crucial times, as it did in 1905–1906, and engaged in 'repression amid mutiny' (to paraphrase John Bushnell) then the Provisional Government – and perhaps even the tsarist regime – might have survived.

The armed forces were clearly a crucial factor in the overall dynamics of the Bolshevik seizure and consolidation of power in 1917–1918. Most interesting to study would be the role of the garrisons in the so-called 'triumphal march of soviet power' in the last months of 1917. The general fate of the army may also show how the Bolsheviks were able to 'ride the tiger'. One force that was dominant in 1917 but absent for most of 1918 was the army; and the demobilisation of the old army perhaps made possible the survival of the Bolshevik government.

Moreover, the role of young men in uniform was a wide-ranging and long-term one.[37] The shock-troopers (*udarniki*) of the Provisional Government led to the White Guards in 1918–1920, men who had much in common with the near contemporary *Sturmabteilungen*, *Arditi*, and *Freikorps* of other parts of Europe. The Civil War was the golden age of the *praporshchik*. But the spillover did not just affect the counter-revolutionary forces. The Red Guards too, and the early volunteers for the Red Army, often represented young World War soldiers (and officers) who found it hard to return to civilian life and whose love of action led them to fight for the Soviet cause.[38] This theme deserves a place in any history of social change and *mentalité* in the revolutionary era.

There is room for more work on many other aspects of the Russian armed forces in 1905–1921. If access to the army and navy archives (TsGVIA and TsGAVMF) becomes easier in an era of historical *glasnost'*, then it would be interesting to study how one relatively small formation of the army was affected by the revolution. The sources are potentially rich; it is worth remembering that one value of studying armies as social institutions is that military bureaucrats keep relatively good records. (Even without access to archives something might be made of XLII Corps, which was stationed in Finland.) The military effectiveness of the Russian Army might also be assessed from the German and Austro-Hungarian point of view; even their official histories have been relatively little used.[39] There remains also the Black Sea Fleet, which contrasted with the Baltic Fleet in the way it held together – at least until the massacres of early 1918. The national movement in the forces is worthy of a work on its own. Ezergailis has written on the Latvian rifles and Fić on the Czechoslovaks, but 'Ukrainization' deserves serious attention.[40] It would also be interesting to see why the nationalist governments which appeared on the old Empire's periphery in 1918–1920 were (with the exception of Finland and Poland) unable to marshal effective military forces.

The development of cultural life in the Russian armed forces in 1917 is also potentially interesting. Certainly the navy had a spread of clubs and literary magazines and popular 'universities'.

In addition there is no full social history of the Red Army in 1918–1920, which had a decided impact on the later development of Soviet life.[41] John Erickson concentrates on the command issues, and Francesco Benvenuti on the complex relationship between the army and the new socialist state.[42]

Some of the lessons of other disciples might well be applied to the history of the revolutionary army. What about military sociology and its findings on the role of non-commissioned officers and of small groups? The large political-science literature on military coups (mostly those of the post-1945 period) could well be applied to the Russian army high command in 1917, and also to events on the Civil War fronts in 1918–1920.

The Russian military in 1905–1921 was like the military elsewhere. Its dual components, commanders and commanded were products of their society and interacted closely with it. But commanders and the commanded had been absorbed into institutions which set them apart from the rest of society (and from each other), and those institutions deserve full study as separate and distinct entities.

Notes

1.   For a useful discussion see Ronald G. Suny, 'Toward a Social History of the October Revolution', *American Historical Review*, LXXXVIII (1983), pp. 31–52.

2.   George Katkov, *Russia 1918: The February Revolution* (New York: Longman, 1967); Tsuyoshi Hasegawa, *The February Revolution: Petrograd, 1917* (Seattle: University of Washington Press, 1980); Alexander Rabinowitch, *The Bolsheviks Come to Power: The Revolution of 1917 in Petrograd* (London: NLB, 1979).

3.   Israel Getzler, *Kronstadt 1917–1921: The Fate of a Soviet Democracy* (Cambridge: Cambridge University Press, 1983); Donald J. Raleigh, *Revolution on the Volga: 1917 in Saratov* (Ithaca: Cornell University Press, 1986).

4.   Practical considerations confine this article to the late tsarist period, and I exclude John Keep's important *Soldiers of the Tsar: Army and Society in Russia, 1462–1874* (Oxford: Clarendon, 1985).

5.   Allan K. Wildman, *The End of the Russian Imperial Army*; vol. 1, *The Old Army and the Soldiers' Revolt (March–April 1917)*; vol. 2, *The Road to Soviet Power and Peace* (Princeton: Princeton University Press, 1980, 1987).

6.   Vol. 2, p. 402.

7.   Vol. 2, p. 404.

8.   Leopold Haimson, 'The Problem of Social Stability in Urban Russia, 1905–1917', *Slavic Review*, XXIII (1964): 619–42; XXIV (1965), pp. 1–22.

9.   Vol. 1, pp. xvii, 75–80.

10.   Vol. 1, p. 378.

11.   Vol. 2, p. 402.

12.   Vol. 2, p. 405.

13.   Vol. 1, pp. 337, 372, 380, vol. 2, pp. 38, 234.

14.   Vol. 2, pp. ix, 402.

15.   John Bushnell, *Mutiny amid Repression: Russian Soldiers in the Revolution of 1905–1906* (Bloomington: University of Indiana Press, 1985).

16.   Ibid., p. ix.

17.   Ibid., pp. 21, 227ff.

18.   Ibid., p. 226.

19.   Ibid., pp. 101, 104.

20.   *Leninskii sbornik*, vol. XXXVII (Moscow: IPL, 1970), p. 137.

21.   Mikhail Frenkin, *Russkaia armia i revoliutsiia: 1917–1918* (Munich: Logos, 1978); Mikhail Frenkin, *Zakhvat vlasti Bolshevikami v Rossii*

i rol' tylovykh garnizonov armii: Podgotovka i provedenie Oktiabr'-skogo miatezha (Jerusalem: Stav, 1982).

22. Matitiahu Mayzel, *Generals and Revolutionaries: The Russian General Staff during the Revolution: A Study in the Transformation of a Military Elite* (Osnabruck: Biblio-Verlag, 1979).

23. Peter Kenez, 'A Profile of the Pre-Revolutionary Officer Corps', *California Slavonic Studies*, VII (1973), pp. 121–58; David R. Jones, 'The Officers and the October Revolution', *Soviet Studies*, XXVIII (1976), pp. 207–23.

24. William Fuller, *Civil-Military Conflict in Imperial Russia 1881–1914* (Princeton: Princeton University Press, 1985), p. xxiii. The inability of the government to support potential pro-autocracy groups is shown in another book on the pre-1914 situation, Robert H. McNeal, *Tsar and Cossack 1855–1914* (London: Macmillan, 1986).

25. Ibid., pp. 261, 263.

26. Richard Pipes, *Russia under the Old Regime* (Harmondsworth: Penguin, 1977).

27. George Katkov, *The Kornilov Affair: Kerensky and the Breakup of the Russian Army* (London: Longman, 1980). There is also the book by the Danish historian Jorgen Munck, *The Kornilov Revolt* (Aarhus: Aarhus University Press, 1987); I learned of its publication after the original manuscript of this article had been submitted, and have not had the opportunity to see it. Also of note is J. D. White, 'The Kornilov Affair: A Study in Counterrevolution', *Soviet Studies* XX (1968): 187–205, which attempts to put the military plot into political-economic setting.

28. *Miatezhniki: Iz vospominanaii o revoliutsii* (Moscow: GIZ, 1923), p. 33f.

29. Evan Mawdsley, *The Russian Revolution and the Baltic Fleet: War and Politics, February 1917–April 1918* (London: Macmillan, 1978). The Baltic Fleet has received at least as much scholarly attention as any other part of the revolutionary armed forces, partly because of its connection with the central events of the revolution and partly because of the documentation available. For another perspective on the fleet see Norman E. Saul, *Sailors in Revolt: The Russian Baltic Fleet in 1917* (Lawrence: Regents Press of Kansas, 1978).

30. Marc Ferro, 'The Russian Soldier in 1917: Undisciplined, Patriotic, and Revolutionary', *Slavic Review*, XXX (1971): p. 510.

31. Wildman, *The Old Army*, pp. 154f.

32. Bushnell, *Mutiny*, p. 224.

33. Although from time to time Soviet sources have seen fit not to mention the names of some of the activists. One such example was F. F. Raskolnikov, who once again seems to have become a test of de-Stalinization; see V. Polikarpov 'Fedor Raskol'nikov' *Ogonyok*, no. 26 (June 1987): 4–7.

34. Evan Mawdsley, 'The Baltic Fleet and the Kronstadt Mutiny', *Soviet Studies*, XXIV (1973), pp. 506–21. Paul Avrich in *Kronstadt 1921*

(Princeton: Princeton University Press, 1970) also discusses the possibility of conspiracy.

35.　Military history is popular among Soviet historians but it depends on the war; Soviet work on the military history of 1917 is small compared to that on 1941–1945.

36.　Wildman, on the other hand, argued (vol. 1, p. 203) that the army at the front was as badly affected by the revolution as were the units in the rear garrisons.

37.　Admittedly much of the army in the total-war effort of 1917 were older men in their late twenties and thirties, but there were many younger men as well.

38.　See also Rex Wade, *Red Guards and Workers' Militias in the Russian Revolution* (Stanford: Stanford University Press, 1984).

39.　*Der Weltkrieg 1914 bis 1918: Die Kriegführung im Sommer und Herbst 1917: Die Ereignisse ausserhalb der Westfront bis November 1918.* Der Weltkrieg 1914 bis 1918, vol. XIII (Berlin: Mittler, 1942); *Österreich-Ungarns letzter Krieg 1914–1918*, vol. VI (Vienna: BfH und Kriegsarchiv, 1936).

40.　Andrew Ezergailis, *The Latvian Impact of the Revolution: The First Phase: September 1917 to April 1918* (Boulder: East European Monographs, 1983); Victor M. Fic, *Revolutionary War for Independence and the Russian Question: Czechoslovak Army in Russia 1914–1918* (New Delhi: Abhinav 1977).

41.　A start has been made in Mark L. von Hagen, *Soldiers in the Proletarian Dictatorship: The Red Army and the Soviet Socialist State* (Ithaca: Cornell University Press, 1990); and Orlando Figes, 'The Red Army and Mass Mobilization during the Russian Civil War, 1918–1920', *Past and Present*, no. 129 (1990), pp. 168–211.

42.　John Erickson, *The Soviet High Command: A Military-Political History, 1918–1941* (London: Macmillan, 1962); Francesco Benvenuti, *The Bolsheviks and the Red Army, 1918–1922* (Cambridge: Cambridge University Press, 1988).

7 The Landowners

John Channon

The economic significance of the landed class (*pomeshchiki*)[1] had declined considerably by the First World War; but politically they still represented one of the major bulwarks of the autocratic state. The number of landowning families had changed little since the beginning of the century, yet the percentage of nobles belonging to landowning families had declined sharply (from 54–55 per cent in 1895 to 36–37 per cent in 1912) with many nobles now engaged in non-agricultural activities.[2] Moreover, the dynamism of a society undergoing economic and social transformation was reflected in inter-class mobility, clearly apparent in the half century before the revolution when the social composition of the *pomeshchiki* had begun to change. As a result of economic pressures in the late nineteenth century some members of the landlord class had become impoverished or had moved into state service and the professions. The landlord class was simultaneously replenished by an influx of individuals engaged in the new commercial, industrial and financial spheres of society. Thus, with the upsurge of industrial development from the mid-1880s, a new kind of *pomeshchik* had emerged from the indigenous and foreign bourgeoisie. At the time of the February revolution, the landed class still dominated the Russian countryside politically, even though it was now of mixed social composition in terms of origin and estate (*soslovie*).

On the eve of 1917 there were roughly 100 000 landlord families (and about 400 000 individuals including family members). Approximately 39 000 of these were 'new' landowner families (totalling 155 000 individuals including family members) although the majority of *pomeshchiki* still comprised members of the old noble social estate (*dvoryanstvo*).[3] Any statement of the quantitative aspects, however, should be approached with caution. Statistics on the number of *pomeshchiki* by the time of the revolution are a minefield, not least because data usually referred to the number of estates – and not the number of owners who frequently possessed several properties – while the term 'privately-owned' (*chastnovladel'cheskii*) could refer to peasant as well as non-peasant land.

Assessing the cohesion of the *pomeshchiki* as a class is similarly difficult. Although social mobility was in evidence, it is generally assumed that it takes at least two generations before the acceptance of a new class position is achieved. This socio-economic process has given rise to terminological difficulties, not least of which is the problem of how *pomeshchiki* should be translated into English. The two terms commonly used – noble and gentry landowners – are both problematic. The first relates to a legal social estate, the *dvoryanstvo*, but admittedly one which was relatively open and fluid. The gentry, on the other hand, has the advantage of implying a landed class whose primary income derived from the land; but it underplays the element of heredity and privilege. Yet the Russian landed class by 1917 comprised members of both an hereditary class imbued with prestige, exclusiveness and aristocratism and newer members who had bought into land in more recent years.[4] The term *pomeshchiki* clearly included both these groups. Thus the term landed class probably serves best to describe the *pomeshchiki* in our period.

Evidently the *pomeshchiki* were not a unified class. They were differentiated both vertically and horizontally: vertically in terms of class (between large, middling and small landowners as well as between those from different social backgrounds); and horizontally through regional and ethnic divisions (in areas of agriculturally advanced and backward estate practices and among Russian and non-Russian landowners, respectively). In practice, of course, these categories often overlapped.[5]

In recent years there has been no shortage of Western studies on the landed class in the decades before 1914, most of which have contained an argument for or against the 'decline of the gentry' thesis.[6] These have served to complement the investigations of Soviet historians.[7] When we come to 1917, however, Western studies are notable for their absence. This might seem surprising in the light of the interest displayed in landowners before the Revolution and the frequent statements in textbooks on 1917 about the demise of the landlord class, quite apart from the role played by émigré scholars in the Western historiography of the Revolution. It should come as less of a surprise when viewed against the background of the new social history exerting such an influence on studies of 1917. Western historians writing from such a perspective have attempted to dispel notions of 'the masses' and have have laid emphasis on workers, peasants and others as social groups worthy of study in their own right. These studies have enabled significant advances in our understanding of 1917. Yet a lack of cohesion among the practitioners of this new social history, and especially the absence of discussion of its theoretical application, has led to an over-concentration on certain social groups at the expense of others. Little consideration has been given to the 'losers' – the middle classes, the landowners or the industrialists – either during or after 1917. It is therefore very fortunate that Soviet historians have not been so remiss.[8] Their studies, together with Soviet works that appeared during the Revolution and the 1920s, form the core of the material on which this chapter is based; and my aim is to provide an interpretative overview of the current state of the debate and to indicate areas that would benefit from future investigation.

A thorough assessment of the role and activities of the landed class in 1917 has yet to be undertaken. But various parts of the story may be pieced together. Among the most interesting of these is the theme of those landowners who opposed the peasant revolution by setting up their own organisations and creating a landowners' movement. This affected only some landowners, and they tended to be those still resident on their estates and chiefly the largest and wealthiest. In other words, they were the ones who by and large had the greatest say and wielded the most power. The currently available evidence is concentrated on landowners resident in the central regions of European Russia. The activities tell us something about both landowners' politics in 1917 and the social revolution in the Russian countryside. Neither social and cultural aspects of landed class life nor the economic condition of the *pomeshchiki* and the fate of their estates – confiscation, inventorying or destruction – are the subject of investigation here.

With the worsening of the economic crisis towards the end of 1916, a number of large *pomeshchiki* (the so-called land magnates), among them Orlov-Denisov, Obolenskii, Shcherbatov and Balashov, suggested to the Minister of Agriculture that they should form a Union of Landowners (*Soyuz zemel'nykh sobstvennikov*), with the 'patriotic aim' of helping the army and supplying the state with grain and other agricultural products. Furthermore, they argued, it would help to consolidate 'individual land ownership' as well as more generally defend 'the interests of landownership and agriculture'. [9] In accordance with the rules drawn up, landowners could be members of the Union, regardless of social estate (*soslovie*), so long as they possessed at least 50 desyatinas (114 acres) of land. A minimum of ten persons was required to create a local division of the Union.[10]

In fact, only five such divisions were set up at this time but the Union of late 1916 marked the revival of the All-Russian Union of Landowners that first appeared in 1905. The initiators of the Union lost interest in it when the revolutionary threat subsided after 1907.[11] Since the moves to recreate the Landowners' Union were made several months before the February revolution, it seems probable that its objectives were different from those after February. The Union wanted to help the war effort and prevent the overthrow of tsarism in late 1916, whereas it aimed to develop a strategy for the landowners' own survival after February. It is true that peasant unrest had grown considerably in the years immediately before the First World War and continued during the War, albeit to a much reduced degree, not least because of the conscription of many millions of peasant males.[12] Landowners, too, were obviously aware of this situation. Yet the propertied classes clearly had little idea of the fury of the social and economic forces that would be unleashed by February while their socialisation and *Weltanschauung* poorly equipped them to comprehend the events they saw or heard reported.[13]

The picture of impassive landowners being violently thrown off their estates has undoubtedly been overdrawn despite the fact that such instances indeed occurred. But few appeared to believe that their situation was hopeless. They prepared to take on the peasant movement and believed it could be defeated. A network of organisations, coordinated from the centre, was created throughout the country, developing gradually but, by summer 1917, flourishing to such a degree that it touched a large majority of the provinces in European Russia. It is not fanciful to speak of a landowners' movement in 1917, developing as a counter to that of the peasantry and responding to the pattern of agrarian unrest. Based on criteria derived from the Union's activities, this landowners' movement may be divided into two main phases. The first lasted from March to June, the second from July to October.

The development of the peasant struggle for land after February led to the spread of the Union's activities. In March and April divisions of the Union were created in the provinces of Tambov, Penza, Kazan, Simbirsk, Samara, Poltava, Kherson, Ekaterinoslav and Ufa, all Black-Earth provinces with the exception of the latter.[14] It is not coincidental that many of these were provinces with a large number of separator peasants.[15] The first information on local organisations of the Union came from Ufa province in March while the following month, on 7 April, seventy people gathered for a congress of landowners (*zemledel'tsy*), in Morshansk district of Tambov province. The participants sent a telegram to the President of the Council of Ministers, Prince L'vov, and the Minister of Agriculture, Shingaryov, reporting their difficult situation due to the 'unfounded demands' of the peasantry. The congress requested that the government explain to peasants 'in no uncertain terms' about the need for reaching agreement on questions of land, rents and wages.[16]

The end of April saw the First Provincial Congress of Landowners in Voronezh. Its social composition was revealing. N. P. Makarov, the Popular Socialist and former member of the congress noted that a significant number of the participants (about 300–400) were peasant-owners possessing between 30 and 100 desyatinas (71 and 270 acres), mainly land purchased from *pomeshchiki* or consolidated allotment land. The size of these peasant holdings was greater than that deemed appropriate for the households' labour power, but less than that of large capitalist agriculture.[17] The remainder, a 'smallish group', were small leaseholders, barely engaged in agriculture and 'people without roots'.[18] This composition formed the basis for Makarov's assertion that his party's agrarian programme should prove attractive to the delegates. He was to be proved mistaken. The majority of the congress rejected the Popular Socialists' programme in favour of that of the Kadets, evidently establishing the Union's political allegiance.[19] Although small in numerical terms, the *pomeshchiki* were still influential in the congress. They represented a much larger land area than the peasants, and were the initiators and organisers of the congress. The *pomeshchiki* placed their wager on the 'strong large peasant – owners', on their aspirations to protect private land from seizure by peasant communities in the face of the forthcoming agrarian reform. The inclusion in the Union of peasants possessing partially as well as fully enclosed holdings (*otrubniki* and *khutoryane* respectively) enabled organisations to be created in 24 volosts.[20]

At the beginning of May there occurred in Moscow the Constituent Congress of the All-Russian Union of Landowners and Farmers (*sel'skie khozyaeva*). This was an attempt to link up these various local organisations with a national centre. The 300 delegates came from 31 provinces (including Voronezh, Ryazan, Tula, Penza, Simbirsk, Kazan, Samara, Saratov, Moscow and Ufa) and included *pomeshchiki*, *khutoryane*, *otrubniki*, leaseholders and other categories of landowners. After learning that landowners were being excluded from attempts to decide local issues, the Congress resolved to create divisions of the Union everywhere.[21]

The basic aim of the Union remained to defend private property in land. Fearing for the future of private landownership and appreciating the need to increase the Union's peasant base, it was deemed necessary to increase the land area of peasants who lacked enough for their families' sustenance, though the rules gave no indication of the categories of land from which this increase could be made.[22] Provision was made for the compulsory alienation, under exceptional circumstances, of privately-owned land, though this was to be executed 'cordially' and in accordance with the 'actual value' of the land, a seeming contradiction in terms. In the rules of the Union, as in the Kadet programme, it was emphasised that 'under no circumstances is land belonging to those who toil on the land subject to alienation'.[23]

Striving to attract to the Union as many peasant-owners as possible, the Rules abolished the 1916 property qualification whereby Union members had to possess at least 50 desyatinas (114 acres) of land. New members could include the following three categories: 'all land owners, owners of estates, irrespective of size of property, of sex, *soslovie*, religious belief, nationality and political persuasion; leaseholders and all those sharing the basic position of the present rules; and all institutions, societies and unions, pursuing similar objectives'.[24]

The rules established the form that the landowners' movement would assume in this phase, emphasising its legal character, manifested in the defence of landowners rights through the courts as well as through representation in public organisations and government institutions. In the spirit of the Kadets, the Union strived to create a 'peaceful solution to all land disputes'. The basic tenets of the rules were repeated in the rules of the local organisations, with variations depending on the time they were passed. In the spring, when peasant unrest was only just developing, the rules were limited mainly to the general aim of defending 'the interests of private ownership', as an 'indispensable part of the contemporary state structure'. In the summer, when peasants were carrying out their threats to eliminate *pomeshchik* landownership changes appeared in the rules of local unions. In Belozersk district union (Novgorod province), for example, the rules now stated that the union aimed at 'the preservation of the interests of private and peasant landownership in the district, the defence of property in land from seizures and confiscation, the conducting of legal affairs on behalf of union members and the presenting of petitions in their names'.[25]

The last point of the Union's rules declared that its name should be preserved. This was not always accepted in local congresses and the diversity of names by which the local divisions were known is striking: 'unions of farmers' (*soyuzy sel'skikh khozyaev*); 'union of farmers and sowers' (*soyuz sel'skikh khozyaev i posevshchikov*);[26] 'union of farmers and landowners' (*soyuz sel'skikh khozyaev i pomeshchikov*);[27] 'union of landowners and leaseholders' (*soyuz zemlevladel'tsev i arendatorov*) and agricultural unions (*ob'edineniya*) and societies (*obshchestva*); 'union of sowers' (*soyuz posevshchikov*); 'union of grain farmers' (*soyuz khleborobov*); 'the party of cultivator-owners' (*partiya khleborobov-sobstvennikov*). Several names emphasised the peasant composition of the organisation, such as the 'union of khutoryane' (*soyuz khutoryan*), the 'peasant union' (*krest'yanskii soyuz*), the 'union of small landowners' (*soyuz mel'kikh sobstvennikov*); and 'peasant unions' (*krest'yanskie soyuzy*).[28]

After the May Congress the founding members created a Union Council in Moscow, to which were accorded the following activities: literary and oral propaganda to deal with questions on the socialisation and nationalisation of land as well as various political issues of the moment; legal help to landowners; the task of publishing a series of agitational brochures with help from professors of folklore *au fait* with peasant language and customs. It was suggested that the Council should devote most attention to publishing activity, devolving to local departments the task of selecting agitators. Daily newspapers were set up by the local divisions of the Union in the provinces of Ryazan, Penza and Kazan.[29] For working out questions on particular aspects of agriculture a number of corresponding sections were also created.[30] The president of the Union was N. N. L'vov (brother of the ober-procurator of the Holy Synod), while K. I. Kozakov, known for his work as a member of the Moscow District Land Reorganisation Commission under Stolypin, was chosen as the Council's secretary.[31] This marked a move to strengthen the Union's appeal to separator peasants.

After the Congress, *pomeshchiki* and peasant owners in some districts indeed displayed a unity of interests. This occurred in reaction to resolutions of peasant congresses and soviets and volost executive and land committees to transfer privately-owned land to peasant organisations, and to limit private landownership to the so-called labour norm, namely, the amount that could be worked by the labour power of the household. At this time, unions of landowners were created in Belgorodsk, Dmitrievsk, Fatezhsk, L'govsk and Putivl'sk districts (Kursk province), in Ranenburgsk and Ryazhsk districts (Ryazan province), Kirsanovsk district (Tambov province) and in Epifanovsk district (Tula province), interestingly all Central-Black Earth provinces.[32]

In the Central Industrial region, the *pomeshchiki* of Moscow province also organised a union and peasants who had property (*sobstvennost'*) were invited to become members.[33] The appeal to *khutoryane* and *otrubniki*, written by the secretary of the Chief Council of the All-Russian Union, Kozakov, was circulated widely in the district by the *pomeshchiki*. Kozakov appealed to the 5000 *khutoryane* and *otrubniki* whom he had helped with the consolidation of communal land as their property. 'Allocating you to *otruba* and *khutora*, I said that no-one would ever take away that land from you,' he wrote. 'In this free republican system, the right of property in land is inviolable . . . And you believed me. Now I consider it my duty to speak the truth to you, as I spoke it earlier. *Khutora* and *otruba*, your property, your labours and your expenditure, are in danger (threatened).' He summoned *khutoryane* and *otrubniki* to unite with *pomeshchiki* in the Union for the defence of the rights of private ownership of land. At the Congress of land owners (*zemel'nye sobstvenniki*) of Moskovsk district, in June 1917, *khutoryane* and *otrubniki* comprised 25 per cent of delegates. Such unions were also created in Klimsk, Podol'sk and eight other districts of Moscow province. The social composition of these organisations was characterised by a correspondent of *Zemlya i Volya* as follows: '. . . unions of kulaks, *pomeshchiki* and large *otrubniki*, coming together in order to resist the imminent threat to them: the alienation of all land which is someone else's property for the use of toilers'. The article emphasised the class unity of kulaks and *pomeshchiki*. The aim of these unions, continued the newspaper, was not patriotism or a desire to be of use to the state, but to preserve the right of property.[34]

Reporting on congresses of landowners (*zemlevladel'tsy*) in Saratov, Tula, Moscow and other towns, another newspaper emphasised that not only *pomeshchiki* joined the unions: 'They attract to their ranks en passant that part of the Russian peasantry which, possessing their land through right of private ownership, is a miniature likeness of *pomeshchiki*, on account of their agrarian and economic interests.' The All-Russian Union strives, the paper continues, 'to attract those peasants who, through the Stolypin land reorganisation, consolidated allotment land for themselves according to the Law of 14 July 1910 or separated from the commune to *khutora* and *otruba*'.[35]

Under the threat of losing land, there was an acceleration in the creation of local divisions of the Union. There was also an increase in the flow of peasant landowners (*sobstvenniki*) to the *pomeshchik* unions. Thus in the Zaraisk district congress (Ryazan province), a majority of delegates (150 out of 200) were small owners (*melkie sobstvenniki*) and *otrubniki*. A similar composition was noted in Egor'evsk district congress, where, it is claimed, *otrubniki* sided with *pomeshchiki*.[36]

Between spring and summer 1917 the communal peasantry's movement against separator peasants increased in intensity and the number of complaints to provincial commissars by *khutoryane* and *otrubniki* concerning committees which had seized their lands rose. Developments in Saratov province were characteristic.[37] At the Saratov District Congress of Land Owners, 135 out of the 150 present were peasants.[38] At the Saratov Provincial Congress in May 1917 a majority of the 200 delegates were *khutoryane* and *otrubniki*.[39] The Second Provincial Congress of Landowners (*zemlevladel'tsev*) which followed in June was characterised by a Bolshevik newspaper as an assembly of peasant-owners and *pomeshchiki*: 'The spectacle was extremely instructive. Economic interests were much stronger than the old enmity between peasants and the *pomeshchik* masters. The economic development led to a pathetic unity of peasant separators with oppressor *pomeshchiki*'.[40]

Similarly in the Central Black-Earth region, the seizure of separators' lands and fear of losing land (especially that which had been purchased) pushed some peasants towards these *pomeshchik* organisations. The situation in Tambov province is illustrative here. Among the 400 present at

Kozlovsk District Congress of land owners (*sobstvenniki*), there were many leaseholders together with *khutoryane* and *otrubniki*. A similar situation prevailed elsewhere in the province. The chairman in Usmansk district, at a meeting of soviets of peasants deputies noted that, as a rule, *otrubniki* and *khutoryane* spoke together with *pomeshchiki*. Similar occurrences were reported from the Urals. In Krasnoufimsk district (Perm province) many *otrubniki*, *khutoryane* and other peasants were members of the Union of Landowners.[41]

Striving to attract peasants to local divisions of the Union, *pomeshchiki* adopted a variety of methods. Each issue of the Ryazan provincial newspaper, for instance, reported advice given by the division to its members and the applications and petitions compiled for them. These provided general illustrations of how to defend the interests of those under attack. On other occasions landowners resorted to bribes. Sometimes *pomeshchiki* 'cordially' allotted land to peasants, though even this might have strings attached. In Tolkovsk volost (Ostrovsk district) in Pskov province, *pomeshchiki* declared their willingness to 'forgive' the surrounding peasants (presumably for their 'illegal' activities) and allot to them five desyatinas (about 13.5 acres) per household, on condition that they agreed to join the union. In other localities, *pomeshchiki* reduced rent payments or sold peasants land at knocked-down prices, while a volost union of landowners in Opochetsk district sold grain to needy local inhabitants.[42]

The spread of the Union's organisations gave renewed hope to the large landowners and their conduct changed noticeably. The *pomeshchiki* had often been in no position to resist the resolutions of the peasant committees. Now, large landowners began to tamper with (and destroy) documents containing their signatures and to threaten peasants using non-peasant land, accusing them of illegal seizures. In spring 1917, when the All-Russian Union was still 'gathering strength', complaining to both central and local organs of government and public bodies was the main method employed in the struggle with peasant organisations. At the first session of the Chief Land Committee, in May 1917, the Minister of Agriculture, Shingaryov, reported that up to a hundred telegrams and petitions from *pomeshchiki*, *khutoryane*, *otrubniki* and unions of landowners were received daily by the Committee, with requests to defend them from 'the arbitrary rule' of the peasant committees.[43]

In response, the Provisional Government wrote to its commissars requesting them to explain to the local inhabitants that 'legal action must be taken against . . . seizures of land and property'. It was occasionally recommended that chairmen of volost committees be taken to court.

Similar telegrams were sent to a number of other districts inthe region.[44] Complaints increased. On 10 May, the presidium of the Union declared that volost executive committees 'are little informed about their rights and obligations, and sometimes neglect the demands of legal order and necessity'. Everywhere, it continued: the working of landowners' estates was disrupted, their land, cattle and equipment seized, workers taken away, taxes imposed and arrests made, while *pomeshchiki*, *khutoryane* and *otrubniki* were all subjected to violence. The Union stressed to the government the 'direst consequences for the army and the towns' of the destruction of privately-owned properties.[45]

On 12 May the Minister of Internal Affairs, Prince L'vov, circulated to provincial commissars a telegram complaining that the illegal activities of the committees were intolerable and that arrests, searches, plundering and the imposition of taxes were inadmissible since they undermined the new order. On several occasions the Union complained about the actions of individual members of the government. Landowners were especially antagonistic towards Chernov when he replaced Shingaryov as Minister of Agriculture. Such sentiments came from the localities too. Typical was the accusation made by the union of farmers (*soyuz sel'skikh khozyaev*) of Simbirsk province in May 1917 that several declarations of the Minister of Agriculture 'go against the resolutions of the Provisional Government', and 'since the agrarian question will be decided by the Constituent Assembly, all land seizures regardless of their subdivision into organised and disorganised, must be viewed as offences and consequently, punishable as such'.[46]

The wrath of the *pomeshchiki* was especially provoked by the draft law of 23 May prohibiting land transactions, the inheritance of land and the use of land as collateral. The Union organised protests against the law which would delimit landowners' rights to property. The protests were supported by the Provisional Committee of the State Duma, by the Ministries of Justice, Internal Affairs and Finance and by the Council of Banks. A report from the Council of Banks came out decisively against any suspension or cessation of land transactions, warning that the 'extreme complications' and 'shocks' arising from it would threaten the national economy. Not surprisingly bank representatives considered the prohibition of land transactions dangerous to fiscal interests, emphasising that it was inadvisable to forbid peasants who possessed the means from purchasing land: in their view a 'large part of the toiling population' were discontented with the draft law.[47]

A letter from landowners to the Ministers of Agriculture and Justice asserted that L'vov had effectively abolished the right of ownership of land.

Yet this, it pointed out, stood in defiance of his own logic. Lvov's stated intentions were alleged to be not only unjust but also contradictory to the principle of general equality so fundamental to the new order. Furthermore, to pass the law would be to contradict the government declaration on the inviolability of private ownership up to the convocation of the Constituent Assembly. Following the line taken by the bank representatives, L'vov asserted that forbidding land transactions would disrupt bank operations, deprive *pomeshchiki* of credit and bring dangerous consequences for the entire economy.[48] The draft law was then effectively abandoned.

By the beginning of June the Union existed in dozens of provinces, chiefly in three regions, the Central Black-Earth, the Volga and the West, where large landownership was greatest, where remnants of serfdom still persisted and where land hunger was most acute.[49] By the end of July reports presented at the Plenum of the Chief Council of Landowners revealed that divisions existed in at least thirty provinces. More divisions were created at province level after July though in several provinces only district organisations existed.[50]

In recent years more information has come to light on the number of local divisions of the Union. Such calculations reveal 337 local divisions of which 45 were provincial and regional, 167 district, and the remaining volost. Although divisions of the Union had not been created in all provinces of European Russia where *pomeshchik* landownership existed, they functioned in more than one-third of all its districts (167 out of 470).[51] Organisations of the Union were created in 11 districts of Moscow province, 10 districts each in Penza and Novgorod provinces, 8 districts of Tambov, Tula, Kursk, Pskov and Smolensk; 7 districts in Yaroslavl', Tver', Vladimir, Chernigov and Khar'kov provinces; 6 districts in Ryazan and Oryol provinces; 5 districts in Saratov provinces. The largest number were created in April to July 1917. Although precise data on the numbers belonging to the Union are still uncertain, some idea can be gleaned from information on the delegate composition of its local congresses as well as the number of its organisations. Congresses of local divisions often had up to 600 delegates Some even comprised more than 1000 *pomeshchik* and peasant land owners – such as those in Sychevsk district, Smolensk province, Poltava provincial congress (where 1200 delegates participated) and in Ekaterinoslav (where 1273 gathered, representing 3470 landowners (*zemlevladel'tsy*). In addition, data from the press on local divisions in Penza and Pskov provinces, Krasnoufimsk district (Perm province) and several southern provinces reveal tens of thousands of members. In Novgorod-Seversk district (Chernigov province) by the beginning of July there were 3500 union members and in Samara province, 4000.

The majority of the local divisions of the Union included peasants owning land privately. In a number of districts this included middling and even small peasant owners, possessing anything from one to ten desyatinas of purchased land.[52]

That these middle and small peasants owners were being attracted to the Union was of concern to district soviets and land committees. Peasant congresses from June to August passed resolutions forbidding the activities of the unions of landowners on the grounds that they were counter-revolutionary organisations.[53] A particularly fierce struggle over the middle and small peasant owners developed in Ryazan province where the union was especially active. A meeting of the province's representatives of public organisations and district commissars on 22–24 July, resolved 'to split away small owners from the union of large landowners by providing for the defence of the individual and the individual property of small owners via the land committees, and where these do not exist, volost committees'. In opposition to the union, the Ryazhsk district soviet convoked a congress of petty landowners, at which 400 peasants were present. The Congress resolved that such peasants should 'not join the union with the large landowners', claiming that this would lead to a split in the peasantry. More concrete action was taken in the province too. The presence of representatives from the Zaraisk district soviet at the local congress of the union of landowners was sufficient to provoke the departure of 150 small landowners.[54]

Soldiers from local garrisons also became involved in the struggle, disrupting congresses of landowners.[55] Such soviet interference prevented union congresses in Kursk, Bogoroditsk and other towns from agreeing on resolutions. In Voronezh, Tula, Ryazan and Penza provinces, soldiers succeeded in getting small and middle peasant owners to leave the unions. In Kashirsk district congress of landowners (Tula province) on 9 July, where two-thirds of the 150 delegates were peasant representatives, small and middle peasant owners vacillated over which path to choose. In Biryuchensk district (Voronezh province) small peasant owners were also warned against association with *pomeshchiki*.[56]

In sum, there was a definite correlation between the increase in intensity of the agrarian revolution and the upsurge in activities of the landowners' unions. As peasant organisations moved against the *khutoryane* and *otrubniki*, so the latter were drawn to the unions. March and April witnessed the creation of many provincial divisions, mainly in the Black-Earth provinces, and many of their members were peasant owners. The *pomeshchiki* might have been few but their influence was considerable. Early May saw the convocation of the Union's Constituent

Congress, providing a vital link between the centre and local organisations. (Later that month a Council was established to head the Union in Moscow; 300 delegates attended from 31 provinces.) New rules reduced the property qualification for membership. The Congress planned to engage in 'legal' activities to oppose the Provisional Government and to stress the idea that a unityof interest existed between *pomeshchiki* and landed peasants. This was taken up at the Second Congress in June where various ways to attract peasants to the Union were explored. As the Union's local branches increased from the early summer, the *pomeshchiki* felt more confident to try and halt the peasant revolution as well as to criticise the government for doing too little to protect private property.

The next stage in the attempt to consolidate the alliance between *pomeshchiki* and peasant proprietors came with the All-Russia Congress of the Union of Landowners, between 1 and 8 July 1917. Four hundred delegates attended representing mainly peasant owners.[57] V. V. Meller-Zakomel'skii (from Petrograd) was elected President by Kindyakov, a member of the State Duma (from Saratov), N. A. Mel'nikov (from Kazan'), Andrievskii, a member of the State Council (from Tambov) and P. I. Raevskii (from Tula) among others. The Congress discussed reports from the localities, passed a resolution on the land question and sent a delegation to the Provisional Government to protest about agrarian disorders.[58] The Congress met under the slogan of uniting *pomeshchiki* and kulaks for the struggle with the revolutionary peasant organisations and sharply criticised the coalition government for not fulfilling its promise to preserve as inviolable the former basis of landownership until the Constituent Assembly. The resolution of its legal section, affirmed by the Congress, noted that if the government wanted landowners to 'fulfil their duty to the motherland and to hand over the harvest to it, then it should categorically forbid land committees to take away land, equipment and livestock and to deprive them of labour'. Clearly they wanted the preservation of private property. The Congress demanded that the Provisional Government should immediately confirm and publish the draft project of the former Minister of Internal Affairs, Prince G. E. L'vov, forbidding the illegal activities of the volost executive and land committees.[59]

The Congress delegates spoke of the necessity to propagandise in the army, among the clergy and also in regions where there were non-Russian nationalities. The army was of particular concern. At the beginning of July an ensign named Klepov sent a petition to the War Minister and Supreme Commander-in-Chief requesting the organisation of a congress of 'warrior-cultivators'. This was an attempt to wean 'pure' peasants, namely those cultivators who were permanent residents in the countryside, away from the influence of the All-Russian Congress of Peasants' Deputies. The request was refused on the grounds that no congresses were permitted which involved military personnel.[60] The Congress attached great significance to preparations for the Constituent Assembly. Entrusted to its Main Council was the task of forming an electoral bloc with all organisations which acknowledged the right of private ownership. The largest section at the Congress was the 'third section' which discussed the agrarian question. More than forty people spoke at these sittings. The discussions revealed differences between the views of the hereditary nobles, who were willing to sacrifice a part of their estates on the understanding that the basis of their private ownership would be preserved, and representatives of the 'bourgeois' *pomeshchiki* and peasant owners. The peasant deputies were keenest to reduce estate holdings so as to spread the opportunities for the development of *khutora* and *otruba*. Fear of the developing revolution and the danger of isolation compelled the hereditary nobility to make concessions to the peasant representatives and, after lengthy discussion, a resolution was passed which was based on the Kadet agrarian programme.[61]

In the subsequent struggle with the peasant movement an important role was assumed by the Plenum of the Main Council of the All-Russian Union of Landowners on 29–31 July 1917. The programme and the intention to cultivate public opinion before the convocation of the Constituent Assembly, as suggested by N. N. L'vov, received the approval of the Plenum.[62] Lvov as President of the Union quite openly revealed the counter-revolutionary aims of the Union. Earlier, the Union had emphasised its aspiration to preserve by legal means the right of private ownership. Now the leaders saw the struggle as fundamentally one against the 'destructive beginnings of the socialist tendency', the struggle against revolution proper. In L'vov's words, 'We must do everything, right up to risking our lives, but we must conquer it.' The Union, he noted, had already begun work on uniting with groups of bankers and industrialists, making contact with Kadets and other parties.

Within a week or so, a Council of Public Figures was created in Moscow. Twenty five places were allotted to the Union. At the meeting of 8–10 August, a firm government was demanded together with the dissolution of revolutionary organisations. At the State Conference, in mid-August, at which twenty delegates represented the Union, a strong government was again demanded as was the immediate closure of the soviets and peasant committees. Members of the Union expressed doubt in the ability of a Provisional Government guided by SRs and Mensheviks to re-establish order and give guarantees of safety, accusing it of not fulfilling the promises given to landowners while conniving at the 'criminal', 'anti-state' activities of the soviets and land committees.[63]

On 18–19 August there occurred a gathering of legal advisers of the local organisations of the Union. In the spirit of the State Conference, they proposed to all local divisions of the Union that both individuals and entire committees should be held criminally responsible for the disruption of owners' rights. They also urged both appeals against the actions of committees and civil actions against them concerning losses.[64] This was the next turning point in the landowners' struggle, the increased use of legal measures and armed force against the peasantry and their supporters.

Between July and September prosecutions of peasant committees were widespread, twice as many occurring in the first two of these months as in the previous four. The vast majority of these occurred in the eleven provinces most affacted by peasant unrest. In the provinces of Mogilyov and Pskov, landowners prosecuted the entire staff of volost committees.[65] Large numbers of prosecutions of land committees occurred in Smolensk, Moscow, Kursk, Voronezh, Tula, Kazan and Simbirsk provinces, to name just a few.[66] Everywhere the number of complaints from *pomeshchiki* about peasant activities increased. Demands were made that provincial commissars punish peasants and return confiscated property. On some occasions, land and other property were indeed returned; and land committees were prosecuted for exceeding their authority. In 26 provinces of central Russia, in July and August, 155 instances of arrests and other acts of official coercion have been discovered; seven of these affected members of district soviets and 104 those of volost committees. At this same time, more than 2000 members of land committees were arrested.[67]

The Union's provincial and district divisions by then acknowledged only harsh means of struggle with the peasantry: arrests, the dissolution of peasant organisations and armed resistance. In the middle of September, the Tambov provincial union and the Marshal of the Nobility, Prince Cholokaev, protested to the Provisional Government and the Chief Land Committee about the instructions issued by the province's public organisations stating that estates should be transferred to the land committees for registration. Although the instructions envisaged only the establishment of formal control over estates in order to defend them against the peasantry – and not the liquidation of private ownership – landowners considered it illegal and demanded its immediate rescindment, insisting that persons infringing laws were criminally responsible and that martial law should be established in the province. Law suits were subsequently brought by landowners and the instruction rescinded on 7 October on the grounds that it was at variance with the laws and instructions of the government.[68]

On 1 October 1917, the Main Council of the Union organised a conference on the revolutionary situation in the countryside. Representatives
from 25 provincial divisions attended. *Pomeshchiki*, it was noted at the
conference, were not the only victims of the agrarian disorders which had
now seized much of the country. The better-off peasants were affected
too. In a telegram to the government the Main Council demanded that
it 'immediately and urgently circulate the harshest of instructions to
provincial commissars and garrison commanders as regards the need for
early, decisive suppression of agrarian disorders by armed force'. The
Council insisted that cavalry units be despatched to particularly troubled
areas. If transgressors were treated with impunity and the government failed
to act, the Union then threatened 'to embark on retribution and summary
justice'.[69]

On 21 October, the Main Council held a second conference of legal
advisers of local divisions. This time, representatives of ten district
divisions were present.[70] Three main questions were discussed: measures for combatting the agrarian disorders and illegal activities of local
organisations; the rising number of new draft land laws; the elections to
the Constituent Assembly. The conference acknowledged that the measures
taken in the struggle with peasant organisations – protests, complaints and
legal prosecutions – 'had been ineffective, and resolved again to petition
the government to halt the activities of the volost land committees and limit
the power of the district and provincial committees'. In general, however,
the land owners considered that force should be the main means of struggle.
They hoped that the government would introduce martial law in a number
of provinces.[71]

Opinions became inflamed. The Moscow lawyer, I. P. Kupchinov, a
member of the Main Council, compared the agrarian movement and
its consequences with an 'unfriendly invasion' and the situation in the
localities with a 'war zone'. It was argued that the Minister-President, as
Supreme Commander-in-Chief, should himself take extraordinary measures
and submit to a military tribunal those persons not executing the instructions
of the government. Effective results, it was said, could only be achieved by
a military government. Kupchinov believed that martial law in localities
already seized by agrarian uprisings, as well as those where unrest was
increasing, would not meet opposition from the leaders of the SRs and the
Mensheviks.[72]

The Provisional Government's use of regular units in the countryside
in September and October have been interpreted by Soviet historians as a
shift towards military dictatorship. On 8 September, Kerenskii announced
that the plan to suppress the peasant movement, as worked out by General

Kornilov, was to be applied to all provinces.[73] On 28 September, the government set up 'special committees' for this purpose. On 12 October it discussed a draft law giving powers to provincial commissars to deal with disturbances. On 20 October, the commission of Pre-Parliament examined the Menshevik draft law for the creation of 'committees of public organisations' to carry out a 'centralised struggle' to impose order on the villages.[74]

In accordance with the demands of the landowners, martial law was introduced in 4 Central Black-Earth provinces (Tambov, Oryol, Tula, Ryazan), two Volga ones (Penza and Saratov) and many districts of other provinces. In September and October, armed action was taken against the peasants on 112 occasions. But soldiers in the rear garrisons frequently refused to fire on peasants. Provincial and district commissars, garrison heads and regimental commanders besieged the government with telegrams reporting the intransigence of the rear units. On 19 October the Minister of Internal Affairs requested that the War Minister immediately deploy cavalry regiments, still loyal to the government, against the peasantry.[75]

The Main Council of the Union immediately refused to acknowledge the October Land Decree and, throughout November and December, emphasised to local divisions that, as with all other instructions of the Soviet government, the Union should consider them illegal. The Union's main task, it stressed, was to organise a planned, mass struggle against the Bolsheviks. The Council recommended protests against the Land Decree as an illegal act; agitation for the prosecution of Lenin; and organisation of mass protests.[76] It placed its hopes in the Constituent Assembly, certain that there would be a return to the former political situation. Thus confiscated estates would be fully or partially returned to their legal owners or expropriated with just and proper compensation. The Council recommended that owners of confiscated estates should cease payments to the land banks, in order to force them into active defence of their debtors – a very unrealistic prognosis.[77] Land owners were urged to take precautions during any confiscation of estates, with the aim of ensuring their preservation. It was suggested that a detailed inventory of the estate property be compiled so that when property was returned, the owners could calculate the extent of the losses suffered.[78]

After October the Bolsheviks' passed legislation permitting some former *pomeshchiki* to remain on their estates although the land area of the latter was to be considerably reduced in accordance with allocations worked out on the basis of the local land norms. Neither the October Land Decree nor the Fundamental Law of February 1918 excluded former *pomeshchiki* from the right to use land if cultivated by their own labour. In November and December, the Union's legal section explained to *pomeshchiki* that the Land Decree of the Bolsheviks and other such declarations from the Soviet government did not make one's home, the area around the dwelling (*usad'ba*) – which owners were advised not to leave (presumably to keep alive the hope of a return to earlier days) – and one's personal belongings subject to confiscation. Owners could also keep for their own use a plot of arable land.[79] Some *pomeshchiki* chose to remain on their estates and farm the area apportioned to them or served as managers of the socialist farms, usually engaged in specialised farming, recently created on their estates.[80]

After the dissolution of the Constituent Assembly, some *pomeshchiki* joined the anti-Bolshevik armies, believing that only civil war could now enable them to repossess what they had lost.[81] The Main Council of the Union remained in Moscow and attempted to maintain links among local organisations. From January to March 1918 it issued the newspaper *Golos zemli*. It also propounded the notion, common among the opposition at the time, that the Soviet regime would not last for long. A. Vorms, member of the Main Council and chairman of the legal section, summoned landowners to prepare themselves to give support for counter-revolution.[82]

In March 1918 the Main Council sought support from Russia's former Allies.[83] The call went out to 'all true patriots' to rise up against 'soviet power'. Three members of the Main Council participated in the creation of a new counter-revolutionary organisation, 'The Right Centre', which aimed at the overthrow of the Soviet government with the help of the German armed forces.[84] The spectre of famine may even have served to raise the Union's hopes further and its leaders spent much time organising opposition to the food measures of the Bolsheviks.

The Bolsheviks at last moved to suppress the Union's activities. On 16 March the Union was evicted from its Moscow premises and at the beginning of April the People's Commissariat of Agriculture instructed soviets to expel from their estates *pomeshchiki* suspected of counter-revolutionary activities. Such attempts to expropriate landowners' property and expel them from their estates sometimes met with armed resistance.[85] On 9 June 1918 the ruling board of the People's Commissariat of Agriculture handed over responsibility for investigating the Union's affairs to the Cheka. On 16 July the Cheka reported with grim satisfaction that the Union was liquidated.[86]

In conclusion, it is vital to provide a corrective to the established view that the landowners were a passive social group in 1917; and, as we have seen, this can be done by focusing on a little-studied aspect of their activities: the development of their own organisations to combat peasant revolution. No longer is it possible to see the fate of the landowners as similar to that of the Pompeians in the face of an erupting Vesuvius. Russian landowners did not accept that their destiny was, in Trotsky's words, to be confined to the dustbin of history. It is therefore not fanciful to speak of a landowners' 'movement', which developed in opposition to that of the peasantry and responded to the pattern of agrarian unrest. This movement may be divided into two phases: first, growth and consolidation between March and June; second, the maturation in July and August, leading to a decisive break with past strategy and tactics in September and October with the resort to armed force. There was a shift away from 'concessions'; and calls for the establishment of martial law can be seen as a measure of their eventual desperation. A change in the attitude of the landowners is visible, too, in the reduction in the property qualification (to almost a nominal figure), the wooing of the peasant – separators and those peasants who had individually purchased land. All this was designed to strengthen the campaign to retain private ownership.

Meanwhile the increased politicisation of land owners also acted to push the Kadets to the right. And the Union, perceiving the Provisional Government as moving towards conciliation with the peasantry, came into conflict with Kerenskii. Eventually landowners' calls for arrests of peasants and their supporters and armed intervention to suppress rural unrest to protect *pomeshchik* interests were answered positively by the actions of the Government. With the October revolution the Landowners' Union carried on the struggle against Bolshevism, refusing to accept the new land laws until the Union was finally suppressed in July 1918. Thus the attempt of the *pomeshchiki* to resist the October revolution was in vain and their active struggle to protect their properties from seizure and destruction (and thus maintain some economic power) eventually resulted in their elimination as a political force in the early summer of 1918. Far too little is known about this landowners' movement and its local activities in particular. To what extent the movement was representative of landowners in general and of the role of private property-minded peasants remains to be seen. It is to such questions as these that attention needs to be directed in the future.[87]

Notes

1. Originally a service class which acquired land in return for its services to the state, the *pomeshchiki* by the nineteenth century had become synonymous with landlords.

2. Data are taken from Seymour Becker, *Nobility and Privilege in Late Imperial Russia* (Illinois: Northern Illinois University Press, 1985).

3. Information on the 'new' landowners is taken from V. M. Selunskaya, *Izmeneniya sotsial'noi struktury sovetskogo obshchestva okt. 1917–1920* (Moscow, 1976), p. 182 and A. P. Korelin, 'Rossiiskoe dvoryanstvo i ego soslovnaya organizatsiya (1861–1904 gg.), *Istoriya SSSR* (1971) no. 5, p. 59.

4. For a recent discussion see Hans Rogger, *Russia in the Age of Modernisation and Revolution, 1881–1917* (London: Longman, 1983), pp. 67–8, 88–95, and Becker, *op. cit.* See also the recent review article by Theodore Taranovski, 'Nobility in the Russian Empire: Some Problems of Definition and Interpretation', *Slavic Review*, vol. 47, no. 2 (1988): 314–18

5. There might also be differentiation both according to gender and between those who were farming and those who were absentee landowners.

6. Apart from Becker (*op. cit.*), see for instance G. M. Hamburg, *Politics of the Russian Nobility, 1881–1905* (New Brunswick, N.J., 1984); Robert Edelman, *Gentry Politics on the Eve of the Russian Revolution: the Nationalist Party, 1907–1917* (New Brunswick, 1980); R. T. Manning, *The Crisis of the Old order in Russia: Gentry and Government* (Princeton, 1982). Becker takes issue with Manning, in particular, over her interpretation of the 'decline of the gentry' thesis, offering contrary data on many points

7. See for example the works by A. M. Anfimov: 'Pomeshchich'e khozyaistvo Rossii v gody pervoi mirovoi voiny', *Istoricheskie zapiski*, vol. 60 (1957): 124–75; 'Khozyaistvo krupnogo pomeshchika v XXv.', *Istoricheskie zapiski*, vol. 71 (1962): 47–55; *Krupnoe pomeshchich'e khozyaistvo Evropeiskoi Rossii (konets XIX – nachalo XX veka)*, Moscow, 1969; by Yu. B. Solov'ev: 'Samoderzhavie i dvoryanskii vopros v kontse XIX v.', *Istoricheskie zapiski*, vol. 88 (1971): 150–210; *Samoderzhavie i dvoryanstvo v kontse XIX veka* (Leningrad, 1973) and *Samoderzhavie i dvoryanstvo v 1902–1907gg.* (Leningrad, 1981); and by A. P. Korelin, 'Dvoryanstvo v poreformennoi Rossii 1861–1904 gg.', *Istoricheskie zapiski*, vol. 87 (1970): 91–173; 'Rossiiskoe dvoryanstvo i ego soslovnaya organizatsiya (1861–1904 gg.), *Istoriya SSSR*, no. 5 (1971): 56–81; *Dvoryanstvo v poreformennoi Rossii 1861–1904 gg.* (Moscow, 1979).

8. Some interesting comments on this question may be found in the early sections of an unpublished paper by S. G. Wheatcroft, 'Towards an Analysis of the Class Divisions in the USSR in the 1920s and the 1930s

with special reference to the Non-Agricultural Non-Labouring Classes', SIPS paper (CREES, University of Birmingham, November 1984). It should also be borne in mind that social history in Britain and France has been focused on 'the people' as distinct from the élites. Thus Western social historians, working with this paradigm, have concentrated on the urban workers and the peasantry when researching the Russian Revolution. Perhaps unconsciously, the élites – the industrialists and landowners – have not been their primary concern. (For a recent discussion of trends in social history see the chapter by E. J. Hobsbawm, 'History from Below – Some Reflections', in Frederick Krantz (ed.), *History From Below* (Basil Blackwell, 1988). One curious aspect about Soviet work on the landowners is that it appears to be dominated by female historians: Osipova more recently (see n. 9 below) and Chaadaeva in the 1920s (see n. 11 below).

9.   T. V. Osipova, *Klassovaya bor'ba v derevne v period podgotovki i provedeniya velikoi oktyabr'skoi sotsialisticheskoi revolyutsii* (Moscow, 1974), p. 97; Osipova, 'Vserossiskii soyuz zemel'nykh sobstvennikov (1917)', *Istoriya SSSR* (1976) no. 3: 116; *Sovety krest'yanskikh deputatov i drugie krest'yanskie organizatsii*, vol. 1, pt. 2, p. 137.

10.   *Sovety krest'yanskikh deputatov v 1917*, p. 140

11.   Chaadaeva claims that the Union emerged because landowners were frightened of the developing agrarian movement and created an organisation for the immediate defence of the interests of large landownership. See O. N. Chaadaeva, Introduction to material relating to the Plenum of the Main Council of the Union of Landowners, *Krasnyi Arkhiv* (1927) vol. 2, 21: 97–9. The first public proposal for such an organisation came at a gathering in Moscow of 203 individuals (consisting almost exclusively of nobles) from 33 provinces in November 1905. The initiators of the Union were principally landowners from provinces such as Samara and Saratov where the peasant threat was most acute. The winter of 1905–1906 witnessed a growing feeling that a permanent national organisation, comprising certain delegates elected from the provincial noble societies, was necessary to defend the interests of the landed nobility against threats from the peasantry and 'misguided liberal bureaucrats'. The more conservative provincial landowning nobles, active in local affairs, like those who formed the Union, were prominent supporters of actions which led to the emergence of the United Nobility. According to Chaadaeva, the Union's rules were worked out by the central organisation of the United Nobility. See Becker, *op. cit.*, pp. 160–1; G. Hosking, *The Constitutional Experiment: Government and Duma, 1907–14* (London, 1973), and G. Hosking and Roberta Thompson Manning, 'What Was the United Nobility ?' in L. Haimson, ed., *The Politics of Rural Russia* (Bloomington, Indiana, 1979); and Chaadaeva, *op. cit.*

12. Some 17 000 agrarian disturbances were recorded in European Russia during 1910–14 and 537 from January 1914–1916: A. M. Anfimov, *Rossisskaya derevnya v gody pervoi mirovoi voiny* (Moscow, 1962), ch. 5. Citing this same source (though giving the number as 557), Keep suggests that these latter figures should be seen not as evidence of revolutionary stirrings but rather as part of the 'normal fabric of rural life': see J. L. H. Keep, *The Russian Revolution* (London, 1976), pp. 40–1.

13. This is neatly encapsulated in what Stites has called the revolutionaries' struggle 'for the dignity of the lower classes'. See, for example, the noblewoman who 'became hysterical' when a tram conductor referred to her as comrade: Richard Stites, 'Utopias in the Air and On the Ground : Futuristic Dreams in the Russian Revolution', *Russian History/Histoire Russe*, vol. 11, nos 2–3, Summer–Fall (1984): 252. For other examples see Douglas Brown, *Doomsday 1917. The Destruction of Russia's Ruling Class* (London, 1975).

14. More accurately this was noted in 'a number of districts of these provinces': see Osipova, *Klassovaya bor'ba*, p. 97.

15. This referred to peasants who had individually consolidated land outside the commune, some of whom adopted such a form of land tenure as a consequence of the Stolypin land reforms after 1906.

16. *Khronika revolyutsionnykh sobytii Tambovskoi gubernii*, p. 10.

17. No evidence is provided, though, to show that labour was hired in order to work this land.

18. *Vlast' naroda*, 20 May 1917; Osipova, 'Vserossiskii soyuz', p. 117 and *Klassovaya bor'ba*, p. 98.

19. Makarov writing in *Vlast' naroda*, 20 May 1917, cited in Osipova, *Klassovaya bor'ba*, p. 98.

20. Osipova, *Klassovaya bor'ba*, pp. 98–9 and 'Vserossiskii soyuz', p. 117.

21. Osipova, *Klassovaya bor'ba*, p. 99.

22. *Ustav Vserossiiskogo soyuza zemel'nykh sobstvennikov*, Moscow, 1917, p. 1. Another set of rules was published at this time with the same title but does not correspond with these points. Osipova (*Klassovaya bor'ba*, p. 99) is evidently discussing the former.

23. *Ustav*, p. 2

24. *Ustav*, p. 2; together with *Ustav Lebedyanskogo soyuza zemlevladel'tsev*, Lebedyan, 1917 and *Ustav Belozerskogo uezdnogo otdela soyuza zemel'nykh sobstvennikov*, p. 1 cited in Osipova, *Klassovaya bor'ba*, p. 100.

25. In her article Chaadaeva gives this as 'soyuz krupnykh i melkikh sobstvennikov' and argues that this emphasised the 'class unity of pomeshchik and peasant landowners' ('Vserossiskii soyuz', p. 117). For Stavropol' see O. Chaadaeva, *Pomeshchiki i ikh organizatsii v 1917 godu* (Moscow-Leningrad, 1928), p. 86.

26. For Osipova, this emphasises class unity (*Klassovaya bor'ba*, p. 99)

while Chaadaeva gives this as '*posevshchiki*' (*Pomeshchiki*, p. 86).

27. *Spisok gubernskikh i uezdnykh otdelov Vserossiskogo soyuza zemel'nykh sobstvennikov 1917 g.* cited in Osipova, *Klassovaya bor'ba*, pp. 99–100 and 1976, p. 117; for Bessarabiya province see Chaadaeva, *Pomeshchiki*, p. 86.

28. Chaadaeva, *Pomeshchiki*, pp. 82–3.

29. The Ryazan' newspaper may well have been typical. It discussed the advantages of private property (*sobstvennost'*) and its solidity compared to socialisation; it urged *pomeshchiki* to use the rights allotted to them by the Provisional Government resolution (on preserving sowings) of 10 April and to ensure that 'only good, efficient farmers (*del'nye khozyaeva*)' were elected in the volosts. (Initially the newspaper was called *Izvestiya Ryazanskogo gubernskogo otdeleniya Vserossiiskogo soyuza zemel'nykh sobstvennikov* and then *Zemledelets*. For details see Chaadaeva, *Pomeshchiki*, pp. 86–7. It was also proposed to publish newspapers in Stavropol' and Vitebsk.

30. These sections were several in number.

31. On N. N. and V. N. L'vov see K M. Astrakhan, *Bol'sheviki i ikh politicheskie protivniki v 1917 g.* (Moscow, 1973), p. 366. Some sources note that they were related to Prince G. E. L'vov, premier of the Provisional Government until July.

32. Osipova, *Klassovaya bor'ba*, pp. 100–1.

33. A peasant from Troitsko-Golenishchevsk (Moskovsk district), a volost where 42 householders had joined the Union, wrote: 'Those who did not have property were not admitted.'

34. *Zemlya i Volya*, 19 May 1917 and 25 May 1917; *Sovety krest'yanskikh deputatov*, vol. 1, pt. 2, p. 157; Osipova, *Klassovaya bor'ba*, p. 101, citing archives.

35. *Narodnoe slovo*, 8 June 1918 (the newspaper of the Popular Socialist party) cited in Osipova, *Klassovaya bor'ba*, p. 102.

36. *Sovety i krest'yanskikh deputatov*, vol. 1, pt. 2, p. 172 (for Egor'evsk); *Ryazanskie gubernskie vedomosti*, 3 August 1917 (for Ryazan) cited in Osipova, 1974, p. 102

37. Osipova, *Klassovaya bor'ba*, p. 102 citing Kosenko; Osipova, 'Vserossiiskii soyuz', p. 118 states 'land committees'. Between April and July *khutoryane* and *otrubniki* in Saratov province sent 439 complaints to the provincial commissar about the activities of the committees which took away their land. In Vol'sk district alone, 24 volosts passed resolutions calling for the division of *otrub* land.

38. *Sovety krest'yanskhikh deputatov*, vol. 1, pt. 2, p. 177; Osipova, *Klassovaya bor'ba*, p. 102. Osipova also states ('Vserossiiskii soyuz', p. 118) states that these were rich (*bogatye*) peasants but offers no evidence to support this.

39. *Vestnik vremennogo pravitel'stva*, 24 May 1917

40. *Privol'zhskaya pravda* (Samara), 22 June 1917, cited in Osipova, *Klassovaya bor'ba*, pp.102–3.

41. In Tambov province, for instance, there were 196 land disturbances between March and June while in Malo-Pupovsk volost (Kozlovsk district) alone 1 200 desyatinas belonging to 80 *khutoryane* were divided (*Krest'yanskoe dvizhenie v 1917 g.*), p. 212; for purchased land see Osipova, 'Vserossiiskii soyuz', p.119; *Khronika revolyutsionnykh sobytii v Tambovskoi gubernii*, p. 15; Osipova, *Klassovaya bor'ba*, p. 103.

42. *Izvestiya Vserossiiskogo soveta krest'yanskikh deputatov*, 16 August 1917; and *Narodnoe slovo*, 29 June 1917, cited in Osipova, *Klassovaya bor'ba*, p. 103.

43. *Izvestiya Glavnogo zemel'nogo komiteta* (1917) no. 1: 14.

44. Similar telegrams were sent to Ranenburgsk, Venevsk, Mtsensk, Ostrogozhsk, Karsunsk, Penzensk, Spassk, Laishevsk, Saratovsk, Ostashkovsk and Vladimirsk districts.

45. Osipova, *Klassovaya bor'ba*, p. 104, citing archives.

46. *Zemlya i Volya*, 18 May 1917; *Sovety krest'yanskikh deputatov*, vol. 1, pt. 2, p. 155; Osipova, *Klassovaya bor'ba*, p. 105.

47. *Zemlya i Volya*, 17 June 1917; *Narodnoe slovo*, 7 June 1917 cited in Osipova, *Klassovaya bor'ba*, p. 105. It is not clear who was to be included under the term 'toiling population' (*trudovoe naselenie*).

48. Osipova, *Klassovaya bor'ba*, pp. 105–6, citing archives.

49. Chaadaeva, *Pomeshchiki*, p. 82.

50. For the Plenum reports see *Krasnyi arkhiv* (1927), vol. 2 (21): 97–121; Chaadaeva, *Pomeshchiki*, pp. 83–4.

51. Osipova, 'Vserossiskii soyuz', pp. 119–21 for sources. See also A. D. Malyavskii, *Krest'yanskoe dvizhenie v Rossii v 1917g., mart – oktyabr'* (Moscow, 1981), p. 244.

52. Osipova, 'Vserossiskii soyuz', p. 120.

53. In the provinces of Kaluga, Voronezh, Ryazan', Kursk, Tula, Penza and Simbirsk as well as in the districts Vyaznikovsk, Sychevsk, Shatsk and Tversk.

54. *Zemlya i Volya*, 19 July 1917 and 25 July 1917; *Ryazanskaya zhizn'*, 27 July 1917, cited in Osipova, 1976, pp. 120–1.

55. This occurred, for example, in Penza, Narovchat, Gdov and Opochka.

56. *Zemlya i Volya*, 19 July 1917; for sources on soldiers and Voronezh see Osipova, 'Vserossiskii soyuz', pp. 121–2.

57. *Sovety krest'yanskikh deputatov*, vol. 1, pt. 2, p. 161.

58. Chaadaeva, *Pomeshchiki*, p. 83.

59. *Vserossisskii soyuz*, no. 1 (July 1917) cited in Osipova, 'Vserossiskii soyuz', pp. 122–3.

60. Osipova, 'Vserossiskii soyuz', p. 123.

61. Ibid.

62. Chaadaeva, *Pomeshchiki*, pp. 83–4; *Krasnyi arkhiv* (1927) no. 2 (21): 119–20; Osipova, 'Vserossiskii soyuz', p. 123.

63. I. I. Mints, *Istoriya Velikogo oktyabrya*, vol. 3 (Moscow, 1970), pp. 713–14. Involvement of *pomeshchiki* in the Kornilov revolt is

still a contentious issue. Chaadaeva, for instance, sees counter-revolutionary landowners as the prime movers behind the Kornilov revolt: *Kornilovshchina* (Moscow-Leningrad, 1930). For alternative explanations see the recent review of the literature in John W. Long, 'Kornilov Redivivus: New Data on the Prelude to Bol'shevism', *Russian History/Histoire Russe*, vol. 11, no. 1, Spring 1984. James White and Marc Ferro have more recently argued that the Kornilovites were a 'shaky amalgam of counter-revolutionary industrialists, financiers and landowners': see Long, *op. cit.*, p. 105.

64. Osipova, 'Vserossiskii soyuz', p. 124.
65. A. V. Shestakov, *Bol'sheviki i krest'yanstvo v revolyutsii 1917g.*, p. 16 for the figure of 17. This is further cited in Osipova, 'Vserossiskii soyuz', p. 124 and Malyavskii, *op. cit.*, p. 244. In Pskov such activity occurred, in particular, in Ostrovsk and Toropetsk districts where district and volost land committees were especially active.
66. Osipova, 'Vserossiskii soyuz', p. 124. Similarly Borovitchsk and Starorussk district land committees of Novgorod province provoked the wrath of land owners: see *Delo naroda*, 27 September 1917 and *Krest'yanskie dvizhenie*, p. 193.
67. Malyavskii, *op. cit.*, pp. 244–5. See also Chaadaeva, *Pomeshchiki*, pp. 115–17 for further evidence.
68. *Khronika revolyutsionnykh sobytii v Tambovskoi gubernii*, pp. 28–9.
69. Osipova, 'Vserossiskii soyuz', p. 125, citing archives.
70. The ten divisions were: Oryol, Voyansk, Petrograd, Tver, Shuisk, Bronnitsk, Sychevsk, Venevsk, Efremovsk and Kozlovsk.
71. *Idem*, pp. 125–6.
72. *Idem*, p. 126.
73. For a discussion of the *pomeshchiki* and the Kornilov revolt, see n. 63 above.
74. *Revolyutsionnoe dvizhenie v Rossii v sentyabre 1917 godu, Dokumenty i materialy* (Moscow, 1961), pp. 221–2; *Revolyutsionnoe dvizhenie nakanune oktyabrya*, pp. 202–3.
75. Shestakov, *op. cit.*, p. 17; *Revolyutsionnoe dvizhenie v sentyabre*, p. 459.
76. Osipova, 'Vserossiskii soyuz', p. 127, citing archives.
77. *Loc. cit.* A special letter regarding this was sent by the Soviet to the banks on 13 November.
78. Osipova, 'Vserossiskii soyuz', pp. 127–8.
79. *Idem*, p. 128 citing archives. For a more detailed discussion of landowners who were allocated land and remained in the countryside after October see John Channon, 'Former Landlords (*Pomeshchiki*) in Rural Russia after the Revolution: some economic and social aspects', *Discussion Paper no. 85/6* (Department of Economics, University of Lancaster, 1985); *idem*, 'Tsarist Landowners after the Revolution: Former Pomeshchiki in Rural Russia during NEP', *Soviet Studies*, vol. 39, no. 4 (October 1987): 575–98.

80. Osipova, 'Vserossiskii soyuz', pp. 128–9; Channon, 'Former Landlords'.
81. For a list of uprisings in which landowners are alleged to have participated see Osipova, 'Vserossiskii soyuz', p. 128.
82. For details of what Vorms wrote see *Golos zemli*, 30 January 1918 (cited in Osipova, 'Vserossiskii soyuz', p. 128).
83. *Golos zemli*, 20 March 1918 cited in *loc. cit.*
84. D. L. Golinkov, *Krakh vrazhskogo podpol'ya* (Moscow, 1971), pp. 62-3.
85. Few such organisations existed after the early summer of 1918 although some lasted until the autumn when they were suppressed by the committees of poor peasants (instituted in June). See, for example, the activities of the Voronezh Landowners' Union discussed in V. M. Fefelov, *op. cit.*, pp. 72–3.
86. Mints, *op. cit.*, vol. 3, pp. 109–10; *Golos zemli*, 20 March 1918, cited in Osipova, 1976, p. 129.
87. For a discussion of recent work by Soviet historians on the peasantry see John Channon, 'The Peasantry in the Revolutions of 1917': paper presented to a conference on 'The Revolutions of 1917: 70 years after', Hebrew University of Jerusalem, January 1988. In the 1920s Chaadaeva was much more cautious with regard to statements about a 'pomeshchik-kulak' alliance, suggesting that the policies directed towards this goal achieved only limited success.

APPENDIX

Table 1.   Estimate of number of landlord (pomeshchiki) families and total number of pomeshchiki, including family members, by 1917

Number of landlord families (A)	Total number of pomeshchiki (incl. family members) (B)
30 000 [1]	120 000
85 000	340 000 [2]
94 500–96 500 [3]	378 000–386 000
100 000 [4]	400 000
110 000 [5]	440 000

Notes

(i)   All figures in (A) have been × 4 or in (B) ÷ 4 since we know that, on average, there were approximately four members pers *pomeshchik* family (excluding hired labour which includes domestic servants). For an explanation of this derivation see John Channon, 'Tsarist Landowners . . . ' *op. cit.*, p. 596, n. 48.

Sources

1. Alexandra S. Korros in L. Haimson, ed., *The Politics of Rural Russia*, p. 293, also cited by T. Shanin in *Russia 1905–7: Revolution as a Moment of Truth*, Macmillan, 1986, pp. 203–4, 349, n. 36, though he appreciates that this figure seems rather low.
2. Derived by the present writer from the following sources: On the assumption that the population of the Russian Empire in 1913 was 170.1 million and that pomeshchiki would be 340 000. (For population see M. E. Falkus, *The Industrialisation of Russia, 1700–1914*, Macmillan, 1972, pp. 17, 34; for 0.2 per cent figure see V. S. Nemchinov, *Vsemirno – istoricheskoe znachenie velikoi oktybr'skaya sotsialisticheskoi revolyutsii*, Moscow 1957, p. 63.
3. Seymour Becker, Nobility and Privilege in late Imperial Russia, Dekalb., Ill., 1985.
4. John Channon, 'Tsarist Landowners . . . ' *op. cit.* This was an 'approximate' number.
5. Robert Conquest, *The Harvest of Sorrow* (Hutchinson, 1986), p. 43, citing David Mitrany, *Marx Against the Peasant* (Chapel Hill, 1951), p. 59 and John Maynard, *The Russian Peasant and Other Studies* (London, 1943), p. 120; and N. Jasny, *The Socialised Agriculture of the USSR* (Stanford, 1949), pp. 144–45.

    These were 110 000 *'large'* owners (my emphasis) who lost 108 million acres plus 2 million peasants who lost 140 million acres during the reign of the Provisional Government in 1917. J. L. H. Keep, *The Russian Revolution* (1976, p. 208) similarly notes that there were 2.4 million peasants on individual farms.

8   The Industrial Workers

Robert Service

Studies of the workers of the former Russian empire in 1917 have not always been plentiful. Barely any were published from the late 1920s through to the late 1950s in the Soviet Union and to the late 1960s in the West. How urban labourers lived, how they worked, what they thought and what they did: such questions failed to be addressed. It was the apex of Russian politics which pre-occupied writers, and the struggle among the parties was the transcendent theme. Not even the central party bodies attracted much investigation. Instead, the leading politicians in these bodies commanded attention. What might be called an historiographical leaderology – to appropriate Lenin's term – dominated descriptions and analyses of revolutionary Russia. Here, then, a rare armistice existed in the disputes that prevailed generally among scholars. Dissension about the rights and wrongs of the Bolshevik seizure of power in October 1917 remained furious. The variety of militant positions was large: all Soviet and a few Western historians welcomed the fact that a Bolshevik-led government had been installed;[1] other foreigners, while not greeting it so warmly, felt that the creation of a Soviet régime, had to be accepted as a long-term fact of political life.[2] Still others entirely denied the legitimacy of the Bolshevik claim to governmental authority.[3] Yet all of them, stretching from Trotskyists on the left to conservatives on the right, implied that the burden of investigative effort should be placed on high politics and that our knowledge of the working class was more or less adequate.

The truce extended to terminology. Virtually all books on 1917 spoke about 'the workers' as a more or less undifferentiated mass. This reflected usage by contemporary politicians in 1917 of every party affiliation and was not the only instance of Soviet and Western historians finding themselves in accord. 'The workers', furthermore, were often used as a synonym for 'the urban masses' or the 'street crowd'. Sociological casualness is a euphemism for such an approach. Nor has it yet entirely disappeared from influential studies of the Russian Revolution.[4]

Treatments of the Revolution postulated a set of relationships which had an almost catechistic rhythm and predictability. Lenin led the Bolshevik Central Committee. The Central Committee led the party. The party led the workers. Such treatments reduced the role of the working class in the fall of the Provisional Government to a low plane of significance. Workers supposedly had an impact on 1917 mainly inasmuch as they followed the Menshevik Tsereteli and the Socialist-Revolutionary Chernov in the months after the February revolution and then transferred their allegiance to the Bolsheviks before the October revolution. Several Western writers in particular stressed that factory labourers understood extremely little or even nothing about their country's politics; and that, apart from choosing representatives in the various mass organisations, their political participation failed to extend beyond occasional street demonstrations. The impression was given, both in the Soviet Union and in the West, that workers had a negligible impact upon the running of soviets, trade unions and factory-workshop committees (and even less upon the internal party affairs of the Bolsheviks). There was a widespread perception that nearly all debates and actions were undertaken by tiny, rival groups of prominent politicians, and that middle-class intellectuals dominated everyone and everything in 1917.

This dismissiveness was first abandoned, cautiously, not in the West but in the USSR. Nikita Khrushchev's campaign for de-Stalinisation yielded much scholarly fruit in official historiography. From the late 1950s a fresh emphasis was placed upon the social classes which were in the foreground of support for or opposition to the Bolsheviks. For example, P. I. Leiberov, A. G. Rashin and O. I. Shkaratan produced works on the numerical strength and social composition of the working class.[5] Much fundamental enquiry was initiated in the Khrushchev era and was continued under the harsher conditions for Soviet scholars following Khrushchev's replacement as party leader by Leonid Brezhnev. Books by V. Z. Drobizhev, L. S. Gaponenko and E. V. Gimpel'son have continued the investigative tradition re-inaugurated under Khrushchev.[6]

The last comprehensive census under Romanov rule appeared in 1897; but, after the industrial recession around the turn of the century and the revolutionary upheaval of 1905–1906, there had been a considerable expansion in manufacturing and mining output. The Great War, too, witnessed a further increase in the material indices. The size of the work-force rose simultaneously. Soviet scholars, bringing together disparate data, have published figures suggesting that there were around 3.5 million labourers in factories and mines at the time of the February revolution. As Lenin had insisted since the 1890s, this was not the full extent of the urban working class. He added railwaymen, construction-site workers, general manual labourers in various occupations and town artisans. By taking Lenin's approach as a basis and by incorporating previously unavailable data on the period through to 1917, the same scholars have maintained that around 18.5 million wage workers of all types existed by the end of 1916.[8] This was in line with the wish of official Soviet historians to demonstrate that, although Russia was far from being a fully industrialised country before the Bolshevik seizure of power, its level of industrialisation could not reasonably be assessed only on the basis of the number of factory workers.[9]

Sociological research on the workers was also resumed. Those workers who had employment at large-scale factories, who had gone through some schooling and had industrial skills and whose parents, too, had been factory employees were regarded as the vanguard of the Russian working class.[10] Studies were undertaken to correlate a number of criteria: size of factory; level of skill; educational training; familial connections with factories and with town life. Those workers who scored highly on all these counts were claimed to have come over to the Bolsheviks earlier in 1917 than the other sections of the working class. The less skilled, less educated and less urbanised workers were thought to have been less 'conscious', less capable of understanding the 'correct' political line; but historians in the USSR affirmed that even this section of the working class, through the stimulus of Bolshevik party propaganda, came to accept the need for a further revolution to get rid of the Provisional Government and establish a Bolshevik-led socialist régime.[11]

Leiberov, Rashin and Shkaratan were essentially resurrecting a long-buried Soviet historiographical tradition; and indeed Rashin, years previously, had helped to found the tradition.[12] In the 1920s historical journals and indeed contemporary trade union publications like *Vestnik truda* had produced a vast amount of statistics on the size and composition of the Russian working class in the revolutionary period.[13] Only gradually, from the late 1950s, did the choice of themes expand. Not just the numerical size and social composition but also the nature of its activities started to be investigated. The incidence of strikes in 1917 became a major topic.[14] Works were also published on membership of mass working-class organisations like the trade unions and the factory-workshop committees.[15] In addition, two outstanding books were written by P. V. Volobuev: the first considered the Provisional Government's economic policies and their implications for all sections of society, especially the working class; the second looked at the relations between industrialists and factory workers.[16] All such works have increased our knowledge of the Russian Revolution. Without them, the birth of Western scholarship on the workers of the former Russian empire in 1917 would have been immeasurably more difficult.

But Soviet scholarship has yet to recover the thematic range it possessed in the decade after the Revolution when research on the working had a vibrant contemporary importance. Studies of the household budgets of workers remain scanty. Little is known in detail about the working-class diet in Petrograd and the rest of the country. In addition, factory workers continue to attract immensely more published work than do the other segments of the urban working poor. The contacts between workers and the non-Bolshevik parties in 1917, furthermore, are virtually ignored. The writers of the 1920s did not confine themselves, or were not constrained to confine themselves, quite so narrowly.[17] It must also be noted that Soviet historians traditionally have largely adhered to the catechistic triad of Lenin, the party and the masses. No major empirical enquiry has yet challenged its validity. The claim is maintained that the workers acted on instructions or at least through the encouragement from the Bolshevik party. Consequently the workers' 'consciousness' is judged by the extent to which it reflected the will of Lenin and the Central Committee. The officially-sanctioned monographs still imply that Russian workers did little independently to 'make' the very revolution which is supposed to have been a 'workers' revolution'.[18]

Western scholarship on the Russian working class has meanwhile grown at a fast rate. Various articles and monographs appeared, especially from the 1960s,[19] and John Keep's study of 'mass mobilisation', published in 1976, is generally acknowledged to have constituted a landmark in historiography.[20] His underlying interpretation derived its ancestry from Leonard Schapiro and Merle Fainsod. Keep asserted that the Bolshevik assumption of power in October 1917 was a violent and illegimate conspiracy, based on months of manipulation and mobilisation of popular opinion and perpetrated by a numerically insignificant minority of the urban population. Unlike Schapiro and Fainsod, however, his chapters described and analysed the economic and social conditions which provoked so much working-class unrest. He also traced the unrest to objective difficulties in the running of a war effort by an inadequately-developed industrial and military power. His book broke new ground in Western scholarship by focussing attention on the internal workings of the soviets, trade unions and factory workshop committees. Data on the elections and social composition of functionaries, on inter-committee relationships and on operational methods were provided; and the evolution of mass organisations between February and October was delineated. John Keep agreed with Soviet historians that the Bolshevik party and its Central Committee guided and directed such organisations; but he insisted that this process was manipulative, hypocritical and malign.[21]

In particular, he argued that the main political and ordinary technical functions were arrogated by and stayed with the intellectuals.[22] Secondly, mass participation in debate and decision at open meetings declined gradually after the February Revolution. Politics increasingly took place behind closed doors, and the committee men and women used democratic procedures exploitatively: merely in order to rubber-stamp their wishes.[23] The principal sinners in his book are the Bolsheviks. Each chapter offers a compilation of the variety of flexible and cynical strategems whereby the Bolshevik party, in the provinces as well as at the centre, seized and secured power in 1917–1918. Sometimes this was done with the unwitting collaboration of other socialist parties, which later were extruded from authority. On other occasions a military solution was adopted and the Provisional Government's supporters were overwhelmed by armed might.[24]

Furthermore, Keep's book traced how quickly the principles of election and accountability were ignored after October 1917. The mass organisations which had been used to mobilise 'the masses' against the Provisional Government were transformed into mere conveyor-belts of the Bolshevik Central Committee's wishes; and, as in his other works, Keep highlighted the prominent and decisive part played by Lenin and his associates, especially Trotskii and Sverdlov, in producing this dénouement.[25] His book represented a more sophisticated version of one of the long-held Western traditions. Social and economic conditions and organisational vicissitudes were introduced; but the primacy of causation was still given to the decisions taken at the apex of politics. Lower-level politics were incorporated, but treated as ancillary to central events. Lenin remained in his conventional portraiture as the single major force in the undermining of Kerenskii's authority, in the demoralisation of the Mensheviks and Socialist Revolutionaries and in the setting up of the Soviet state. Like official historical textbooks in the USSR, Keep's path-breaking investigation of 'mass mobilisation' tended to conceive the workers predominantly as the objects, not the subjects of their history. Central control and direction from above were crucial aspects of his interpretation.

A challenge to basic aspects of John Keep's book has come from Soviet historians, bridling at the perjorative connotations of an interpretation which lays almost exclusive stress on the 'manipulation' of popular opinion and organisational procedures. Nevertheless the fact that his work has been reviewed and its contentions described so extensively is an index of the acceptance of the seriousness with which the author is treated.[26]

Yet another challenge to the book as well as to both Soviet and Western scholarship in general has been mounted by a number of historians, based mainly in the USA and Western Europe, who have expressed doubt that the workers were really so tightly controlled from above in their thought and action in 1917. The French scholar Marc Ferro, looking at telegrams sent into the Provisional Government in March, found that workers already had several definite ideas on the best future course of public affairs and that demands for a democratic republic and the eight-hour working day were prominent.[27] This undermined the contention that such ideas had to be carefully inseminated and cultivated over several ensuing months. Subsequent detailed accounts of Petrograd workers by Stephen Smith and David Mandel and of Moscow workers by Diane Koenker examined the motivations of the working class.[28] All three laid stress on the living and working conditions of workers as being the crucible of rising working-class radicalism; and, incidentally, they supported the tenet of the Soviet historians that the workers with skills, education, lengthy urban residence and relatively high wages were in the vanguard of opposition to the authorities. Moreover, the rivalries among the various sections of the working class did not cease. Smith has shown in detail that unskilled and less 'urbanised' workers resented the better conditions of the skilled workers; and that they were also slower to support radical policies or to become involved in politics. Many skilled workers in their turn wanted to maintain wage differentials.[29]

There was, however, growing unity within the working class as the general crisis of the economy pressed hard on all workers. Nor was millenarianism the predominant stimulus to action. Smith has indicated that the movement towards 'workers' control', whereby the labour force established supervision over management, was initiated largely as a practical defence against likely lock-outs or even permanent closures by employers. The absence of social-security benefits turned continued employment in a working factory into a prospective matter of life and death. Thus the activity of the labour movement in 1917 was perceived to have had an inherent 'rationality' as well as an 'autonomy' from middle-class intellectual influence.[30] Similarly, Rex Wade in his study of the Red Guards indicated that a popular concern about law and order, as much as a campaign by party-political activists, stimulated the formation of militia units.[31] The workers themselves became radical without much prodding or even guidance from the intellectuals who served as the country's leading politicians.

It has become clear, in addition, that workers took an active part in the establishment of their mass sectional organisations. Analyses of the pre-revolutionary period are helpful. The labouring poor of towns and cities were not without experience in self-mobilisation. The memory of the soviets (or class-based sectional 'councils') of 1905 was undimmed;

and many workers, in Petrograd and then elsewhere, were quick to call for their re-establishment after the February revolution.[32] Furthermore, legal trade unions had existed after 1905 in major urban centres, despite many institutional restrictions and police harassment, and gave invaluable organisational training to activists; and the Romanov imperial government, by insisting that trade-union officials should themselves be workers, ensured that the working class had thousands of its own experienced representatives.[33] There were also sickness-insurance committees, Sunday schools and the informal *zemlyachestva* (which were geographically-based associations of workers coming together for work in particular towns).[34] Notions of mutual help and collective control were strong. After the quiescence of the years immediately following the 1905–1906 revolution, there was also a resurgence of radicalism before the First World War.[35] The slogans supported by workers in the street demonstrations of 1914 tended to be near to those proposed by the Bolshevik faction; but the Bolshevik underground leadership was keenly aware that this stemmed more from the workers' response to their own social and material circumstances than to leadership and instruction from the faction's local bodies. Proof came in February 1917: workers found that Bolshevik slogans currently failed to correspond to their wishes and voted majorities to the Mensheviks and Socialist Revolutionaries in the soviets.

A comprehensive analysis of the social composition of soviets and other working-class sectional organisations has yet to be made; but Koenker, Mandel and Smith provided much material on the participation of workers in the running of soviets, trade unions and factory-workshop committees. Negative evidence reinforces the point. Bolsheviks in several regions complained about the absence of middle-class intellectuals who might be able to fulfil the technical tasks in the organisations which workers found difficult because of inadequate leisure time or education.[36]

The working class used its organisations with discrimination. Paul Avrich has emphasised that the factory-workshop committees gave backing to the Bolsheviks earlier than did the soviets.[37] Power in revolutionary Russia, being weak at the centre, was devolved to the lowest units of administration; polyarchy was prevalent. Factory-workshop committees could respond very rapidly to specific local conditions; and, likewise, suburb soviets could become important when town soviets were impervious to the current demands of local workers.[38] Institutional freedom of choice was exercised. Workers made use of the mass organisations deemed by them most likely in a given situation to fulfil their wishes. A sort of institutional leap-frogging was common.[39] There was a widespread feeling that each community, and part of the community, had the right to protect its interests and to decide how best to ensure this protection. The idea that workers were 'dark masses', inactive in the making of their own history, has to be dropped. Politics were participatory as well as representative. Open-air meetings, at factory gates or on street corners, were frequent. Such was the trend towards taking part in public life that the Provisional Government used the perjorative term 'mitingovanie' to designate the problems caused by the outbreak of democracy.[40]

But what were the political ideas of the working class in 1917? A. F. Butenko's collation of answers to a questionnaire issued at the Second All-Russian Congress of Soviets of Workers' and Soldiers' Deputies revealed that workers, when they voted for Bolsheviks in the autumn, were voting for 'soviet power' rather than a Bolshevik-dominated political system.[41] Alexander Rabinowitch's account of Petrograd politics has confirmed this finding in relation to the country's capital.[42] Other impressionistic evidence indicates that workers had turned decisively in favour of policies favouring the immediate initiation of overtures for peace.[43] Furthermore, Smith's account of the 'workers' control' movement in Petrograd demonstrates that a demand for greater influence over conditions at the workplace was growing strongly (even if we as yet do not know enough about other localities).[44]

Evidently the workers were not devoid of ideas about the country's needs. Nor were their ideas static. Workers in the February Revolution had not aimed at 'soviet power', contenting themselves with electing soviets to put pressure on the liberal-led Provisional Government to promulgate a régime of civic freedoms and to fight a defensive war. Distrust of the cabinet grew when Foreign Minister Pavel Miliukov was shown to have advocated an expansionist war policy. It increased again with the Russian military offensive on the Eastern front in June 1917. The possibility that even the Kerenskii cabinet, emerging in July, might not have dropped a commitment to a military struggle for complete victory over Germany was not dispelled. Working conditions also failed to improve. M. I. Skobelev as Minister of Labour had made noises about reform of regulations on safety standards; but little resulted in workplaces from his efforts.[45] The Provisional Government's hostility to demands for higher wages, and the fact that the state was a major employer in armaments plants, turned increasing numbers of the factory labour-force against the state authorities. Food supplies to the towns fell in the summer, and the doubling of state-fixed prices paid to the peasants in August 1917 brought about no improvement.[46] It is hardly surprising that the judgement was made that a government which consistently refused to stand firm against urban and rural middle-class interests no longer suited the interests of the working class.

Nevertheless our information is based on fairly narrow primary sources. The most intensive study of the 'workers' control' movement, for example, is exclusively and avowedly a Petrograd study and makes no claim to cover the rest of the former Russian empire.[47] Regional factors have yet to be investigated extensively. In 1917 the general perception was that Petrograd workers were politically more 'conscious', more radical and more active than those of Moscow; and that those of Moscow were in advance of those in the rest of the country.

Moreover, Diane Koenker has agreed with John Keep that the fervour for participation in politics waned in the course of the year.[48] 'Absenteeism' was a worrying phenomenon even for the Bolsheviks despite their electoral gains in summer and autumn. Furthermore, Keep's figures on the significance of middle-class activists have not been wholly refuted. Such activists, mainly being 'intellectuals', were more prominent in Petrograd and the major urban centres than in the general run of towns and cities;[49] and the incidence increased at each successively higher step of the hierarchy of each organisation. Their concentration in the Central Executive Committee of the Congress of Soviets of Workers' and Soldiers' Deputies was strong.[50] In addition, Ferro has suggested that 'bureaucratic procedures' were evident even where working-class activists were involved.[51] The mass organisations of 1917 should therefore not be idealised. Consequently, while recent writings have convincingly put the workers back into the story of the labour movement, a complete rejection of the older tradition would not be in order. In several respects the problem has been that writers engaged in controversies have inadvertently been aiming their arrows past each other. A fusion of the two traditions would appear to be both possible and desirable.

This is all the more plausible since, except for official Soviet historians and their Western supporters or Trotskyists, most writers since the late 1960s have agreed that the October revolution did not produce a 'workers' state', did not initiate a socialist order, did not keep its promises to its own working class. The workers lost their revolution quickly after October 1917; and it would be difficult to explain such a dénouement if the workers really had utterly dominated the labour movement and its politics throughout the pre-October months.

This never appeared as a mystery for historians like Leonard Schapiro, Merle Fainsod, E. H. Carr and Isaac Deutscher; none of them rated the strength of working-class independence of thought, organisation and activity highly in the first instance; and John Keep, indicating the manipulative techniques of the Bolsheviks in 1917 in the upper and middle ranges of the labour organisations, has reinforced their analysis.[52] And yet, if the newer writings are correct in contending that workers nevertheless had some active impact on their own history, why did it all go wrong? The Bolsheviks themselves, especially Lev Trotskii and his sympathisers attributed the onset of political authoritarianism and economic hardship to unpredicted and changing circumstances. A European socialist revolution did not take place and the Soviet state remained ringed by hostile powers. A lengthy bloody civil war ensued. Food supplies dropped disastrously. Industry collapsed. This had fundamental social repercussions. Workers in large numbers returned to their villages; the working class contracted. There can of course be debate about each of these factors. Would it really have helped a lot if Germany had had a revolution? Would there not have been a further European war?

The contention may be reasonable that such difficulties made a 'workers' state' more likely to come to grief. And yet, as the Menshevik writers emphasised in their earliest accounts, the inherent authoritarianism of Bolshevism was also an important factor. The installation of the Cheka; the shooting of workers demonstrating in favour of the Constituent Assembly; the armed dispersal of the Petrograd Assembly of Plenipotentiaries: all were acts of wilful violence. Lenin and his associates were never slow to increase the intensity of coercion, both reactively and pre-emptively, in the first weeks of the October Revolution.[53]

This is not to say that Lenin did not believe in 'mass self-activity' (as contemporary Russian socialists described autonomous activity by 'the masses'); on the contrary, he was precisely such a believer, and his belief had been strengthened by the experience of 1917.[54] But he also believed in ideas which were in tension with ideas of mass action. He was a severe centraliser, an authoritarianist; and he had no doubts about his party's right and duty to hold power even in the teeth of the evidence from the Constituent Assembly elections that only a minority of the population wanted the Bolsheviks in power. He consequently wanted 'mass self-activity' only on his own terms.[55] Even so, it seems genuinely to have disconcerted him and his adherents that the 'triumphal march' of Bolshevism faltered in 1917–1918 and that the previous steady accumulation of working-class support for his party began to be reversed. Bolshevik (and general contemporary Marxist) sociological theory was weak; and Lenin in particular took it for granted that the working class had undifferentiated interests in political and economic life.[56] There was an assumption among Bolshevik leaders that, once the party had attracted working-class support, it would not lose it. They were aware that workers did not automatically move towards far-left socialist notions. Lenin's *What is to be Done?* in 1902, the founding text of Bolshevism, had postulated that the workers would develop a mere 'trade union consciousness' unless socialist intellectuals inseminated Marxism;[57] and Bukharin and Trotskii had subsequently declared that the German ruling classes had prevented revolution in Germany by propagating a virulent nationalism among the working class.[58]

The historian William Rosenberg has examined how the economic crisis of 1917–1918 rendered workers defenceless against the Bolshevik central leadership's authoritarian measures after October 1917. As factories were threatened with closures, so the divisions within their respective work-forces widened – and the more skilled workers sought to ensure that the less skilled should be the first to lose their jobs. Within working factories, furthermore, labour forces looked after their own interests regardless of the policies of the Soviet state, the Bolshevik party or the mass labour organisations. A disintegration of the feelings of solidarity exhibited in the months before the October revolution occurred. The prospect of unemployment and hunger, as the urban sector of the economy collapsed, had its repercussions. Only a minority of the working-class supporters of Bolshevism remained actively pro-Bolshevik.[59]

'Objective' economic pressures were plainly of great significance; but certain 'subjective' aspects of the politics of the Russian Revolution require equal attention. Stephen Smith has stressed that the mass organisations of the working class lacked a 'theory' about the construction of a socialist order which would have prevented the emergence of the centralist authoritarianism which subverted the self-governing characteristics of the organisations themselves.[60] This is negative evidence for the weakness of the mass organisations after October 1917. Yet the nature of working-class politics in the pre-October months needs to be taken into account. It is possible to draw up a list of workers' demands in summer and autumn 1917; but we need also to enquire which of those demands counted for most in the minds of the workers. The available sources are not informative here; but clues can be culled from the minutes of gatherings such as the First All-Russian Congress of Trade Unions, held in Petrograd in late June 1917. The Congress delegates were mostly workers themselves, and their presence from all over the country offers opportunities for insight into working-class attitudes.[61] The Congress was preoccupied by the threat of national economic collapse. The gathering ruin of industry in particular was discussed. The rights of workers at the place of work had been a strong demand since the February revolution and were aired throughout the Congress proceedings. 'Workers' control' as an objective had considerable appeal in the workforces of large factories in Petrograd.[62]

And yet practical measures to confront the crisis in food supplies were not the subject of deliberation. Nor was land ownership debated; this is especially astonishing in a population whose massive majority lived on the land. Millions of workers themselves retained ties with their native villages. In the end, however, only a highly abstract resolution on the economy was passed. To be sure, this was a trade union congress and not a congress of soviets or of a political party. But it is striking that neither the war question nor the question of state power entered the agenda even though the solutions to all economic questions were intimately connected with these other questions.[63]

Accordingly Russian workers were mentally exercised more firmly by some political questions than by others. There are grounds for supposing that the working class displayed an especially deep interest in what might be called social politics, especially in relation to themes of direct concern to the lives of the workers. 'Political' politics at a national level were obviously not ignored; the calls for a democratic republic in March 1917 and for a socialist coalition government in September and October 1917 were important. Yet it would have been surprising if the anticipation of hunger and unemployment had not pushed workers increasingly towards highly local remedies. Feeding oneself and one's family was bound to become the priority.[64] This does not mean that Russian workers were 'unpolitical'. Rather it hints that the scope of the politics of most of them was not comprehensive. Moreover, the policies brought forward at soviet, trade union and factory-workshop meetings were frequently ill-formulated. Often the policies were not detailed policies or schemes for action, but rather statements of objectives. To be in favour of peace or the transfer of land to the peasants was to have a broad preference. The mechanisms of implementation were a crucial omission.

The problem arises whether the Bolsheviks, being aware of these inadequacies of working-class thought, did not manipulate their way to power. Quickly after the October revolution, Lenin and Trotskii showed that they had not the slightest intention of sharing power with any of the other soviet-based parties except the Left Socialist Revolutionaries.[65] They knew that they were cutting across the widely-found working-class opinion that all socialist parties should be included in the post-Kerenskii coalition.[66] Similarly, the Bolshevik party's policy on the land as pronounced by the April Party Conference was to nationalise it; and the ultimate goal of the party was collectivisation.[67] This did not accord with peasant aspirations and there is no evidence that workers approved either. Most Bolshevik leaders, furthermore, wished to engage in a 'revolutionary war' if a 'democratic peace' without indemnities and annexations was not swiftly arranged after the anticipated socialist seizure of power in Russia. And yet the war-weary workers (especially those who were not employed in factories producing armaments) seem to have wanted peace more or less at any price.[68]

Such disjunctions seem at first sight to confirm that older tradition of Western historical thought that the Bolsheviks simply hoodwinked 'the masses' about their true intentions by tossing up a few vivid slogans like 'Peace', 'Bread', 'Freedom' and 'Land'. But the matter is more complex. In the first place, Bolshevism was a political trend replete with ambiguities and tensions in 1917. Lenin was not the entire Bolshevik party; and it is possible that, like the workers, Bolshevik activists in the party as a whole wanted a socialist coalition government to replace the Kerenskii cabinet. The cheers that greeted Martov's speech in favour of such an outcome at the Second Congress of Soviets of Workers' and Soldiers' Deputies in October 1917 help to corroborate this.[69] Secondly, the Bolshevik Central Committee did not campaign actively for land nationalisation or indeed agricultural collectivisation in 1917. The simple transfer of land to the peasants was the party's slogan in its political campaigns, and numerous activists may well have disliked the policy of nationalisation on intrinsic grounds. Thirdly, revolutionary war was a contingency policy which the Bolsheviks believed would never need to be implemented: most of them really thought that multilateral peace was about to break out, induced by a pan-European socialist revolution.[70]

So that the concordance between the goals of many party activists and the working class's aspirations was closer than might seem from an examination of statements made by Lenin. This was particularly obvious in a manifesto issued by the Central Committee in May 1917 as material to be used for local electoral campaign in Petrograd. The Central Committee advised lower-level activists to talk about the iniquities of the liberal ministers; about the war being a ploy by kings and the bourgeoisie in quest of imperialist gains; about the need to transfer the land to the peasants and to obtain public control over the industrial sector.

No doubt this reflected the cunning of many leading Bolsheviks who did not want to spell out policies which might lose votes in the soviets. Lenin tended to drop words like dictatorship from his vocabulary after April. He used them in lengthy texts, most notably in *The State and Revolution*. But for popular consumption he largely avoided them until after the Kornilov mutiny, when he took the line that only a workers' dictatorship would be able to stave off a right-wing military dictatorship.[71] His avoidance of talking about land nationalisation had a similar purpose; and he, like many other Bolsheviks who no longer spoke openly about revolutionary war even as a contingency policy, were adapting their remarks to their audience.[72] Few workers wanted to risk dying in another war, be it described as 'revolutionary' or not. The central party leaders' selectivity was manipulative. Exact and frank as they were about much, they were also obfuscatory about much. They wanted power. They thought that their policies were more adequate to the solution of the country's woes than were the policies of other parties. They operated in a competitive multi-party environment where votes in the soviets as well as direct action on the streets counted; they could not win and hold power merely by conspiracy. Hence they fudged: and they fudged efficiently.

Whether they liked it or not, furthermore, they had to simplify. The Central Committee faced a public which understood the questions of current politics only to a limited extent. The February revolution had increased 'political consciousness'; but a broad understanding of most questions did not result. Russian workers were not unusual in this. For example, surveys of British elections since the end of the Second World War have indicated the slightness of understanding evinced by most electors. Parties have to introduce simplicity and vividness to their policies. The invention of slogans becomes a key art. So it was in Russia in 1917. The Bolsheviks, like their rivals, knew that the electorate was very variegated in its appreciation of the current issues. The problem was especially bad in Russia because the Romanov monarchy had severely inhibited public debate. Print journalism had been hobbled. The consequences of decades of rule by an absolute monarchy could not quickly be surmounted.[73]

Yet it was not only for such reasons that the Bolshevik central leaders altered their policies and invented their slogans. They themselves shared several working-class enthusiasms of the months between February and October. A dichotomy between the history-from-above tradition and the history-from-below tradition is to be avoided: the Bolshevik Central Committee simultaneously manipulated and yet also reflected working-class opinions. Even Lenin, a highly authoritarian socialist, shifted towards his own variant of support for 'primitive democracy' and mass participatory politics. His authoritarianism was not so much abandoned as removed from the foreground of his attention. If Lenin fooled the workers in 1917, it was partly because he fooled himself to a considerable extent. The same could be said for many other leading Bolsheviks.[74]

Their policies stemmed from a development of their pre-revolutionary notions in the light of the circumstances prevailing after tsarism's collapse. Yet to some extent they were also bowing to working-class pressures. For a time the division of the Bolsheviks and Mensheviks into separate parties was prevented by rank-and-file Bolsheviks who saw no need for the working class to have more than one party to represent the interests of the working class.[75] The formation of an exclusively Bolshevik organisation was delayed until the summer in many localities. It is likely, too, that workers entering the ranks of the Bolsheviks in spring 1917 gave considerable strength to those radical activists campaigning in favour of Lenin's *The April Theses*.[76] And, when working-class issues were debated, workers themselves made a contribution to policy. The classic instance is the adoption of the 'workers' control' commitment. The Bolshevik Central Committee, so far from inventing this policy, took it from the Petrograd factory-workshop movement.[77] It is claimed that three-fifths of the Bolshevik party was working-class in origin and, for the most part, occupation in 1917: this would have given force to the working-class influence in a party which was organised largely on democratic lines in 1917.[78] Nor were workers debarred from official party posts. In Petrograd and Moscow there were many intellectuals on Bolshevik committees; but in some localities, such as the Donets Basin, there were scarcely any Bolsheviks of middle-class origin.[79]

It would consequently be fatuous to postulate a one-way traffic in ideas and instructions from middle-class Bolshevik leaders to the mass base of the party. A complex picture emerges. Rationality and perceptiveness characterised the workers' movement in 1917. Organisations were set up by the workers; and factory labour-forces fought for and defended working-class interests with ferocity. Workers joined and affected the functioning of the party that took power in their name in October 1917. And yet it is also beyond dispute that they failed to get the revolution that most of them appear to have wanted.

Not that it is entirely clear what revolution they wanted. We cannot even be sure that absolutely all workers who voted Bolshevik were consciously voting for 'socialism' and its philosophical principles. Concrete particular policies, promises or slogans may have motivated them to a greater extent. Nor is it plain, as regards workers who indeed voted consciously for 'socialism', what they meant by the term. Be that as it may, the working class fast lost nearly all its gains. Bolshevik party functionaries guided them to that end. Whether another result was possible is a moot point. The labour organisations in 1917 were strong, temporarily, in comparison with the forces which they confronted. But they were weak when judged alongside analogous organisations elsewhere. Their levels of communication, co-ordination and awareness was not consistently high. Moreover, they faced unenviable political tasks. Circumstances were exceptionally volatile. Much political compromise was required if civil war was to be avoided and dictatorship averted. The skills and will to deal with these problems were not abundant in Russia in 1917. Lenin and his associates were more than willing to apply force in pursuit of their objectives. The use of forceful methods was not in itself sufficient to keep him in office. His policies continued to appeal to a segment of the working class, and the promotion of thousands of skilled workers to administrative posts in governments enhanced the Bolshevik party's grip on power.

But post-October developments lie beyond the scope of this chapter, and the scope of the historiographical agenda merely on 1917 remains considerable. In the first place, we need more studies of the economic possibilities in 1917. How much did the industrialists and the bankers contribute to their doom by intransigence? As yet we simply do not know, not least because studies of the working class have been located between social more than between economic parameters. We also need to know much more about the general living and cultural milieu of workers. Life-styles have been less adequately researched than working conditions.

There is a great deal to be discovered about the non-metropolitan areas. The politics of Baku, Riga and Saratov have been examined.[80] But such cities are the exceptions, and local studies of the old Russian empire are in their infancy. The labour movement in the Ukraine has been covered mainly by Soviet scholars;[81] but the range of questions asked by them has, as yet, been extremely limited. In addition, more needs to be known about workers other than those employed in factories. A monograph on railwaymen or on builders, for instance, would be very helpful. Meanwhile the need for research on gender divisions persists. What did women workers do in politics after their initial spectacular contribution to the February Revolution? And why, as the queues got still longer, did they not figure prominently in further events? (Was it the lengthening nature of the queues they had to stand in?) As yet we do not know. And what about that vast legion of house-servants? What happened to them in 1917? How much change entered their relationships with their employers? There is also a pressing requirement for research on Russian, and indeed non-Russian, working-class attitudes in general. Little is ascertained about the workers' feelings about socialism, capitalism, religion, civil rights and private property.[82]

All this work will surely reveal that the workers of Russia and its subject areas in 1917 achieved much to better their plight, but not for long; that they perceived that radical policies were needed to improve their conditions; and that they turned to the Bolsheviks for assistance. They were subjects in their own history. But they were also objects of the actions of others. The Provisional Government and the leading bodies of all the parties, including the Bolsheviks, competed in trying to guide the working class down prescribed political channels. So it has always been in great revolutionary conturbations. It is only because writers have claimed either that all was manipulation (or, in its less malign form, guidance) that such a judgement has strenuously to be insisted upon.

Notes

1. See *Istoriya vsesoyuznoi kommunisticheskoi partii: kratkii kurs* (Moscow, 1938); and I. Deutscher, *Trotsky: The Prophet Armed*, 1879–1921 (London, 1954).
2. See E. H. Carr, *The Bolshevik Revolution*, vol. 1 (London, 1950).
3. See M. Fainsod, *How Russia is Ruled* (Harvard, 1953), and L. B. Schapiro, *The Origin of the Communist Autocracy. Political Opposition in the Soviet State* (London, 1955).
4. See in particular L. B. Schapiro's epilogue to his 1917. *The Russian Revolutions and the Origins of Present-Day Communism* (London, 1984).
5. See I. P. Leiberov and O. I. Shkaratan, 'K voprosu o sostave petrogradskikh promyshlennykh rabochikh v 1917 g.', *Voprosy istorii*, no. 1 (1961): 42–58; A. G. Rashin, *Formirovanie rabochego klassa Rossii* (Moscow, 1958); and O. I. Shkaratan, 'Izmeneniya v sotsial'nom strukture fabrichno-zavodskikh Leningrada, 1917–1928 gg.', *Istoriya SSSR*, no. 5, (1959): 21–38.
6. See V. Z. Drobizhev, A. K. Sokolov and V. A. Ustinov, *Rabochii klass Sovetskoi Rossii v pervyi god proletarskoi diktatury* (Moscow, 1975); L. S. Gaponenko, Rabochii klass Rossii v 1917 g. (Moscow, 1970); E. V. Gimpel'son, *Velikii Oktyabr' i stanovlenie sovestkoi sistemy narodnogo khozyaistva, 1917–1920 gg.* (Moscow, 1977). See also I. P. Leiberov, *Na shturm samoderzhaviya: petrogradskii proletariat v gody pervoi mirovoi voiny i fevral'skoi revolyutsii* (Moscow, 1979).
7. See *PSS*, vol. 3, pp. 581–3.
8. See Gaponenko, *op. cit.*, chap. 2.
9. For a recent example of this idea, stated forcefully, see P. V. Volobuev, *Vybor putei obshchestvennogo razvitiya: teoriya, istoriya, sovremennost'* (Moscow, 1987).
10. See Shkaratan, *op. cit.*; and Gaponenko, *op. cit.*
11. See Drobizhev, *op. cit.*
12. See his 'Demobilizatsiya promyshlennogo truda v Petrogradskoi gubernii za 1917–18 gg.', *Materialy po statistike truda*, issue 5 (Petrograd, 1919) as cited by S. A. Smith, *Red Petrograd. Revolution in the Factories, 1917–18* (Cambridge, 1983), p. 323.
13. See, above all, the 1920s trade-union journal *Vestnik truda*.
14. A. M. Lisetskii, *Bol'sheviki vo glave massovykh stachek (mart – oktyabr' 1917 goda)* (Kishinev, 1974).
15. See Yu.Biblikov, V. Malyshkin and E. Malaeva, *Profsoyuzy do*

velikoi oktyabr'skoi revolyutsii, 1907–1917 gg. (Moscow, 1957); A. G. Egorova, *Profsoyuzy i fabzavkomy v bor'be za pobedu oktyabrya* (Moscow, 1960); M. L. Itkin, 'Tsentral'nyi sovet fabzavkomov Petrograda v 1917 g.', in *Oktyabr'skoe vooruzhyonnoe vosstanie v Petrograde. Sbornik statei* (Moscow, 1980).

16.   *Ekonomicheskaya politika Vremennogo pravitel'stva* (Moscow, 1962); *Proletariat i burzhuaziya v 1917 g.* (Moscow, 1964).

17.   See note 13.

18.   The beginnings of a professional questioning of this position does not even arise in the interesting collection of reports in P. V. Volobuev (ed.), *Rossiya 1917 goda: vybor istoricheskogo puti* (Moscow, 1988).

19.   On the sources of this re-orientation of Western scholarship see Chapter IX by Edward Acton.

20.   J. H. L. Keep, *The Russian Revolution. A Study in Mass Mobilisation* (London, 1976).

21.   See *idem*, chapters 21–7.

22.   See *idem*, pp. 122–5.

23.   See *idem*, pp. 90–5.

24.   See *idem*, pp. 358–82.

25.   See *idem*, pp. 288–339.

26.   See G. Z. Ioffe, 'Velikii Oktyabr': transformatsiya sovetologicheskikh kontseptsii i ego klassovo-politicheskaia sut'', *Voprosy istorii KPSS*, no. 6 (1985): 72–86; V. P. Buldakov and A. Iu.Skvortsova, 'Proletarskie massy i Okt'iabr'skaia revolyutsiia (Analiz sovremennoi zapadnoi istoriografii)', *Istoriya SSSR*, no. 5 (1987): 149–63.

27.   See M. Ferro, *The Russian Revolution of February 1917* (London, 1972: translation of French edition of 1967), pp. 112–21 and especially p. 115.

28.   See S. A. Smith, *Red Petrograd*; D. Mandel, *Petrograd Workers and the Soviet Seizure of Power from the July Days, 1917 to July 1918* (London, 1984); D. Koenker, *Moscow Workers and the 1917 Revolution* (London, 1981).

29.   See Smith, *op. cit.*, pp. 14–34, 121–8 and 192–9.

30.   See Smith, *op. cit.*, pp. 145–8.

31.   R. A. Wade, *Red Guards and the Workers' Militia in the Russian Revolution* (Stanford, 1984).

32.   See T. Hasegawa, *The February Revolution: February 1917* (Seattle, 1981), pp. 330–1 and 337–8.

33.   See R. Service, *The Russian Revolution, 1900–1927* (London, 1986), p. 20.

34.   Such organisations have as yet attracted much less attention than the larger and more formal organisations of the labour movement.

35.   See L. H. Haimson, 'The Problem of Social Stability in Urban Russia, 1905–1917', *Slavic Review*, no. 4 (1964) and no. 1 (1965).

36.   See R. Service, *The Bolshevik Party in Revolution: A Study in Organisational Change* (London, 1979), p. 47.

37. See P. Avrich, 'The Russian Factory Committees in 1917', *Jahrbücher für Geschichte Osteuropas*, no. 11 (1963): 161–82.
38. See R. Wade, 'The Rajonnye Sovety of Petrograd: the Role of Local Political Bodies in the Russian Revolution', *Jahrbücher für Geschichte Osteuropas*, no. 2 (1972).
39. See the argument in R. Service, *The Russian Revolution*, p. 43.
40. This term was also bandied about by the Bolsheviks, too, quickly after they themselves formed the government.
41. A. F. Butenko and D. A. Chugaev (eds), *Vtoroi s'ezd sovetov rabochikh i soldatskikh deputatov. Sbornik dokumentov* (Moscow, 1957), pp. 386-97.
42. See A. Rabinowitch, *The Bolsheviks Come To Power* (London, 1976), pp. 211–14 and 291–2.
43. See below, pp. 158–9.
44. See Smith, *Red Petrograd*, pp. 145–8 and 160–7.
45. See W. H. Roobol, *Tsereteli – A Democrat in the Russian Revolution. A Political Biography* (The Hague), p. 130.
46. See P. V. Volobuev, *Ekonomicheskaia politika*, pp. 431 and 442.
47. See Smith, *op. cit.*
48. See Koenker, *Moscow Workers*, pp. 171–83.
49. See, for example, Service, *The Bolshevik Party*, p. 47.
50. See Keep, *The Russian Revolution*, pp. 122–5.
51. See M. Ferro, *October 1917: A Social History of the Russian Revolution* (London, 1980), pp. 184–207.
52. See above, note 22.
53. See G. Leggett, *The Cheka. Lenin's Political Police* (Oxford, 1981), chapters 2 and 3; J. H. L. Keep, *The Debate on Soviet Power. Minutes of the All-Russian Central Executive Committee of the Congress of Soviets. Second Convocation, October 1917 – January 1918* (Oxford, 1979), pp. 25–31.
54. See my *Lenin: A Political Life*, vol. 2, *Worlds in Collision* (London, 1990), chapter 9.
55. *Ibid.*
56. See, above all, his *State and Revolution: Polnoe sobranie sochinenii* (Moscow, 1958–65), vol. 3, especially, pp. 53–9.
57. See his *What is to be Done?*: *idem*, vol. 33, pp. 1–120.
58. See *Lenin: A Political Life*, vol. 2, chapter 8.
59. See W. G. Rosenberg, 'Russian Labor and Bolshevik Power after October', *Slavic Review* (summer 1985): 213–38.
60. See Smith, *Red Petrograd*, p. 261.
61. See D. Koenker (ed.), *Tret'ya konferentsiya professional'nykh soyuzov, 3–11 iyulya (20–28 iyunya st. st.) 1917 goda. Stenograficheskii otchet* (London, 1982), p. xvi (editorial note).
62. See especially *idem*, pp. 324–6.
63. See *idem, passim.*
64. See note 59.

65. Nor did they have them before; but their comments were suitably vague on this: see *Lenin: A Political Life*, vol. 2, chapter 9.
66. See note 41.
67. *Sed'maya (aprel'skaya) vserossiiskaya konferentsiya RSDRP (bol'shevikov). Protokoly* (Moscow, 1958), pp. 246–7
68. See *Lenin: A Political Life*, vol. 2, chapter 8.
69. See Rabinowitch, *op. cit.*, pp. 295–6.
70. See *Lenin: A Political Life*, vol. 2, chapters 7 and 8.
71. This topic is dealt with in detail in *idem*, chapter 7.
72. See *idem*, chapter 8.
73. On the other hand, it should not underestimated how active and free were the publishers of newspapers from the first days of the February Revolution.
74. See note 71.
75. See R. Service, *The Bolshevik Party in Revolution*, p. 43. In this book I allowed an error to be printed about the number of activists who became Bolsheviks between the outbreak of the First World War and the Sixth Party Congress in August 1917 as judged by a questionnaire to the Congress delegates. The proportion should be nine, not ninety-nine per cent: see *Shestoi s'ezd RSDRP (bol'shevikov). Avgust 1917 goda. Protokoly* (Moscow, 1958), p. 296.
76. See *idem*, pp. 53–4.
77. See S. Smith, *Red Petrograd*, pp. 153–4.
78. See Service, *The Bolshevik Party*, p. 43.
79. See *idem*, p. 47.
80. See R. G. Suny, *The Baku Commune, 1917–1918. Class and Nationality in the Russian Revolution* (Princeton, 1972); A. Ezergailis, *The 1917 Revolution in Latvia* (Boulder, 1974); D. Raleigh, *Revolution on the Volga: 1917 in Saratov* (Cornell, 1986).
81. A useful recent exception is T. Friedgut, *Iuzovka and Revolution* (Princeton, 1989).
82. For a start in the direction see S. A. Smith, 'Workers and Civil Rights in Tsarist Russia, 1899–1917' in O. Crisp and L. Edmondson, *Civil Rights in Imperial Russia* (London, 1989), pp. 145–70.

9 Epilogue

Edward Acton

Recent trends in the historiography of the Russian Revolution may be assessed in a variety of ways. One would be to highlight the way in which the canvas of 1917 has been expanded, reaching far beyond the two capitals to out-lying regions, cities, towns and villages. A second would be to review the treatment accorded distinct themes – social and economic, political and institutional, military and diplomatic, cultural and intellectual. A third would be to sub-divide recent work in terms of separate phases of the revolution – the pre-revolutionary period, the February revolution, the April crisis, the first Coalition, the July days, the Kornilov rebellion, October, the period of military and industrial demobilization, Brest-Litovsk, and the outbreak of civil war. But each of these strategies runs the risk of degenerating into annotated bibliography, rather than taking stock of the overall pattern and broad implications of new research. Because the ramifications of the Revolution have been of such profound importance, different interpretations of the events of 1917 continue to inform different views of the modern era as a whole, and the Revolution remains one of the most heavily politicised of all fields. In a very real sense, the Revolution is at the strategic centre of contemporary history, a centre besieged by groups of historians belonging to conflicting interpretative schools. The most illuminating way to review recent historiography is to place it in the context of this struggle.

Until the 1970s it was possible to view most of the work done on the Revolution in terms of three long-established historiographical traditions: Soviet, liberal and 'libertarian'. During the last decade or so, however, the most innovative and arresting work has been done by 'revisionist' scholars consciously detaching themselves from each of these three traditions. The purpose here will be to outline some of the main themes in revisionist work – specific areas of which are discussed elsewhere in this volume – and then consider how the established traditions have reacted to it. This approach will pigeon-hole historians in a way that does individuals less than justice. Yet, bearing in mind Bacon's reassuring maxim that 'the truth proceeds more easily from error than confusion', it may provide the best way to gain a sense of what has been happening.

Already in the early 1950s, a few major historians had distanced themselves from the prevailing view in the West. Carr had begun his massive 14-volume history of the early Soviet period; Deutscher had begun his great trilogy on Trotskii.[1] They were untypical in their belief that the general direction of the revolution was the inexorable product of Russia's earlier history, and in their willingness to stress positive repercussions of October. But neither concentrated on the events of 1917 itself and both tended to view those events 'from above', through the eyes of the leading Bolsheviks.[2] What opened the way for the emergence of a substantial 'revisionist' school, at once indebted to and reacting against the work of Carr and Deutscher, was the easing of tension between East and West from the late 1950s. Western historians of Russia began to break out of the attitudes encouraged by the Cold War. To question the liberal account was no longer tantamount to condoning Communist rule. Disenchantment with the liberal establishment characteristic of the 1960s began to find expression in the work of a new generation of scholars at universities and research institutes. They began to apply to the revolution the techniques and approaches, the concern with social history and with quantitative methods, already being widely applied in less sensitive fields. Moreover, following the Second World War, there was a great expansion of Russian studies in the West – in the US, Britain, France, Germany, and rather later, in Israel and Japan. In no country was a concerted research plan adopted, but there was a rapid increase in the number of Russian and Soviet specialists. Western research gained the resources for more detailed social, economic and institutional research on the revolution. Western scholars began to make full use of the primary material published in the Soviet Union in the 1920s; the cultural thaw within the Soviet Union increased Western readiness to take seriously new research by Soviet scholars; from the late 1950s a series of cultural exchange agreements between the USSR and the major Western democracies facilitated Western scholars' access to Soviet libraries and, to a much more limited but still significant extent, to archives.[3]

As yet, the 'revisionists' have set about dismantling separate aspects of the traditional interpretations rather than replacing them with any comprehensive new synthesis. The major thrust of revisionist work has been in two directions. First, it has challenged the assumption that the revolution can be understood by viewing it only through the eyes of prominent actors on the political scene. It has begun to examine the revolution 'from below', to penetrate beneath the world of high politics to developments in the factory, in the village, among the rank and file of the armed forces. To reconstruct the changing perceptions and goals of the masses, a wide range of sources has been sifted – private correspondence and letters to the press, contemporary reports in the metropolitan and local press and the myriad publications put out by the new organizations which sprang to life after February, memoirs and official reports, conference protocols and records of the countless resolutions passed in grass-roots meetings in the villages, at the factory gate, in soldiers' committees and local soviets.[4] Detailed monographs have appeared seeking to trace the way in which the Revolution was experienced by workers, peasants, soldiers and sailors.

The burden of this work has been the need to take seriously the aspirations of the masses themselves. It credits them with values, goals and a sense of direction of their own. The more closely the behaviour of workers, soldiers and peasants is examined, the less wild and gullible, the more rational and autonomous they appear. It did not require external propaganda to inspire the workers' demand for improved working and living conditions and guaranteed employment, the soldiers' demand for peace, or the pressure from peasants both in the army and in the villages for drastic land reform. Nor did it require outside prompting for workers, soldiers and peasants to assert their human dignity and challenge any authority not directly responsible to them – in the factory, in the army and in the countryside. Moreover, the steps they took to realise their goals, and their increasing radicalism, emerge as an essentially rational reaction to their experience. Politically, the most radical workers were precisely the most educated and most skilled, the section of the proletariat with the strongest tradition in working-class organizations. The less skilled and educated were initially motivated primarily by direct economic concerns, but in the course of 1917 social and political consciousness developed rapidly. And it was above all their own ordeal during 1917 – the struggle over wages and 'control' in the factory, over peace and authority within the army, over land and the apparent prevarication of the Provisional Government – which heightened the consciousness of workers, soldiers and peasants. The sense of a profound clash of interest between privileged society and 'toilers' gradually permeated both the cities and the army, paralleling a sense of 'them' and 'us' deeply rooted in peasant culture. By the autumn, the demand for Soviet power, for the overthrow of the Provisional Government and the creation of a new order based upon the popular institutions which mushroomed during the year commanded widespread support among the lower orders.

Viewed from below, the political history of the Revolution emerges in a new light. The overthrow of the tsarist regime and the breakdown of the authority and coercive power of 'census society' had opened the way to mass intervention in public affairs. And the masses proceeded to act upon the political leaders as much as being acted upon by them. It was this intervention which defined the parameters within which public institutions and political parties operated and in large measure dictated the political course of the revolution. When the moderate socialists failed to articulate and respond to the demands from below they forfeited their popularity and prominence in trade unions, soldiers' committees, peasant committees and soviets. The masses sought alternative routes towards their goals, and the Bolshevik party was the main beneficiary. As Allan Wildman remarks of the soldiers, Bolshevik popularity rose not because they held out 'a new vision of the revolution' but rather because they seemed to provide 'a more speedy realization of the original one'.[5] While the peasants undermined the authority of the Provisional Government in the countryside and took matters into their own hands, a growing proportion of workers and soldiers shifted their support to the Bolshevik party because it espoused the very goals towards which they strove.

The implications of this work are far-reaching. The root cause of both the fall of tsarism and the failure of the liberals and moderate socialists must be traced to deeper causes than in the traditional liberal interpretation. The radicalization of the masses is to be seen as a product more of their own experience – of tsarism, of factory life, of war, and of economic break-down – than of Bolshevik propaganda. The view of October as the product of a truly mass revolutionary movement, and of widespread support for the Bolsheviks both in the cities and in the army, is not so wide of the mark. Equally, there is a need for a far-reaching reappraisal of the traditional image of the Bolshevik party in 1917. The dislocation of that year and the party's hectic growth, with membership multiplying tenfold between February and October as tens of thousands of workers and, to a lesser extent, soldiers enrolled, was conducive neither to clear lines of authority nor to the imposition of discipline from above. Instead of the centralised and tightly-knit body envisaged by Lenin in *What Is To Be Done?* there emerged a 'relatively democratic, tolerant and decentralized' party of 'essentially open and mass character'.[6] It was precisely because it responded to and espoused the goals of the masses that the party attracted such a groundswell of support in the months leading up to October.

At the same time, however, the revisionist scholars hold no brief for the régime which emerged from the revolution. The second major thrust of their research is in part addressed to this problem: it has begun to analyse in detail the mass organisations – soviets, soldiers' committees, trade unions, factory committees, peasant committees, Red Guards, and the major socialist parties themselves – which burgeoned during the revolution. It explores the role played by these organisations – in February, during the July Days, in October, and amidst the economic collapse of 1918. It traces the relationships between them. It examines the way in which their democratic processes worked; the similarities and differences in power and outlook between their executives and their rank-and-file membership; the potential power in the hands of the executive committee or presidium to control the flow of information, the timing of elections, the agenda, the alternatives presented to the plenum. It examines, in short, their strengths and weaknesses: the genuine expression they gave to pressure from below, but also their fragility, the ebb and flow of popular interest in them, and the imperfect way in which they mediated mass aspirations. This facet of revisionist work is at a less advanced stage than that dealing with 1917, but it has begun to unravel the disastrous impact upon the democratic upsurge of 1917 of precipitate industrial and military demobilisation; of the break-down of the urban-rural trade nexus and the desperate struggle for grain; of the rapid dispersal of large sections of the working class; and of civil war.

Until very recently, the revisionists seemed to be taking the field by storm. Their work stood out as the most innovative and arresting in the field – Mandel, Koenker, Smith, Hogan, Bonnell, Rosenberg and Flenley on workers in Moscow and Petrograd;[7] Shanin, and from a rather more traditional viewpoint, Gill on the peasantry;[8] Renehan and Rabinowitch on the local soviets;[9] Wildman, and for an earlier period Bushnell on the army;[10] Mawdsley and Saul on the navy;[11] Wade on the Red Guards and workers' militia;[12] Mercedal on the Left SRs;[13] Service on the Bolsheviks;[14] Galili y Garcia on the Mensheviks;[15] Suny, Raleigh, and Getzler on the revolutionary process outside the two capitals;[16] Hasegawa and Rabinowitch on the dynamics of February and October respectively.[17] Their work has begun to find reflection in introductory sketches.[18] But it has yet to be drawn together into a major new synthesis, a full-scale and full-blooded account, and its wider impact has been limited. Part of the explanation, no doubt, is that the more sensitive and detailed the treatment of broad social categories, the closer the examination of the differences between skilled and unskilled workers, between men and women, between peasants in grain deficit areas and those in grain-surplus areas, between soldiers at the front and those in the rear, the harder it is to present an integrated narrative of the Revolution. The task is all but beyond the scope of one scholar and yet, despite the pressure in Britain and elsewhere for collaborative and group research projects analogous to those in the sciences, joint authorship has not caught on in the West. A second factor is that the 1980s saw a sharp contraction in funds available for Russian research, especially in Britain.[19] In the Anglo-Saxon world there has been a drastic decline in the study of the Russian language, and the number of doctoral theses and of new scholars entering the field has fallen sharply from the peak of the 1970s. A third cause is the staying-power shown by the traditional interpretations. And it is to them that we must now turn.

The tradition commanding the biggest battalions is that of Soviet historiography. Although they have bemoaned a decline in output in the past decade, Soviet historians continue to account for the overwhelming majority of works on the revolution, and they have made use of incomparably more archival material than is available to Western historians. There is some truth in the view, echoed in recent Soviet discussion, that after the Khrushchev thaw, a new orthodoxy tended to descend from the late sixties and early seventies.[20] Certainly there were fewer breakthroughs – and scandals – *à la* Burdzhalov and Volobuev. But few of the underlying trends of the sixties were quickly reversed. Independently-minded scholars attacked for work which shakes the Soviet consensus have tended, especially since Brezhnev's death, to resurface.[21] Contacts with Western historians have continued to develop. Attention to the scholarly apparatus, to footnoting and source criticism has continued to increase, and even the luxury of an index appears to be spreading. Although Lenin's works still adorn every argument, there has been strong criticism, led by the doyen of specialists on the Revolution, Academician I. I. Mints, of the absurd lengths to which this is often taken, and the principle though not the practise of quoting Lenin *in context* has been urged with increasing insistence.[22] Moreover, there has been skilful exegesis of specific moments in his corpus – the debate over his attitude to the possibility of peaceful transition to soviet rule after the Kornilov affair is a striking example.[23] Behind the monolithic image which Soviet historiography still projects, controversy between specialists flourishes. The more closely western scholars delve into specific problems, the more conscious they become of this variety. By 1979, it was no longer incongruous to hear a Soviet scholar proclaim: 'It is precisely through controversy that the truth emerges.'[24]

The treatment of a whole host of questions has benefited from this improvement. Much of Burdzhalov's work on the February revolution has been incorporated into conventional Soviet wisdom. The notion that Russia was socially and economically 'multi-layered' on the eve of the Revolution has been taken on board and the door reopened to controversy over the pre-revolutionary economy.[25] This has provided a potentially fruitful context for the massive work on the rural economy by the pioneering team of quantitative historians led by I. D. Koval'chenko.[26] Kir'yanov's work on the evidence of material improvements in working-class life before 1914 shows the same willingness to look anew at old assumptions which sparked the debate in the seventies over the cultural poverty of the working class.[27] The archival evidence adduced in tracing the 'crisis at the top' has brought home much about the old regime, about inter-ministerial conflict and the extent of conservative discontent with the Tsar, which it is difficult to gainsay. There is a willingness to examine how things looked from the point of view of Witte, Stolypin and at times even Nikolai II which, though not always directly challenging the orthodox view of the *objective* historical process at work, does reveal much greater subtlety and self-confidence.[28] For liberal reviewers, indeed, the work on pre-war developments by Leopold Haimson and Roberta Thompson Manning is *more* structurally determinist, leaves *less* room for the role of chance and the individual than that of Soviet scholars like Startsev.[29] Another area where there has been measurable progress is in acknowledgement of the role played by non-Bolshevik revolutionaries, especially during the war. Certainly the Bolsheviks always emerge in the vanguard, but the Left SRs, in particular, are given more attention than before – and more than they tend to receive in the West.[30] Equally striking is the greater interest shown in the motives of the moderate socialist leaders, notably in the first weeks of dual power.[31] And in the range, if not in the investigative quality, of regional studies Soviet historians are years ahead of the West. Soviet historiography has long ceased to be the laughing stock it became under Stalin.

Against this background, it is not surprising that Soviet historians have closely watched the work of Western revisionists. Their explanation for the progress they see in it may lay undue emphasis upon new respect in the West for the achievements of the USSR and the impact of their own staunch work in the field. But the quality of Soviet reviews of Western research has gradually improved. Although articles on recent Western publications tend to begin and end on a note of condemnation, they show an increasingly firm grasp of the theses being argued. The British-based Study Group on the Russian Revolution has been picked out as a focal point for revisionism and, in a guarded, qualified way, Soviet historians have welcomed it. There is much in it that they could hardly fail to welcome – the newfound emphasis on the radical leadership provided by skilled, urban, educated workers, on the increase in class-consciousness, and on the mounting popularity of the Bolshevik party; the shift away from the notion that the party 'manipulated' the masses; the recognition of widespread support for the October revolution.

Yet there is much, too, in revisionist work that remains unacceptable to most Soviet historians. Most fundamental is its supposed failure to do justice to the role of the working class and of its vanguard party. Revisionist stress on the autonomous radicalisation of soldiers and peasants implicitly denies the 'hegemony of the proletariat'. Similarly, in the Soviet view, one-sided preoccupation with the way in which the workers' own experience moulded their consciousness obscures the crucial role of the party. Revisionist treatment of the party's structure suffers from the same 'undialectical' approach. While belatedly recognising that the party was open and democratic, Western revisionists purportedly cannot grasp that it was also disciplined, unified and centralised. They thereby fail to appreciate that the party was guided throughout by Lenin's 'scientific socialism' and underrate the critical leadership role played by the vanguard party from the February revolution onwards. And, instead of recognising the thorough interpenetration between party and class, ideology and psychology, they set up an artificial opposition between them. They assume a fictitious tension between the Bolshevik party and its goals, on the one hand, and the aspirations and organisations of the masses on the other. Even those revisionists who acknowledge a certain coincidence between the goals of the masses and the goals of the party in October continue to treat the two as if they proceeded along quite separate paths. They supposedly fail to appreciate the depth and permanence of working-class and poor-peasant commitment to 'their' party, soviet power and socialism. They thus distort post-revolutionary history, overlooking the fact that it was only because of foreign intervention that the triumphant spread of soviet power after October gave way to devastating civil war. They purportedly remain captive to the traditional Western 'myth' that after October there emerged a party dictatorship divorced from the proletariat.[32]

Secondary questions have been treated by Soviet historians with a closer eye on the evidence, but their basic tenets remain unaltered. The Revolution continues to provide irrefutable proof of the laws of history discovered by Marx and 'creatively developed' by Lenin; it continues to present the prototype of the transformation for which all capitalist societies are destined. Almost stronger is the insistence that, just as Lenin had argued, the success of the Revolution depended on the presence of the Bolshevik party, of this Marxist party 'of a new type'. It is the image of the party's structure and role which renders so much Soviet work wooden – the heroic portrait of the homogeneous Bolshevik party, raising the 'spontaneous' protest of the proletariat into a fully class-conscious and organised socialist revolutionary movement, drawing on Lenin's scientific understanding of the historical process and the objective interests of the proletariat to provide unerring strategic and tactical guidance, establishing hegemony over the mass movement which brought the tsarist régime to its knees in 1905 and overthrew it in February 1917, foredooming the attempts of the Provisional Government to consolidate the rule of the bourgeoisie, and during 1917 opening the eyes of the more backward sections of the proletariat and the working masses to the reactionary nature of the petit-bourgeois and liberal parties, drawing the poor peasants in the army and the countryside into alliance with them, and carrying through the epoch-making October Revolution. Where 1917 is concerned, it is the veneration of the party and the grossly disproportionate attention devoted to it which most severely restricts the vision of Soviet historians. It guarantees that Western revisionist work is still rejected as being in the last analysis merely a new, more sophisticated version of 'Menshevik' or 'Trotskyist' accounts. Allegations of 'bourgeois falsification' are nowadays rarely made; but the general indictment remains in force.

The tantalising question is whether Gorbachev's invitation to extend *glasnost'* to the past, which has already found such dramatic response in the journalistic world, in literature and the cinema, heralds a real departure among professional historians. Some of the demands for historiographical *perestroika* are breathtaking: witness the passionate demand in *Izvestiya* from a history teacher from Riga for new works which tell the unvarnished truth, appealing to the example of none other than Chaadaev, an early victim of censorship under Nicholas I: 'I do not know how to love my country with closed eyes . . . mouth shut . . . I think the time for blind affection has passed, that now for our country's sake our first duty is to the truth.'[33] An optimist would have it that the far-reaching reappraisal of the 1930s now under way will soon envelop 'Great October' itself, that we stand on the brink of a dazzling revolution in Soviet historiography. Breast-beating by leading figures in the historical establishment appears to be gathering pace: there have been repeated calls to make the flow of works on 1917 less boring, not only by enlivening their style and titles, but also by treating history less schematically, curbing excessive concern to demonstrate sociological laws, and highlighting what was unique in the Russian drama.[34] Greater willingness to air the blemishes on the Soviet record may encourage freer discussion of the 'social and economic pre-conditions' for October, and it is even conceivable that current emphasis on devolving initiative and democratisation will open the door to more nuanced treatment of the party's leading role in 1917.[35] Yet the constraints remain. Greater frankness about the legacy of Stalin's crimes and methods may actually intensify concern to reaffirm the glories of Lenin and the old Bolsheviks. The Jubilee edition of *Istoriya SSSR*, marking the seventieth anniversary of the October revolution, opened with a thoroughly traditional celebration of the party's role.[36] While the legitimisation of Gorbachev's own rule remains so closely linked to the heroic image of the party in 1917, there is likely to be some foot-dragging across the Rubicon.

Turning now to 'liberal' historiography, its resilience in the face of the revisionist challenge has been quite remarkable. The staying-power of the traditional western approach is one of the most striking features of recent trends. After all, somebody *au fait* with the doctoral research in progress ten years ago might confidently have expected that by 1987 the liberal view of 1917 would have been banished among specialists. He would have predicted that by now it would be rapidly disappearing from undergraduate textbooks and that already the ripples would be reaching A level and GCSE levels, even if it would take a few decades longer before it ceased to inform the columns of *The Times*. But instead, benefiting no doubt from the shift to the Right in the whole intellectual climate of the West in the late seventies and eighties, it has survived and flourished.

Historians whose general approach remains loyal to the liberal tradition have produced a wide variety of political, institutional and biographical studies – on subjects ranging from the case for the defence of Kornilov,[37] to the urge among educated Russians, transcending ideological divisions, to 'mobilise' the peasantry,[38] the early years of the Cheka,[39] and the later career of Struve.[40] Rather than attempting to grapple with the revisionist case, much of this work has tended to proceed without reference to it. Ulam's study of Russia's 'failed revolutions', for example, seems impervious to revisionist research. He sees the Bolsheviks in mid-1917 almost engulfed by what he calls a 'tidal-wave' of nationalism and chides the leaders of the Provisional Government for the lack of skill and realism which prevented them from harnessing nationalist sentiment to put the Soviets in their place.[41] Besançon's study of Leninism sees Bolshevik success in 1917 in terms of 'infiltration' of the soviets, whose unstable nature made them vulnerable to 'Bolshevik penetration'.[42] For Conquest, the main aim of revisionist work is 'to re-establish old pro-Bolshevik legends about the period'.[43]

Ulam, Besançon and Conquest, it might be objected, are maverick outriders in relation to the main body of liberal historiography. But the work of two of the most influential and respected western authorities on the revolution brings home the limited impact of revisionist work. Just over a decade ago, John Keep published a major study which, on the face of it, seemed designed to accommodate the first tranche of revisionism.[44] The sub-title – *A Study in Mass Mobilization* – suggested that he would incorporate into the liberal perspective the view of the revolution from below. But in fact he had in mind mobilisation *of* the masses rather than *by* the masses. He moved the focus down from the dizzy heights of Lenin and Trotskii to the institutional machinery, the mass organisations, soviets, trade unions, factory committees and militia bands; he widened the circle of leaders; and his sustained effort to survey the scene outside Petrograd and Moscow was a major service. But the essential format remained thoroughly loyal to the liberal tradition. And the flow of revisionist publications which appeared after his own study has done little to alter his view – indeed he has warned since then of the danger that 'radical social historians' will 'resurrect some hoary myths about the nature of Bolshevik popular support in the fall of 1917'.[45]

Liberal reluctance to accept the findings of revisionist work is reinforced by scepticism about the sources on which it is based. Documentary collections are liable to reflect Soviet bias, the range of memoirs by ordinary workers and soldiers is narrow and suspect on similar grounds, while direct access to archives remains severely restricted. Moreover, according to Keep, the influence of activists in guiding and drawing up the resolutions of the lowest strata of factory committees, village assemblies and soviets – the supposed mouth-pieces of rank-and-file opinion – makes it impossible to tell how faithfully they represent mass opinion.[46] In Keep's book, therefore, attention is focussed without further ado upon intermediate and higher organs. Viewed from this perspective, the masses remain ignorant, disoriented, the prey to manipulation. The ideas of the peasants are naive and utopian; workers are 'intoxicated by hopes of a golden age'; 'driven to near-despair by the economic crisis,' he remarks, 'their nerves kept on edge by incessant propaganda, they responded uncritically to the appeals of a party that promised untold blessings once "soviet power" had been achieved'.[47]

What Keep seeks to show is the manner in which mass organisations were used for the purposes of the leadership. So far as the socialist parties are concerned, they are not even included among the mass organisations. Indeed, the image of them that emerges from Keep's pages – especially in the case of the Bolsheviks – is entirely traditional. At the outset we are told that 'their active membership consisted in the main of intellectuals'.[48] But it is not only the political parties which were at the disposal of the élite. So too were the factory committees, the workers' militia, the trade unions and above all the soviets. Their tendency to concentrate power in the hands of officials, their inadequate electoral rules and the feeble control by the plenum over the executive, opened the way for the leadership to manipulate the rather simple-minded masses. The expanding ranks of activists in these institutions, Keep dubs 'junior cadres'. The junior cadres are creatures of the senior cadres, less educated, less sophisticated, but made in their own image and likeness, imbibing what he calls their 'jargon' and 'world view'.[49] And a thick line is drawn between these would-be intellectuals and the rank-and-file masses who followed them 'out of a vague sense of solidarity, without any clear idea of the objectives pursued by those who aspired to direct them.[50]

The process of 'bureaucratisation', whereby there was a tendency for power to pass from the hands of the mass electorate to that of officials, is a vital variable in understanding 1917 and 1918. What distinguishes Keep's view from the picture that emerges in revisionist work is that he dates the process from as early as the spring of 1917.[51] Some of Keep's strictures on the democratic processes of the mass organisations in 1917 are perplexing. Discussing the factory committees, for example, he observes that 'at open mass meetings the natural tendency was to support the candidates for office who spoke most persuasively'. This he finds distinctly sinister. 'The situation was generally one which favoured manipulation by the leadership and hindered efforts to assert control from below'.[52] The grounds on which a democratic electorate will ideally exercise its vote became somewhat obscure. But the key point is Keep's scepticism about revisionist emphasis on the countervailing tendencies implicit in direct democracy, on the diffuse structure of the Bolshevik party during 1917, and on the rational and independent nature of intervention from below. 'Fantasies of uninhibited self-rule,' he remarks in a more recent work, 'were combined with unexpressed longings for a firm directing hand . . . (the masses') naive and contradictory outlook gave great leverage to any party which could combine an ultra-democratic image with an authoritarian core.'[53]

The classic reaffirmation of the liberal view came from the late Leonard Schapiro. His study of 1917, published posthumously in 1984 and now being eagerly devoured in a mass edition by new generations of undergraduates, reasserts all the central tenets of the liberal view.[54] Nowhere is this clearer than in his treatment of the political process. True to the liberal tradition, he sees politics and the struggle for power as a more or less autonomous process. As he put it in his renowned earlier study of the party, one must treat 'the principal characters concerned as human beings, and not as exponents of this or that theory, or as representatives of this or that class interest. I have tried,' he wrote, 'without, I hope, ignoring economic and social factors, not to let them obliterate what is after all the key to any historical situation – the men who thought or acted in this way or that.'[55] It is the decisions, the policies, the judgement, motives, principles and ambitions, the skill and lack of it of the leading political actors which are decisive. His 1984 account spelled out his approach in less detail, but the message was exactly the same. Since this is a book mainly about power, he explained, he trusted that he would not be reproached 'for not dealing with such matters as economic problems or social questions'.[56] The liberal and moderate socialists failed because they were men of principle, unwilling to use force against their political opponents. The Bolsheviks, conversely, owed their victory to ruthless determination, skilful manoeuvre, and demagogic appeal to popular ignorance.

As with Keep, the corollary of Schapiro's treatment of the political leadership as relatively autonomous is his approach to the masses. He sees the role of the masses as essentially subordinate. They oscillate between passivity, wild hope and elemental violence. Schapiro's workers appear as an 'anarchical mob . . . with no thought but destruction', the soldiers are hopelessly naive, the peasantry have a 'total lack of understanding of what was happening'.[57] Ignorant, politically immature, with no grasp of the real issues at stake, they were guided not by rational goals of their own but by the vagaries of rumour, the skill of rival political leaders, rabble-rousing, propaganda and demagogy. The vital constituency of the Bolsheviks were, according to Schapiro, 'the more ignorant among the population': indeed, 'their revolution was in large measure that of the *Lumpenproletariat*'.[58] It is a view which basically ignores the labours of the revisionists.

In its treatment of the aftermath of October, too, the approach epitomised by Keep and Schapiro remains impervious to revisionist work. It continues to place primary emphasis on the authoritarian drive from above and to play down the independence of mass organisations including local soviets in the early months of 1918. It is only when treating the period from the summer of 1918 onwards that the distance between the two lines of interpretation narrows, as both bring home the devastating impact of the supply crisis and civil war; the way in which hungry cities and grain-short provinces, once wholesale decentralisation of power had failed them, provided a motley alliance for centralised power; and the inadequacy of a rigid class analysis in a situation of starvation and what Renehan calls 'economic Balkanization'.[59] When analysing 1917, the liberal and revisionist approaches are divided over how far the political process should be treated as relatively autonomous and how far as an expression of class struggle. The relative autonomy of the centralised state structure which emerged during the course of the civil war, however, is widely acknowledged in the West. Indeed, the consolidation of Europe's first Marxist government arguably marks the moment in European history at which the Marxist view of the relationship between state and society loses its explanatory power.

Adherents of the third tradition to be considered here, that of the 'libertarians', have never numbered more than a small minority of historians of 1917. In some respects, however, revisionist work has lent the libertarian interpretation the weight it previously lacked. Early libertarian studies of the revolution, written for the most part by anarchist activists, were impressionistic rather than scholarly.[60] During the 1960s, their approach to the revolution was echoed by the 'New Left' in the West and by dissident critics of the bureaucratic and oppressive nature of Soviet-style 'socialism' in the East.[61] But much of this work remained at a high level of generalisation, and at least one remove from primary source material. The result was to make doubly certain that the libertarian view would continue to be dismissed out of hand by Soviet historians, and to be treated by most western historians as not wholly respectable academically. For its adherents, of course, hostility from the orthodoxies of East and West is no cause for surprise or alarm. In their eyes, it is evidence rather of the common interest of the Soviet and Western establishments in suppressing a revolutionary vision which threatens both. Nevertheless, they could hardly fail to appreciate the fresh ammunition provided by the research of respectable western academics examining the revolution 'from below'.

The driving force behind the libertarian interpretation is an approach to history which entertains a vision of human capacity for individual liberty and fulfilment and social harmony of which the world has seen no more than a glimmer. But the Russian Revolution gave it that glimmer. The rejection by workers, peasants and soldiers of the authority of tsar, bourgeoisie and moderate socialists alike, the sustained assault upon the State and private property, is celebrated as one of the greatest expressions of man's striving for liberty. Libertarians focus attention above all on the activity of ordinary men and women, of anonymous peasants and workers, of the masses. Protest which Soviet historians dismiss as 'spontaneous' and unreflecting, and which liberal historians see as mindless and destructive, libertarians regard as the very stuff of history. The central drama of the revolution was precisely the attempt of the Russian masses to assert direct control over their own lives; its tragedy was their subordination to Bolshevik domination. October marked the moment at which power began to move from the hands of the mass movement, then at full-tide, into those of a new intellectual elite determined to exercise control from above. The Russian vision paled and faded away.

From the libertarian point of view, therefore, much revisionist work has been a bonanza. The woolly generalisations of Volin or Berkman are given flesh and blood, solid documentary backing. The revisionist depiction of the masses pursuing their own goals in a rational and independent fashion corresponds closely to their own view. From Mandel's portrayal of the Petrograd workers' 'initiative and creativity, (their) deep and genuine preoccupation with democracy and freedom', to Shanin's depiction of peasant discipline, idealism, and political wisdom, their concern for self-rule by consensus and their 'craving for political power and civil rights', there is abundant grist for the libertarian mill.[62] Even revisionist insistence that workers moved from a limited notion of workers' control to outright self-management in response to industrial crisis and the threat of unemployment, rather than in pursuit of utopia, can be regarded as merely a refinement of the libertarian thesis. So too can revisionist emphasis on the concern of the factory committees to co-ordinate their efforts and to move towards democratic but central planning of the economy. The acid test of socialism, in the libertarian view of historians like M. Brinton and C. Sirianni, is the distribution of power at the point of production. In their different ways, both workers' support for factory committees and peasant rejection of all authority imposed from outside, reflect a striving to establish just this kind of control over their own lives.[63]

In terms of popularising the insights of revisionist work, of course, endorsement from the far Left has been a decidedly mixed blessing, especially in the climate of the 1980s. In any case, on two major questions revisionist work sharply conflicts with the libertarian interpretation. The first concerns the *fate* of the mass organisations, especially the factory committees. The dénouement of the movement for workers' self-management, in the libertarian version of events, is the elitist drive for centralised and hierarchical control from a monolithic and doctrinaire Bolshevik party. For it was the Bolsheviks who were responsible for destroying industrial democracy by enforcing management appointed from outside the factory. A decade or so ago, a leading libertarian was able to growl that, given the interest of Leninists in obscuring the truth about this struggle, it should come as no surprise that 'we know less today about the early weeks of the Russian Revolution (i.e. after October) than we do, for instance, about the history of the Paris Commune'.[64] But the veil is gradually being lifted. And the picture that emerges is less clear-cut and heroic, the power of the centre to shape developments much more limited, than libertarian accounts assume. The factory committees themselves turn out to have exerted strong pressure for discipline and intervention from above, both to maintain production and to secure food and raw materials from the countryside. As the economic crisis deepened, they found themselves increasingly at odds with their own constituents.[65]

A second facet of revisionist work which meshes poorly with the libertarian view concerns the Bolshevik party itself. For some libertarians the authoritarian drive was rooted in the Bolsheviks' unconscious championing of the interests of a new class, potentially as hostile to the working masses as were capitalists: the class of the intelligentsia.[66] For others, it was rooted in the preoccupation of Lenin and the leadership with the *level* of the productive forces rather than the *relations* of production, and their conviction that nationalisation solved the problem of power in the factory, when in fact it did no such thing.[67] A manager appointed by the state was as offensive to working-class liberty as a capitalist henchman. Yet, if the revisionist point is taken – that until well into 1918 the Bolshevik party itself is to be treated as a mass organisation; that it was as much the product and vehicle of a movement from below as the instrument of manipulative leadership from above; that the leadership itself was riven with divisions; that the party's structure was chaotic, its growth hectic, its lines of authority and communication haphazard, its structure decentralised and even democratic – this picture dissolves. It is as inadequate for libertarians to find the root cause of 'what went wrong' in the Bolshevik leadership as for Soviet historians to explain what in their view went 'right' by the same means, or for liberals to see the revolution in terms of Bolsheviks Bolshevising here, bamboozling there, and infiltrating everywhere.

What then of the future? Even by 1991 the new dispensation in the Soviet Union had brought to light little new archival material on 1917, or much in the way of new monographs or heavily documented articles. The evidence of fresh thinking among Soviet historians is stronger in 'round table' discussions and 'think pieces' than in major works of scholarship.[68] Moreover, the growing number of iconoclastic journalistic pieces denouncing the party, the Revolution and Lenin himself, have provoked a defensive reaction among professional historians. They have closed ranks and poured scorn on these 'informal historians' with their cheap sensationalism, and their utterly ahistorical attempts to trace every evil from the terror of the 1930s to the administrative-command economy back to Lenin and the 'original sin' of October.[69] Although at the end of 1988 the decision was taken not to publish a comprehensive new party textbook, there is still a strong urge among the senior professariat to provide a single authoritative, if no longer compulsory and definitive, viewpoint.

Nevertheless, the essays and sketches on 1917 that they have produced are markedly less dogmatic and triumphalist in tone than their predecessors. They are enriched by recognition, for example, of Trotskii's role in October and the extent of popular disapproval of the dispersal of the Constituent Assembly.[70] Although there is still some way to go in the adjustment to pluralism, the old inhibitions are being shed fast. *Glasnost'* is opening the way for fully free debate not only among Soviet historians but between East and West. Formal exchange agreements, such as that completed in December 1987 between the London School of Slavonic and East European Studies and the Academy of Sciences in Moscow, are becoming more common. A Soviet presence at western conferences is no longer a novelty, and the number of genuinely international conferences organised within the Soviet Union is growing apace. Soviet translations of several western monographs, including Rabinowitch's study of October in Petrograd, have been published.[71] Major Soviet historical journals as well as the press have opened their columns to western historians.[72]

What impact *perestroika* and its repercussions will have upon western views of the Revolution remains to be seen. The effect may be to reinforce the revisionists by attracting fresh blood – and funds – for research on Soviet history. But equally, the spectacle of Communism in dissolution may give yet another lease of life to the traditional liberal view that October was no more than a *coup d'etat* by a tightly-knit group of *intelligenty*. Ask a class of undergraduates studying the Revolution to close their eyes and conjure up a typical Bolshevik of 1917 and what appears is a gaunt, bearded, bespectacled intellectual diligently carrying out Lenin's instructions with a fanatical, even manic, gleam in his eye. It is exactly the same image that would have come to the minds of their predecessors of twenty years ago. After being introduced to works such as those of Service or Rabinowitch, the vision they will summon up may with luck be a worker but he will surely appear just as gaunt, bearded and fanatical (even if not bespectacled) and will seem to hearken readily (even if not uncritically) to Lenin. One is wary of beginning to question the vocabulary in terms of which historians discuss the Revolution, lest the same fate befall treatments of 1917 as threatened 1789.[73] But for the period before the purging and centralisation of the party in 1918, there is a case for avoiding use of the term 'the Bolsheviks', except with heavy and specific qualification. The term is overburdened with connotations of homogeneity, unity, clarity of doctrine, and almost superhuman energy and power. It provides a ready-made explanatory device that fails to do justice to the complex picture of 1917 that emerges from recent historiography.

Notes

1. E. H. Carr, *A History of Soviet Russia. Volume One: The Bolshevik Revolution 1917–1923* (London, 1950); I. Deutscher, *The Prophet Armed. Trotsky: 1879–1921* (Oxford, 1954).
2. Despite their mutual admiration, Carr's approach was significantly more 'patrician' than was Deutscher's. Whereas Carr could remark that 'The Russian revolution was made and saved not by a class, but by a party proclaiming itself to be the representative of a class', Deutscher laid more emphasis on the role of the working class itself: 'No class

in Russian society, and no working class anywhere in the world, has ever acted with the energy, the political intelligence, the ability for organization, and the heroism with which the Russian workers acted in 1917 (and thereafter in the civil war).' On the other hand, in keeping a greater distance than Deutscher from historical materialism, Carr more closely foreshadowed later revisionism. E. H. Carr, *1917: Before and After* (London, 1969), p. 20; I. Deutscher, *The Unfinished Revolution. Russia 1917–1967* (Oxford, 1967), p. 24.

3.   R. F. Byrnes, *Soviet-American Academic Exchanges, 1958–1975* (Indiana, 1976) provides a useful commentary on the first two decades of the exchange scheme.

4.   For discussion of the sources used in revisionist work, see for example, A. K. Wildman, *The End of the Russian Imperial Army: The Old Army and the Soldiers' Revolt (March–April, 1917)* (Princeton, 1980), pp. 381–6; D. Mandel, *The Petrograd Workers and the Fall of the Old Regime, The Petrograd Workers and the Seizure of Power* (London, 1983, 1984), pp. 5–8; D. Koenker, *The Moscow Workers and the 1917 Revolution* (Princeton, 1981), pp. 228–33; T. Shanin, *Russia, 1905–07. Revolution as a Moment of Truth. The Roots of Otherness: Russia's Turn of Century* (London, 1986), vol. 2, pp. 130–4

5.   Wildman, p. 379.

6.   A. Rabinowitch, *The Bolsheviks Come to Power* (New York, 1976), p. 311

7.   Mandel, *op. cit.*, Koenker, *op. cit.*, S. Smith, *Red Petrograd. Revolution in the factories 1917–18* (Cambridge, 1983); H. Hogan, 'Labor and Management in Conflict: the St Petersburg Metal-Working Industry, 1900–1914' (Ph.D. Dissertation, University of Michigan, 1981); V. Bonnell, *The Roots of Rebellion: Workers' Politics and Organization in St Petersburg and Moscow, 1900–1914* (Berkeley, 1983); W. G. Rosenberg, 'Russian Labor and Bolshevik Power after October', *Slavic Review*, 44 (1985): 205–38; P. S. Flenley, 'Workers' Organizations in the Russian Metal Industry, February 1917–August 1918' (Ph.D. Dissertation, University of Birmingham, 1983).

8.   Shanin, *op. cit.*; G. Gill, *Peasants and Government in the Russian Revolution* (London, 1979).

9.   M. M. Helgesen, 'The Origins of the Party-State Monolith in Soviet Russia. Relations between the Soviets and Party Committees in the Central Provinces, Oct. 1917–March 1921' (Ph.D. Dissertation, State University of New York, 1980); T. J. Renehan, 'The Failure of Local Soviet Government, 1917–1918' (Ph.D. Dissertation, State University of New York, 1983); A. Rabinowitch, 'The Evolution of Local Soviets in Petrograd, November 1917–June 1918: The Case of the First City District Soviet', *Slavic Review*, 46 (1987), pp. 20–37.

10.   Wildman, *op. cit.*; J. Bushnell, *Mutiny amid Repression. Russian Soldiers in the Revolution of 1905–1906* (Bloomington, 1985).

11.   E. Mawdsley, *The Russian Revolution and the Baltic Fleet* (London

1978); N. E. Saul, *Sailors in Revolt: The Russian Baltic Fleet in 1917* (Lawrence, 1978).

12. R. A. Wade, *Red Guards and Workers' Militias in the Russian Revolution* (Stanford, 1985).

13. M. S. Melancon, 'The Socialist Revolutionaries from 1902 to February 1917. A Party of Workers, Peasants and Soldiers' (Ph.D. Dissertation, Indiana University, 1984).

14. R. Service, *The Bolshevik Party in Revolution: A Study in Organizational Change, 1917–1923* (London, 1979).

15. Z. Galili y Garcia, *The Menshevik Leaders in the Russian Revolution: Social Realities and Political Strategies* (Princeton, 1989).

16. R. G. Suny, *The Baku Commune, 1917–1918: Class and Nationality in the Russian Revolution* (Princeton, 1972); D. J. Raleigh, *Revolution on the Volga: 1917 in Saratov* (Cornell, 1986); I. Getzler, *Kronstadt, 1917–1921. The Fate of a Soviet Democracy* (Cambridge, 1983).

17. T. Hasegawa, *The February Revolution: Petrograd 1917* (Seattle & London, 1981); A. Rabinowitch, *op. cit.*

18. R. G. Suny, 'Toward a Social History of the October Revolution', *American Historical Review*, 88 (1983): 31–52; R. Service, *The Russian Revolution 1900–1927* (London, 1986).

19. See A. Bucholz (ed.), *Soviet and East European Studies in the International Framework. Organization, Financing and Political Relevance* (Berlin, 1982) for useful discussion of recent trends.

20. J. L. H. Keep, *Moscow's Problems of History: A Select Critical Bibliography of the Soviet Journal 'Voprosy Istorii', 1956–1985* (Ottawa, 1986) pp. 8–15; S. L. Tikhvinsky, 'Yanvarskiy (1987g.) Plenum TsK KPSS i istoricheskaya nauka', *Voprosy istorii* (1987), no. 6: 3–11; V. P. Naumov, 'Sovremennaya istoriografiya Velikoy Oktyabr'skoy sotsialisticheskoy revolyutsii', *Istoriya SSSR* (1987), no. 5 pp. 79, 88.

21. See, for example, the return of P. V. Volobuyev to the pages of *Voprosy istorii* with a lively article, suggesting he has weathered the weighty criticism he endured during the early 1970s, 'Rossiya: bor'ba za vybor novykh putey obshchestvennogo razvitiya', *Voprosy istorii* (1986) no. 5, pp. 42–67. For the controversy of those years, see *Soviet Studies in History*, XXII (1983–84), no. 3.

22. I. I. Mints, 'Iyun'skiy Plenum TsK KPSS i nekotorye problemy razvitiya istoriko-partiinoy nauki', *Voprosy istorii KPSS* (1983), no. 11, pp. 5–6.

23. See the discussion in *Oktyabr'skoe vooruzhonnoe vosstaniye v Petrograde* (Moscow, 1980), esp. pp. 87–101.

24. V. P. Naumov, *Sovetskaya istoriografiya fevral'skoy burzhuazno-demokraticheskoy revolyutsii* (Moscow, 1979), p. 172.

25. P. A. Golub, *et al.* (eds), *Istoricheskiy opyt tryokh rossiyskikh revolyutsiy*. Vol I. *General'naya repetitsiya Velikogo Oktyabrya* (Moscow, 1985), p. 12.

26.   I. D. Koval'chenko, N. B. Selunskaya, and B. M. Litvakov, *Sotsial'no-ekonomicheskiy stroy pomeshchich'ego khozyaistva evropeiskoy Rossii v epokhu kapitalizma* (Moscow, 1982).

27.   Yu. I. Kir'yanov, *Zhiznennyy uroven' rabochikh Rossii (konets XIX-nachalo XX vv.)* (Moscow, 1979).

28.   See, for example, V. S. Dyakin, *et al.*, *Krizis samoderzhaviya v Rossii. 1895–1917* (Leningrad, 1984); V. I. Startsev, *Russkaya burzhuaziya i samoderzhavie v 1905–1917 gg.* (*Bor'ba vokrug 'otvetstvennogo ministerstva' i 'pravitel' stva doveriya'*) (Leningrad, 1977).

29.   W. H. Roobol, 'Reform and Reaction in Russia: Three Studies', *Russian Review*, 39 (1980), pp. 208–19.

30.   I. P. Leyberov, *Na shturm samoderzhaviya: Petrogradskiy proletariat v gody pervoy mirovoy voyny i Fevral'skoy revolyutsii (iul' 1914–mart 1917 gg.)* (Moscow, 1979); much of this work is drawn together in *Neproletarskiye partii Rosii. Uroki istorii* (Moscow, 1984).

31.   Yu. S. Tokarev, *Petrogradskiy Sovet rabochikh i soldatskikh deputatov v marte-aprele 1917 g.* (Leningrad, 1976); V. I. Startsev, *Vnutrennyaya politika Vremennogo pravitel'stva pervogo sostava* (Leningrad, 1980); *Krakh Kerenshchiny* (Leningrad, 1982). Startsev's remarkable series has reached October with *Shturm Zimnego* (Leningrad, 1987).

32.   I. I. Mints, *et al.* (eds), *Kritika osnovnykh kontseptsiy sovremennoy burzhuaznoy istoriografii tryokh rossiyskikh revolyutsiy* (Moscow, 1983); N. V. Romanovsky, 'Istoriya i ideologicheskaya bor'ba. Velikiy Oktyabr' v noveishey burzhuaznoy literature', *Istoriya SSSR* (1984), no. 5, pp. 178–88; G. Z. Ioffe, 'Velikiy Oktyabr': transformatsiya sovietologicheskikh kontseptsiy i eyo klassovo-politicheskaya sut'', *Voprosy istorii KPSS* (1985), no. 6, pp. 72–86; N. I. Kanishcheka, 'Bol'sheviki i massy v Oktyabre. Transformatsiya versiy zapadnogermanskoy burzhuaznoy istoriografii', *Voprosy istorii KPSS* (1987), no. 9: 111–23; V. P. Buldakov, A. Iu. Skvortsova, 'Proletarskie massy i Oktyabr'skaya revolyutsiya. (Analiz sovremennoy zapadnoy istoriografii)', *Istoriya SSSR* (1987), no. 5, pp. 149–63.

33.   *Izvestiya*, 21 July 1983, p. 3.

34.   See, for example, I. I. Mints, 'O perestroyke v izuchenii Velikogo Oktyabrya', *Voprosy istorii* (1987), no. 4, pp. 3–9; S. L. Tikhvinsky 'Yanvarskii (1987g.) Plenum TsK KPSS i istoricheskaya nauka', *Vosprosy istorii* (1987), no. 6, pp. 3–11.

35.   See the comments by Mints in 'O perestroyke v izuchenii Velikogo Oktyabrya', *Voprosy istorii* (1987), no. 4, pp. 4–5; A. Ya. Grunt, 'Istoricheskoye tvorchestvo narodnykh mass v tryokh rossiyskikh revolyutsiyakh', *Istoriya SSSR* (1987), no. 1, pp. 69–91, goes some way towards tilting the balance of initiative away from the party.

36.   I. I. Mints, 'Oktyabr'skaya revolyutsiya – perelomnoe sobytiye vsemir-noy istorii', *Istoriya SSSR* (1987), no. 5: 3–18; for a more aggressive reaffirmation by Mints see 'Oktyabr'skaya revolyutsiya: preemstven-nost' i novatorstvo bol'shevizma', *Vosprosy istorii KPSS* (1987), no. 7,

pp. 3–16.

37. G. Katkov, *Russia 1917: the Kornilov Affair. Kerensky and the break-up of the Russian army* (London, 1980).

38. G. L. Yaney, *The Urge to Mobilize. Agrarian Reform in Russia, 1861–1930* (Urbana, 1982).

39. G. Leggett, *The Cheka: Lenin's Political Police. The All-Russian Extraordinary Commission for Combating Counter-Revolution and Sabotage (December 1917 to February 1922)* (Oxford, 1981).

40. R. Pipes, *Struve: Liberal on the Right (1905–1944)* (Cambridge, Mass., 1980).

41. A. Ulam, *Russia's Failed Revolutions: from the Decembrists to the Dissidents* (London, 1981), pp. 304–391.

42. A. Besançon, *The Intellectual Origins of Leninism* (Oxford, 1981), pp. 260.

43. R. Conquest, 'The inherent vice', *The Spectator*, 5 May 1984, p. 20.

44. J. L. H. Keep, *The Russian Revolution: A Study in Mass Mobilization* (London, 1976).

45. *American Historical Review*, 88 (1983), p. 1138.

46. Keep, *The Russian Revolution*, pp. 114–15.

47. *Ibid.*, pp. 157, 67, 95.

48. *Ibid.*, p. ix.

49. *Ibid.*, p. 141

50. *ibid.*

51. The same point may be made about Marc Ferro's acclaimed but uneven two-volume history, which in some other respects foreshadows subsequent revisionist work: *The Russian Revolution of February 1917* (London, 1972), *October 1917. A Social History of the Russian Revolution* (London, 1980). See the review by S. A. Smith in *Soviet Studies*, 30 (1981), pp. 454–9.

52. Keep, *The Russian Revolution*, p. 82.

53. J. L. H. Keep, *The Debate on Soviet Power. Minutes of the All-Russian Central Executive Committee of Soviets* (Oxford, 1979), p. 18.

54. L. Schapiro, *1917, The Russian Revolutions and the Origins of Present-Day Communism* (Hounslow, 1984).

55. L. Schapiro, *The Origin of the Communist Autocracy. Political Opposition in the Soviet State. First Phase, 1917–1922* (Cambridge, Mass., 1977), p. vii.

56. Schapiro, *1917*, p. x.

57. *Ibid.*, pp. 43, 64, 92.

58. *Ibid.*, pp. 78, 214.

59. The convergence may be seen in the common ground between Rene-han's revisionist approach and that of L. T. Lih, 'Bread and Authority in Russia: Food Supply and Revolutionary Politics, 1914–1921' (Ph.D. Dissertation, University of Princeton, 1981), a lively analysis from a liberal stance. For Lih, the spirit of local soviet power in its heyday was 'cruel', 'undiscriminating', 'parochial', 'self-obsessed' and based

on envy and revenge, while he likens the revolution to latter-day anti-colonial upheavals, pairing Lenin with Nkrumah and Stalin with Amin – an analogy which achieves the remarkable feat of being unfair to all four, p. 220.

60.   Voline, *The Unknown Revolution 1917–1921* (Montreal, 1974); G. P. Maximoff, *The Guillotine at Work. Twenty years of Terror in Russia* (Chicago, 1940); A. Berkman, *The Russian Tragedy* (Montreal, 1976); P. Arshinov, *A History of the Makhnovist Movement, 1918–1921* (Detroit, 1974).

61.   See, for example, R. Gombin, *The Radical Tradition. A Study in Modern Revolutionary Thought* (London, 1978) and G. Konrad and I. Szelenyi, *The Intellectuals on the Road to Class Power* (Brighton, 1979).

62.   Mandel, *The Petrograd Workers and the Seizure of Soviet Power*, p. 419; Shanin, pp. 99, 98–137.

63.   For a broadly libertarian synthesis incorporating much revisionist work, see C. Sirianni, *Workers Control and Socialist Democracy. The Soviet Experience* (London, 1982), Part I.

64.   M. Brinton, 'Factory Committees and the Dictatorship of the Proletariat', *Critique*, 4 (Spring 1975), pp. 78–9.

65.   In addition to Mandel, Smith and Flenley, see W. G. Rosenberg, 'Workers and Workers' Control in the Russian Revolution', *History Workshop*, 5 (1978): 89–97. 'Russian Labor and Bolshevik Power after October', *Slavic Review*, 44 (1985), pp. 205–38.

66.   Konrad and Szelenyi, p. 87ff.

67.   M. Brinton, *The Bolsheviks and Workers' Control* (Montreal 1970), pp. 40–3; Sirianni, pp. 252–60.

68.   See for example V. P. Buldakov, 'U istokov sovestskoi istorii put' k Oktyabryu' *Vosprosy istorii* (19), no. 10, pp. 63–82, and V. V. Shelokhaev, R. V. Filippov, N. V. Blinov and I. A. Aluf, 'Krazrabotke kontseptsii dooktyabr'skogo perioda istorii KPSS', *Voprosy istorii KPSS* (1989), no. 12, pp. 21–50 which reject a host of conventional Soviet assumptions, scathingly dismiss the notion that the prerequisites for socialism were present in 1917, stress that the Bolsheviks and Mensheviks belonged to one party until 1917, and point to Lenin's belated recognition of merit in the populists' respect for the peasant commune. An excellent account of the general impact of *glasnost*' on Soviet historians, and especially on their treatment of the Stalin period, is R. W. Davies, *Soviet History in the Gorbachev Revolution* (London, 1989).

69.   Typical of the articles which have invoked professorial wrath are A. P. Butenko, 'Real'naya drama sovetskoy istorii', *Nauka i zhizn*' (1989), no. 12, pp. 38–42 and V. A. Soloukhin, 'Chitaya Lenina', *Rodina* (1989), no. 10, which blames mass terror in the Soviet period on Lenin's 'intolerance and brutality'. For the response of professional historians, see for example G. A. Bordyugov, V. A. Kozlov

and V. T. Loginov, 'Poslushnaya istoriya, ili Novyi publitsisticheskii rai. Grustnye zametki', *Kommunist* (1989), no. 14, pp. 74–87, and the round-table discussion on Lenin's ideas about socialism reported in *Voprosy istorii KPSS* (1990), no. 4, pp. 26–46.

70. See for example P. V. Volobuev (ed.), *Rossiya: 1917 god: vybor istoricheskogo puti* (Moscow, 1988), and G. A. Trukan, 'Revolyutsiya kotoraya potryasla mir', *Istoriya SSSR* (1990), no. 1: 78–102, the first chapter in a new semi-popular history of Soviet society among whose joint authors are such heavy-weight figures as Yu. A. Polyakov, Yu. S. Borisov, V. P. Danilov and V. P. Dmitrenko.

71. Half a century after Bukharin's show trial and the appearance of Stalin's notorious *Short Course*, one cannot but relish the appearance in Moscow of S. Cohen, *Bukharin and the Bolshevik Revolution: A Political Biography, 1888–1938* and, for its subtitle quite apart from anything else, R. M. Slusser, *Stalin in October. The Man Who Missed the Revolution* (Baltimore, Maryland, 1987).

72. See, for example, A. Rabinowitch, 'Bol'sheviki i massy v Oktyabr'skoi revolyutsii', *Voprosy istorii* (1988), no. 5, pp. 14–27 and R. Service, 'A Saga of Self-Liberation of Workers, Peasants and Soldiers', *Moscow News*, no. 46, 12 November 1989.

73. For the famous controversy over the language used to describe the French Revolution, see A. Cobban, *The Social Interpretation of the French Revolution* (Cambridge, 1968).

Index